Colorado Industries

OF THE PAST

William L. Reich

JOHNSON BOOKS
BOULDER

Published by Johnson Books, a Big Earth Publishing company.
3005 Center Green Drive, Suite 220, Boulder, Colorado 80301.
1-800-258-5830
E-mail: books@bigearthpublishing.com
www.bigearthpublishing.com

Cover and text design by Rebecca Finkel

9 8 7 6 5 4 3 2 1

Library of Congress Cataloging-in-Publication Data
Reich, William L.
Colorado industries of the past / William L. Reich.
p. cm.
Includes bibliographical references and index.
ISBN 978-1-55566-416-9
1. Industries—Colorado—History—19th century.
2. Business enterprises—Colorado History—19th century.
3. Colorado—History—19th century.
4. Colorado—Economic conditions—19th century. I. Title.
HC107.C7R45 2008
338.09788—dc22 2008003121

Printed in the United States of America

Colorado Industries of the Past

Contents

Acknowledgments

The best part of researching Colorado Industries of the Past was meeting and talking to the experts in each industry. A book like this could never have been done without their knowledge and input.

Kenton Forrest suggested the ice industry as a chapter and then buried me with information on the railroad's relationship. The Colorado Railroad Museum also allowed me to use their old catalogs from the Mine & Smelter Supply Co. Peggy Ford retrieved information and photographs on Greeley's ice harvesting activities.

Jennifer Cousino supplied photographs and information on the sugar industry and allowed me to photograph and examine the Millinery and Dressmaking Exhibit in the Loveland Museum. Grace Goss sent me material on each item in that display. The Molly Brown House in Denver allowed me to photograph one of Molly's hats in their collection.

The librarians at the Morgan Library in Fort Collins helped me search records of the Colorado Flower Growers Association and their agricultural databases for information on the carnation industry.

Staff at both the Western Mining Museum in Colorado Springs and the National Mining Museum in Leadville helped with the very important chapter on mining, as did Bill and Beth Sagstetter, authors of The Mining Camps Speak. Author Dan Abbott patiently supplied photographs and other historical artifacts of smelters and railroads.

I was very fortunate to have Chuck Tuthill's help with the Colorado cigar industry. No one knows more about it than he does. Brent Carmack of the Fort Collins Museum found and allowed me to photograph items and business records from one of the last Fort Collins cigar businesses. Professor Patricia Cooper, University of Kentucky, granted permission to use her interview with William Thiesen.

Lee and Roselyn Scamehorn tried to keep me on track with the Colorado canning industry, a subject they are currently researching. They also read the manuscript for the entire book, offering valuable insights. Bob Seifert, a retired Kuner's employee, also helped with Kuner's history.

Bob Sherer, a Colorado saddlemaker, took me through the saddlemaking process in his shop and reviewed that chapter to keep me from any glaring errors. Don Bailey, of Simla, showed me his saddle collection and gave permission to use photographs he had collected during the writing of his book, *Saddle Strings*. That book lists over twelve hundred Colorado saddlemakers in the state and has further information on about one hundred of the best known.

George Williams of the Pueblo County Historical Society also supplied information, particularly about the Pueblo saddlemakers and the story of "Lucky," Pueblo's display horse.

The following librarians and archivists from all over the state supplied learned help and direction:

> Wendy Hall and Marti Anderson at the Carnegie Library in Boulder; the entire staff at the Denver Public Library's Western History Department; the staff at the Hart Library at the Colorado Historical Society, including James Petersen in the Archives and Steve Grinstead, editor of *Colorado Heritage Magazine*; Dave Hays at the Western History Archives in the University of Colorado Norlin Library in Boulder; Robert Sorgenfrei of the History Archive at Arthur Lakes Library at the Colorado School of Mines; Erik Mason at the Longmont Museum; Dan Davidson of Craig's Museum of Northwest Colorado; Tom Vaughn of the Berthoud Museum; Jay Trask of the Bessemer Historical Society in Pueblo; James Prochaska of the Gilpin County Museum; John Seinle of the Hiwan Historical Society; and Johanna Harden of Douglas County Historical Research Center.

There were other individuals who also helped:

> Vonnie Perkins knows more about D. C. Oakes and his family than anyone in the state and graciously supplied a steady stream of information.
>
> Bonnie Szidon gave me an evolutionary history of the Lindell Flour Mill to present-day Ranchway Feed and Supply in Fort Collins.
>
> Blake Mitchell of Western Timber in Mancos gave me a detailed description of the matchmaking process, one of the remaining niche markets for sawmills.

Thanks to my wife, Joy, for reading the manuscript and traveling to deserted places in the state for research, and to Bill Hughes and Bill Benjamin, friends who accompanied me when Joy couldn't. Thanks to Johnson Books and Mira Perrizo for turning this into a real book.

Thanks also to anyone I may have missed. It has taken almost six years to research and write this book, and I am sure I must have forgotten someone who at the time yielded an important bit of information.

Any mistakes still in the book are, of course, mine.

Introduction

Most of our Colorado forefathers came to the Pikes Peak region in 1859, looking for gold. Only a few found enough to live on, as mining in the Rocky Mountains was difficult.

Some of the original Fifty-Niners came to the area with other plans in mind right from the start. Like all successful businessmen and -women, they saw an opportunity based on the ageless principles of supply and demand. And that's what this book is all about. Back in the early 1800s, when the West was being settled, the people of every town had to produce what they needed for subsistence. Transportation was scarce and expensive, so local industries flourished. Once transportation became more accessible, local businesses then had to compete with larger companies elsewhere that could manufacture products less expensively on a larger scale. Sound familiar? Urban and rural areas throughout the world still struggle with the same issues, but on a more international scale.

Remnants of that bygone era are all around us—from coke ovens to foundations, and from wagon trails to railroad tracks—all have come and gone in the past 150 years. Let's take a look at the people and industries that once flourished here in Colorado.

John P. Good, one of Colorado's original beer brewers, immigrated from Germany in 1854 and crossed the plains with three wagons, one filled with hops. Once he arrived in the Denver area, he quickly opened a general store. But soon he sold the store in order to invest in the Rocky Mountain Brewery, which was Colorado's first brewery. Good knew miners would spend their hard-earned gold dust on beer faster than on almost anything else. He even taught local farmers how to cultivate and grow barley. Good was associated with Colorado breweries until his death in 1918, at the age of eighty-three.

They came to the Pikes Peak region in anything they could afford—oxen-powered wagons, mostly, but also handcarts or mule-pulled, two-wheeled carts, in some cases. They brought what they thought would be necessary to start a new life in the region, including a sense of humor, as shown by naming their not-so-speedy wagon "Lightning Express." From Marvels of the New West, by William Thayer.

Other settlers brought mercantile goods and foodstuffs into the area, opening stores to supply those still intent on mining, or for their womenfolk's necessities. Most had farmed at one time or another and saw that the ground, if irrigated, would grow a variety of crops. Soon grains, vegetables, and fruits were locally available. Grains could be locally ground, and grist and flour mills flourished using waterpower from the plentiful rivers and streams (if steam equipment was not available). Hay for horses was at a premium, and some experienced farmers who had bad mining luck quickly supplied the market with local hay that was freighted up to the camps from the Front Range area.

The widely held belief that the Great American Desert was inhospitable to human or beast was obviously false, as livestock abandoned along the Front Range of the Rockies from the trip to the goldfields not only survived but also gained weight and prospered. Soon, cattlemen brought beef on the hoof to supply the miners with steaks and chops. Local butchers prospered in every town.

Frank Kershaw built an icehouse on the banks of a lake he called Crystal Lake, located in Auraria, and in the summer of 1860 began the regular delivery of block ice to local customers. Ice blocks delivered to Denver homes would become part of everyday life, here as well as everywhere in the States, until the refrigerator would replace the icebox.

There were others already in the area who had been selling merchandise to the local Indians before the Fifty-Niners provided a booming market for goods. J. P. Doyle had a flour mill on his cattle ranch, located on the Huerfano River southeast of Pueblo, and he started the J. P. Doyle Mercantile stores in Denver, Pueblo, and Tarryall, quickly becoming the wealthiest person in the territory. Even the well-known Indian trader Jim Baker shoveled coal into a wagon at Baker's home on the west bank of Coal Creek (soon to become Erie) and hauled it to Golden to sell to miners who were headed up the wagon road in Golden Gate Canyon to Central City. Baker asked and received $25 per ton for the coal, which was about five times the 1860 market price back east, but even at that price the coal industry in the area would have to wait for better transportation, in the form of railroads, before that industry could flourish.

Another business that sprang up due to the demand for money was a mint. Austin and Milton Clark and Emanuel Gruber set up a privately owned and operated mint in Denver to turn the local gold into coin and bars that could be used as legal tender. They also printed paper money, backed by Rocky Mountain gold, that retained its

Right: Joseph Doyle was the first successful Colorado businessman, easily surpassing his former employers—the Bents and Ceran St. Vrain. He had, however, the advantage of selling to tens of thousands of Fifty-Niners—who brought cash with them—instead of to the cashless Utes and Arapahos. From Uncle Dick Wootton, by Howard Conrad. Above: Although there was plenty of gold in the area, there was a dearth of money. Clark and Gruber filled the demand by building their own private mint in Denver. Courtesy Colorado Historical Society, 10027924.

value better than the U.S. and Confederate dollar bills printed and used elsewhere. This private mint was later purchased by the government and became the Denver Mint.

Daniel Cheeseman Oakes typified these early entrepreneurs. In March of 1859, D. C. Oakes left his family and home in Pacific City, Iowa, for a return trip to the Pikes Peak gold region. By then he was a seasoned traveler, having gone to California ten years earlier. There, he had been successful, and brought back $6,000 to his Iowa home (a princely sum then), but he still had the western wanderlust and a keen eye for opportunity. In the summer of 1858 he had traveled to the base of the Rockies to scout out opportunities in the Pikes Peak region. He was not alone. There were several parties wandering in the area, mostly looking for gold. One such group was the Russell Party from Georgia. Oakes had joined them only days before they discovered gold in the sands of the Platte River in present-day Englewood. D. C. shared their excitement and optimism.

D. C. Oakes, one of Denver's founding fathers. From *The History of Denver*, by Jerome Smiley.

Immediately after, D. C. returned to Iowa with the journal of Luke Tierney, one of the members of the Russell Party. D. C. also had some ideas about how to cash in on the coming rush of people that he anticipated heading to Colorado. Using information contained in the journal, Oakes wrote a manual for the folks he knew would be moving west the next year. It was precise and detailed, telling a likely gold prospector how to proceed to the goldfields, how to pan for gold, the equipment he would need, the amount of supplies, etcetera. His list of supplies, costing $517.25, was detailed right down to plates, knives, and spoons. The guidebook told where to go and how to get there, and in hindsight it was remarkably accurate for as little time as Oakes had spent in the area in 1858.

From the Tierney and Oakes guidebook History of the Gold Discoveries on the South Platte River by Luke Tierney To Which Is Appended a Guide to the Route by Smith and Oakes:

> The following estimate of outfit for FOUR MEN, with provisions for SIX MONTHS, embraces the usual articles taken; together with the present prices at the Missouri river, near the crossing. Parties can vary the articles to suit their convenience, or can purchase them in a cheaper market, and freight them up the river to the starting point. This estimate is given, however, to show those who are inexperienced in such things, what is likely to be needed, and the cost of obtaining the same. Our own opinion is that persons starting from the east will find it easier and cheaper to purchase their entire outfit at the Missouri river, near the point of starting. By this means, they will be enabled to reach that point sooner, and save the encumbrance and vexation of freighting their goods up the Missouri, or crossing

the State of Iowa with teams. They will be able to start for the mines a great deal earlier in the spring.

Teams, Implements, etc.

3 yoke of oxen, $60 per yoke	$180.00
1 wagon and cover	$85.00
3 yokes, 2 chains	$9.00
1 tent	$15.00
10 pairs of blankets	$40.00
4 steel picks	$6.00
4 steel shovels	$4.00
4 axes	$5.00
4 gold pans	$2.00
3 augers	$1.00
1 inch chisel	$0.35
1 hand saw	$0.60
1 drawing knife	$0.40
1 twelve-inch file	$0.75
Total	$350.95

Provisions and Supplies for Six Months

1000 lbs. flour	$30.00
400 lbs. bacon	$40.00
100 lbs. dried beef	$12.50
50 lbs. salt	$0.75
50 lbs. coffee	$7.00
8 lbs. tea	$5.20
200 lbs. sugar	$18.00
30 lbs. rice	$2.40
150 lbs. beans	$5.25
60 lbs. dried fruit	$4.00
[24] 6 lbs. pepper	$1.20
3 lbs. soda	$0.30
6 lbs. cream of tarter	$3.00
25 lbs. soap	$2.00
25 lbs. gunpowder	$9.00
50 lbs. lead	$5.00
2000 gun caps	$1.20
4 gallons of pickles	$4.00
4 gallons of vinegar	$1.00
6 gallons of brandy	$6.00
2 dozen boxes of matches	$1.00
1 coffee mill	$0.50
1 frying pan	$0.50
1 dutch oven	$1.25
3 camp kettles	$3.00
6 tin plates	$0.50

1 set knives and forks	$0.75
1 set spoons	$0.25
1 butcher knife	$0.25
Total	$166.30
Teams and Implements	$350.95
Grand Total	$517.25

D. C. had other ideas on how to get rich in the new territory, so he included on his 1859 journey west a partner and a steam-powered sawmill. Oakes intended to establish the mill in the forests close to the mining settlements along the Front Range and sell lumber to those moving into the region. At the Missouri River he was the center of attention as people came by wanting to see what was being taken in the oxcarts and talk to D. C. Oakes, the man who wrote the guidebook. Things were good! Imagine his consternation later in the spring as he crossed the prairie near Julesburg, in what is now northeastern Colorado, and passed people returning to the east. They had not found gold as easily as they had expected and were leaving in angry moods. To them, D. C. Oakes was not a popular figure. Oakes was particularly surprised when he observed his own mock graves with epitaphs similar to this one:

Here lies the remains of D. C. Oakes
Who was the starter of this damn hoax!

D. C. Oakes is depicted here confronting his detracters near Julesburg in 1859. From *Marvels of the New West* by William Thayer.

His party was none too happy, either. They wanted to turn back instead of being possibly hanged with their now-unpopular partner. Oakes talked them into camping by the trail near Julesburg while he and another member of the party rode in to reconnoiter the goldfields. Surprisingly, he found the people who had stayed to be optimistic and the area booming. His vision of the future was coming true; only those who were leaving were disappointed.

By July of that year, Oakes and his partner had two sawmills operating. They were very successful in having a product in demand for a growing marketplace. Oakes was not credited for supplying the lumber for the first frame structure in Denver, though, as Cooper and Wyatt were providing lumber to the settlements at the confluence of Cherry Creek and the Platte River in April, when D. C. was still on the trail headed west.

As the initial rush subsided, many people quit mining but stayed in the area to provide a product or services to the growing population.

High-quality clay deposits allowed almost every town in Colorado to have its own brickyard. Fires in Denver in 1862 and 1863 prompted the local town council to pass laws banning the building of wooden structures inside city limits, guaranteeing a steady demand for bricks throughout Denver's history. Invesco Field and the old Mile High Stadium along Clay Street were built on old brickyards. The original grounds of their playing fields were leveled at the beginning of the twentieth century for the clay they contained. That clay was turned into bricks on-site and distributed throughout the city. At least twenty-two individual brickyards furnished the bricks for Denver's growth.

In 1878, Golden was a bustling manufacturing center with flour mills, breweries, three brickyards, three smelters, and a paper mill. This drawing was from the Denver and Rio Grande Railway, even though the only railroad in town was the Colorado Central.

Millinery shops were present in Denver as early as 1860, providing hats and dresses to the women who had come with their men. One was owned and operated by D. C. Oakes's cousin, William Cody.

The developing West was the free-market system in its simplest form. Prices were not restrained by anything but another business down the street or an angry, gun-toting customer. Miners always thought the mill undervalued their ore, mill owners thought the smelters undervalued their concentrates, and smelters believed

The Berthoud Farmers' Mill and Elevator, shown here from an 1894 illustration from the *Fort Collins Express*, was typical of the flour mills and grain elevators built by entrepreneurs and farmer co-ops throughout the state. Every town was proud of its agricultural production as well as its finished products.

their bullion was worth more than current market value. People grumbled about the high cost of goods, and storekeepers complained about the high cost of freight. There was little business insurance, and risks were high. The manager of John P. Good's general store absconded with the merchandise and proceeds while Good was back east purchasing more supplies. The first railroad or freighting company in an area made obscene profits until the second company came along, at which time they both suffered and often went out of business. It was not surprising, then, that buy-outs were common as the inevitable needs caused first the proliferation of businesses, then the consolidation into bigger, more efficient companies.

Labor was cheap and business leaders encouraged immigration by advertising in Europe, then hiring at the lowest possible wages. J. K. Mullen came to the area and offered to work as a miller for nothing but room and board, just to get a start. He soon became the owner of the largest chain of flour mills in the western United States, and one of Denver's wealthiest men.

Almost every immigrant class got a start in the States by accepting work at the lowest rung of the labor ladder and, of course, was despised because of it. But most thrived here and stayed because work at any pay was better than starving in their home countries.

If you owned a horse and wagon, you could be in the freight business, either at the one-wagon level or, with ambition and a little capital from friends or family, at the multi-wagon level, as David Woods did in the southwestern part of the state and Marinus Smith did in Boulder.

Every settlement and town firmly believed that if only they had a railroad, local businesses could flourish, and their town would be destined for greatness. This was particularly true of the mining camps. Miners could usually find mineral veins, but finding veins rich enough to justify the mining, transportation, and processing expenses was a major problem. The San Juan–area mining towns were late to develop, not because gold and silver were late to be found, but because there was no way to economically transport these metals out. So miners begged for outside capital to build local smelters until the railroads could get there.

Local ore processors had a mixed history of success. They had to learn how to efficiently extract precious metal from the ore in that particular location, but usually there was not enough of it to justify a large enough operation for good efficiency.

The mining industry of Colorado built many mostly unsuccessful smelters. The Windham Smelter, four miles north of Ouray, was more successful than most. Bars of lead-silver bullion are stacked in front while slag buttons cool by the creek. Courtesy Colorado Railroad Museum.

There were many who turned Colorado's agricultural bounty into canned food. This photograph, taken inside the Empson Canning Factory in Longmont, shows workers and canning equipment. Courtesy Longmont Museum.

They could only process the richest ore, leaving miners with the same problem: vast amounts of lower-grade ores. When the railroads did come into an area, the smaller, local smelters could not compete with the larger, more efficient ones at the other end of the rail lines. Slowly the smelters consolidated into a few very large, highly efficient ones. Eventually, with the increasing cost of processing and the decreasing quality of the ores, all the smelters closed.

This was a common dilemma for all businesses. Better transportation into an area brought cheaper equipment, more people, and better access to other markets, but it also brought stronger, outside competition. Every town had a local brewery until better transportation brought in a better product from the outside. The same was true of flour mills and sawmills.

Although consolidation caused many factories to close, there were other reasons for failure. Some entire industries were eliminated due to new technology or other factors that made them no longer economically feasible. The charcoal industry in Colorado in the 1870s and '80s was based on the difficulty that silver smelters had in getting coke at a reasonable cost (coke and charcoal were interchangeable fuels for the silver smelters)—not because the coke itself was expensive, but because it was costly to transport. Front Range smelters with inexpensive access to coke used it, while the mountain smelters were forced to use more expensive locally made charcoal, until the transportation cost for coke decreased because of more competition from the ovens at Cardiff, near Glenwood Springs.

In 1918 the Colorado Fuel and Iron steel mill in Pueblo installed Hopper By-Product coke retorts at the steel mill, and put most of the beehive coking camps, such as Tercio, out of business. And finally, the switch from coal to oil and natural gas was the main reason for the shutdown of the coal-mining camps throughout the state.

Ice companies distributed huge quantities of lake ice to the summer populations from large ice storage houses along the railroads or in the towns themselves. Icehouse structures at Lake George, Pactolus, Denver, Longmont, Montrose, Paonia, Grand Junction, and elsewhere became ghost structures when new refrigeration equipment made ice on demand. Then that same technology replaced the icebox with the refrigerator for home owners and supplied chillers for industries.

There was a saltworks in South Park, several match factories in Buena Vista and Golden, a tire manufacturer in Arvada as well as in Denver, and plasterworks all over the state. Market demand eventually prevails, then as now. Victorian dress and hat styles slowly gave way to a less constraining style of clothing that lent itself to ready-to-wear garments, slowly eliminating the custom millinery and dress shops once visited by Colorado's women.

Not all of the industries in Colorado died. Those entrepreneurs who understood their markets and were able to meet national competition are still in business today. Coors Brewery and Coors Technical Products Ceramic Plant are nationally known, for example. Since 1982 the steel mill in Pueblo no longer reduces iron ores to iron in its blast furnaces, but the mill still converts iron to steel and rolls steel products to final shapes and sizes. Robinson Brick Company is the sole surviving brick producer in the state, and is still located in Denver after 123 years.

It is true that many of the old industries still exist in some form. Adolph Coors and Anheuser-Busch would strongly argue against calling the brewing industry a dead industry since, at the turn of the twenty-first century, these two gigantic breweries made Colorado the number one beer-producing state in the country. However, the Coors of today bears little resemblance to its kin of 1874, and even less to the breweries in Lake City, Sedgewick, Fairplay, or any of the small settlement breweries that served the local population with their daily suds. There are still breweries, a sugar beet factory, and saddle makers, but this book is really not about the survivors. It is about their forebears.

What businesses will survive the next 150 years? Who knows? There will always be industry in some form in Colorado, as it will always be a desirable place to live and work, and the fundamental laws of supply and demand will still be in place. But many of the state's original industries are now dead and forgotten, with only abandoned railroad grades and small reminders here and there of their existence, much like headstones in a cemetery. In some respects, this is a graveyard book about those industries and businesses. May they not be forgotten.

CHAPTER 1

Flour Mills

The first item under "Provisions and Supplies" listed by D. C. Oakes in his 1859 guidebook was one thousand pounds of flour. Flour was the most basic necessity for people who were to live and work in the Pikes Peak settlements. When pioneers lacking a personal gold mine looked around for economic opportunities, they saw land that would grow crops, including wheat, if irrigated, and flour selling for $12 to $22 per one hundred–pound sack in the mining camps. One gold seeker who reached Denver early in the spring of 1859 with a sack of flour was offered three lots of prime land in the center of town, which he refused. At the time, there was little flour in the town, but he was concerned about the value of land in so remote a spot. Three to six months later the lots were worth about $10,000.[1]

Because there were people in what would become Colorado, even before the gold rush, there was a demand for such basic necessities as flour. The first wheat crop in the area that would become the Colorado Territory was probably grown in 1846 at Greenhorn, a small trading settlement where the Taos Trail from Pueblo crossed the Greenhorn River at the mouth of the Wet Mountain Valley. John Brown, one of the original founders of Pueblo, started a trading store at Greenhorn, and in 1846 he planted a crop of wheat. The next winter, he built a gristmill nearby and ground and sold flour and cornmeal at his store. The mill was reported to be a building of logs, the machinery rude, and the millstones hewn out of local granite. Local granite was readily available from the Rocky Mountains, and millstones were heavy and expensive to transport from somewhere else. Brown also ground wheat and corn for the farmers from Pueblo and the settlement at Hardscrabble and sold flour for 6¼ cents per pound to others who would bring their own sacks and containers. This flour was not sieved but whole meal, Spanish-style. By 1859, when the gold seekers entered the Pikes Peak region, the mill at Greenhorn had disappeared, but the stones were report-

The mill at Greenhorn, and other Mexican-type mills, were simple affairs for grinding grain. This illustration shows a hopper (1) for dumping and holding grain before allowing it to trickle down between the millstones (2, 3). The shed (4, 8) sheltered the mill from the elements. Water supplied power to the waterwheel (5), which turned the shaft (6). The shaft was attached to one of the stones while the second stone remained stationary. Grain was ground between the two, falling on the gathering cloth and eventually into the basket on the floor. Mexican mills did no sifting of the flour, so flour from the basket was used directly in the kitchen. From *Marvels of the New West* by William Thayer.

edly "still down by the river."[2] There are grinding stones, nowadays, at several museums around Colorado that were left from local early mills.

In the San Luis Valley, José Marie Jacques, founder of the town of Guadalupe, built a mill in 1856 on the southern bank of the Conejos River, two and a half miles east of town.[3] This Spanish-type mill yielded whole-meal flour. H. E. Easterday built another in 1859 in San Luis, also in the San Luis Valley, in partnership with Ceran St. Vrain. This mill was the first in the territory that bolted or sieved the flour, and Easterday advertised it as "American Mill Flour."[4]

American Mill Flour, which was preferred by the northern European immigrants, varied little from the flour used to bake loaves of bread in England, Ireland, or Germany because the method of grinding and sifting was little changed. Even now, the process is essentially the same. Kernels of wheat are cleaned of debris and chaff, ground into very small pieces, and sifted to remove any unwanted parts. Grinding was done by introducing wheat kernels between two millstones and turning the stones with whatever power was available. At Greenhorn and many other places in Colorado that power source was usually water from the creeks and rivers that were close to the settlements. Sifting or "bolting" the flour to remove unwanted pieces was done by forcing the flour through bolts of cloth—the finer the weave the finer the flour, but the slower the process. A slower process increased the cost of the final product.

The Mexican population was more used to whole-meal flour that was hand-ground with *metates*, as well as ground in gristmills without the final bolting step. The Mexican farmers also preferred the softer-grained Sonoran wheat that was readily available and easier to grind by hand.

Another Arkansas Valley pioneer, Joseph Bainbridge Lafayette Doyle, built a flour mill in the early 1860s at his ranch on the Huerfano River southeast of Pueblo. He was born in the Shenandoah Valley, Virginia, on July 10, 1817. When he was a boy, his family moved to the St. Louis area. In 1838 at the age of twenty-one, he began working for William and Charles Bent, and left for Bent's Fort in the summer of 1839. While in their employ, Doyle would meet and trade with most of the principal traders who later founded the settlements along the Arkansas River and its tributaries. He quit the Bents in 1844 to join Alexander Barclay at Hardscrabble, Colorado, and at one time owned part of Pueblo and Fort Barclay on the Mora River. Doyle was a trader and freighter by profession and became one of the territory's wealthiest men by freighting and trading goods to the Pikes Peak Fifty-Niners. He set up the J. B. Doyle and Company stores in Denver, with branches in Cañon City, Pueblo, and Tarryall. In the early 1860s, Doyle sold more than $500,000 worth of merchandise. At his ranch, he grew wheat, potatoes, corn, beans, tobacco, cotton, melons, and other crops. He also herded one thousand head of cattle. Doyle built a large mansion on his ranch, using lumber transported from the east. The ranch also had a large store, a post office, a schoolhouse, the flour mill, a wagon and blacksmith shop, and houses for employees and servants, as well as the family cemetery. He was serving in the Territorial Legislature in Golden when he died of a heart attack on March 1, 1864. Doyle is buried near his ranch site along with his wife and son, his headstone of beautiful Beulah red marble.[5]

A gristmill is a mill that grinds more than one kind of grain.

In 1865, Otto Mears first appeared on the Colorado scene, when he opened a general merchandise store in Guadalupe. He also joined in partnership with Lafayette Head to build a sawmill and a gristmill there. (A gristmill is a mill that grinds more than one kind of grain.) Because the local Mexican farmers could not produce enough grain for the gristmill, Mears moved in 1866, this time to Saguache to raise wheat for the Conejos Mill and to open another store. During the next year, he brought in a mower, a reaper, and a threshing machine for his crops. All were the first such implements in the San Luis Valley. He continued to supply wheat to the Conejos mill until 1873, at which time he built another mill in Saguache.

The mill at Saguache supplied a ready market for the wheat grown in the upper San Luis Valley in the 1860s to 1880s. Otto Mears was an early Colorado businessman there, growing and harvesting wheat that he undoubtedly used to supply Chief Ouray's band of Utes by government contract. From *History of Agriculture in Colorado* by Alvin Steinel.

While Mears was in Saguache, he won a government contract to supply food and supplies to Chief Ouray and the Ute Indians in the San Juan mountains to the west. He developed a strong friendship with the Indians and a firm understanding of the necessity of good roads through the mountains. He later built toll roads and railroads to move supplies and miners into the San Juan region.[6]

Peter K. Dotson, another southern Colorado pioneer, built a mill on the St. Charles River, not very far north of the first mill at Greenhorn. Dotson had come west in 1851, traveling from his home in Independence, Missouri, to Salt Lake City on a family cattle drive. He stayed in Utah until 1859, when he moved to the Pueblo area, operating a hotel there. While in Pueblo he, along with his brother, scouted the land along the St. Charles River and in 1865 leased a nine thousand–acre tract from the Nolan Land Grant, purchasing the land in 1868. In 1879 a reporter and illustrator visited the Dotson Ranch and depicted ranch buildings and a gristmill in a book called *New Colorado and the Santa Fe Trail,* published in 1880. The mill was probably built between 1865 and 1879, though there is no record of the exact date. Dotson called the mill La Maquina de Los San Carlos. When the reporter stopped at the mill in 1879, he found it empty with the miller nowhere in sight. There was a note attached to the door, however, from another potential customer, written with a poetic bend:

> Where, oh, where did the miller go,
> And leave us no sign or trace?
> The next time to mill we must go,
> We will go to some other place.[7]

Today a little settlement called Burnt Mill still stands where Burnt Mill Road crosses the St. Charles River, giving one a fairly good idea of the eventual fate of the structure.[8]

On June 3, 1860, John W. Smith rode into Denver with a wagon loaded with machinery, including the first imported mill burrs (millstones were also called burrs)

Peter Dotson built this mill at the crossing of the Taos Trail and the Rio del San Carlos—now the St. Charles River—around 1870. Notice the flume that brings water for turning the millstones. This illustration was done for *Harper's Weekly* magazine in 1879.

and a steam-powered flour mill. Smith was a visionary who built numerous mills: planing lumber mills, the Excelsior Flour Mill, and a woolen textile mill. Smith had many varied interests, also investing in local transportation. He was president, for a time, of the Denver, South Park, and Pacific Railroad. He organized the Denver Steam Heat Company, a predecessor of Xcel Energy, which still uses some of Denver Steam Heat's equipment and piping to heat Denver's older downtown buildings.

Andrew Douty built a mill below the outcropping of red rocks at the mouth of Boulder Canyon in 1866. After it burned in 1878, it was replaced by the Yount Mill. Water from Boulder Creek supplied the power. Courtesy Carnegie Branch Library for Local History, Boulder, Colorado.

There were many fast, little streams that could nicely turn a millstone in the new territory. Pella, a settlement west of Longmont on the St. Vrain River, had a mill, as did Littleton on the South Platte River and Cañon City on the Arkansas River. Flour mills also were built near the developing settlements of Denver, Pueblo, Grand Junction, Golden, Longmont, Loveland, Del Norte, Montrose, Alamosa, Holyoke, and Wray. There were at least four on the Poudre River, all in Fort Collins, and one on the Big Thompson River at a settlement called St. Louis, near Loveland.

In the Boulder area in 1860, the Wellman Brothers grew wheat on their farm at Forty-eighth Street and Arapahoe Avenue, as did Andrew Douty along South Boulder Creek that same year. In 1861, Douty built Boulder County's first gristmill on South Boulder Creek, carving the stones from local rock. He would build another mill, known as the Red Rocks Mill, on Boulder Creek at the west end of the city of Boulder. Douty then built a mill on the Big Thompson River at St. Louis in 1867, located a mile east of present-day Loveland.

In 1877 E. B. Yount and his wife bought the Red Rocks Mill from Douty and completely rebuilt it. They made it as fireproof as was possible in those days, using an iron roof and stone walls. But it wasn't enough, as the mill burned down in 1900.[9]

Fire was a constant threat to all flour mills. Flour is a highly combustible substance with a low ignition temperature. It is susceptible to spontaneous combustion, and any small spark or source of flame can cause an explosion. Most mills burned down, and some burned more than once, as was reported of the Yount mill.

Wheat was transported to the Yount Mill by Boulder farmers and emptied into a hopper at the front of the building. The wheat dropped down a chute into a bin in the basement, where it was cleaned and scoured. Then the grinding process began,

Three workers stop for pictures inside the Sternberg Mill in Boulder. The wooden chutes brought grain down to the scrubbers and cleaners before it moved along to the crushing rollers. Cleanliness was important in a flour mill, not only for sanitation reasons but also to limit the amount of flour dust that could support spontaneous combustion and fires. Courtesy Carnegie Branch Library for Local History, Boulder, Colorado.

with bran middlings being removed and sold as livestock feed. The remainder was moved by conveyor to the second floor and reground in grinders that were four feet in diameter. The mill had a capacity of 250 sacks of flour per day. The millstones, conveyors, and other equipment were powered by a ninety-eight-horsepower, thirty-six-inch Risdon waterwheel manufactured in Mount Holly, New Jersey. The wheel's design had won honors at the 1876 Centennial Exposition and was the first of its kind used in Colorado. Although the site was known as the Yount Mill, it was officially the Colorado State Flouring Mill. It was destroyed by fire again on July 7, 1905.[10]

Fire was the scourge of flour mills. Almost every mill burned down at least once. In 1931 the Sternburg Mill in Boulder burned and lost sixty thousand bushels of wheat. This fire was not the result of spontaneous combustion, but rather was thought to be of "incendiary origin." Courtesy Carnegie Branch Library for Local History, Boulder Historical Society Collection.

In 1873 the Jay Sternberg family built a flour mill east of Boulder at what is now Folsom Avenue and Twenty-sixth Street. It burned down in 1889. Boulder investors had the mill rebuilt at Eleventh and Water streets (now Canyon Boulevard) next to the railroad tracks. This successful mill sold "Bread King and Lily White Flour" until it was destroyed by arsonists during the Depression, on February 18, 1931.[11]

In 1865 Peter Housel and John Debacker built a flour mill in the community of Valmont, four miles east of Boulder, using water from the Jones-Donnelly ditch. Other small Boulder County mills were built in Canfield and along the White Rocks area farther east on Boulder Creek.[12]

In 1867, Fort Collins pioneers Auntie Stone and Henry C. Peterson began construction of a gristmill to grind both wheat and corn grown by local farmers. Henry Peterson, an Ohio native, was the first civilian to settle at the old Fort Collins, according to Ansel Watrous, a later owner. Peterson, a millwright by occupation, arrived in Colorado in 1859

Lindell Flour Mills,

Wholesale Dealers in

Flour, Grain and Feed.

"Defiance," "Jack Frost," "Queen," "Leader."

Whole Wheat Flour,
Wheatlets,
Graham and Meal.

The highest cash price paid for Wheat.

B. F. HOTTEL, Manager.

FORT : COLLINS, : COLORADO.

This full-page advertisement for the Lindell Mill appeared in the 1898 *Larimer County Business Directory*. The equipment shown in the cutaway would have been described in the 1887 Fort Collins article. The drawing shows the raceway on the Poudre River side providing water to the 140-horsepower turbine. The Lindell was owned by the Colorado Feed and Elevator conglomerate at the time.

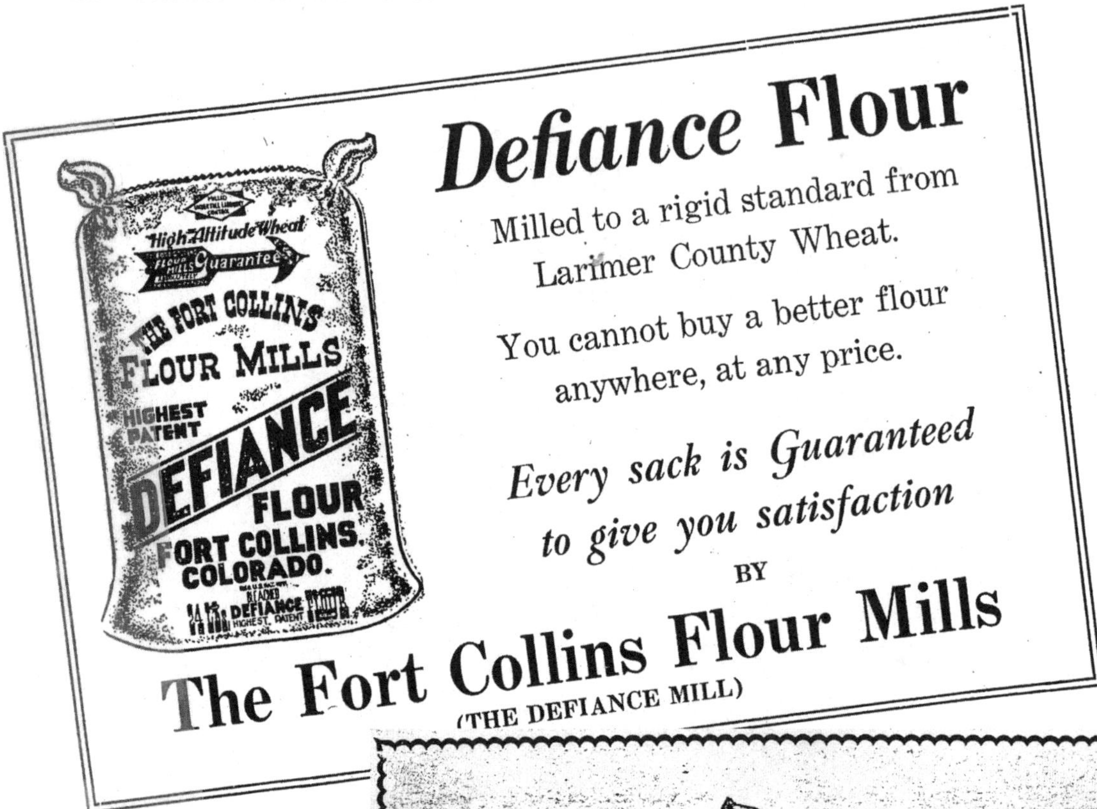

In 1938 the Lindell Mill was still producing Defiance flour, as shown in these advertisements in the *Larimer County Business Directory*.

to pursue gold mining and freighting. In 1864, he became a gunsmith for the soldiers at Fort Collins. Peterson cut logs for and built Auntie Stone's boardinghouse at the fort. Peterson and Stone built and operated a mill until 1873, when Joseph Mason bought the enterprise. According to a Fort Collins *Coloradoan* edition in July 1975, the original mill's equipment was built using machinery from Buffalo, New York. Grain was ground by granite burrs powered by a waterwheel. In 1886 the mill, then known as the Lindell Mill, burned but was immediately rebuilt by the Colorado Milling and Elevator Company.[13] The Fort Collins *Express* gave a glowing account of the new mill and its equipment, which used 437,000 bricks for its 45-by-65-foot, four-story building. A 28.5-foot drop of water from a 40-inch pipe from upstream powered an "improved" 35-inch-diameter Leffell turbine generating 140 horsepower. This turned overhead shafts and belts to all the different equipment requiring power, including rollers instead of stone burrs, and purifiers to separate the bran from the middlings—also known as the Hungarian Process. This mill had a capacity of five hundred sacks of flour every twenty-four hours and cost $50,000 to construct. There were twelve double sets of rolls, one feed roll, three flour packers, and a bran packer on the first floor. The second floor housed two Cyclone dust collectors, one scourer, a receiving separator, and a milling separator. The third floor supported one Eureka separator, five Smith bolts, four Gray scalpers, one cockle reel, one scourer, six Smith middling purifiers, two Smith center reels, and eight Cyclone dust collectors. The upper fourth story contained one B&L separator, one Eureka magnetic cockle separator, one Cyclone dust collector, two Smith center reels, eleven Cray scalpers, one Eureka brush, a Morse bolt, and five Smith bolts. This list from both the 1895 and 1901 Sanborn Insurance maps doesn't quite match up to the more organized but similar equipment in the cutaway advertising illustration in the *Larimer County Business Directory* of 1898.

The Lindell Mill continued to be in use throughout the twentieth century, burning down twice more, each time rebuilt with more modern equipment—an evolving, living phoenix. Although flour production ended in 1948, the company operates today as Ranchway Feed and Supply, milling grain for livestock for the entire Rocky Mountain region. Flour from the Lindell was sold under various names, including Pride of Colorado, Jack Frost, Snowflake, Defiance, and Snow Trader.

During the nineteenth century, there were advances in the method of cleaning the wheat, using screens and air blowers. The smutter was a machine that scoured the kernel with an air blast to blow away the dirt, making the final product cleaner and less gritty. Silk soon replaced bolting cloth as the sifting medium, as it had a much finer weave. Automatic machinery continuously cleaned the bolts or forced more flour through even finer weaves. There was always a desire to have the finished product finer, cleaner, and whiter. Finer, whiter flour made more refined bread, a mark of quality for a baker who often was a housewife as well. Any small advance

The mill in Alamosa produced three hundred sacks of flour a day and could store one hundred thousand bushels of wheat. It was one of J. K. Mullen's mills, part of the Colorado Milling and Elevator Company. Courtesy Denver Public Library, Western History Collection, X-6445.

toward more refined flour was advertised as a major achievement and used to sell more of that brand.

In 1884 farmers in the vicinity of Fort Collins joined together in an effort to improve their livelihood through the organization of a cooperative, the Farmers Protective Association, as did farmers in many other Colorado communities. The group incorporated with the objective of building mills and elevators, manufacturing flour, and buying and selling real estate. The organizers hoped to protect the interests of local wheat growers against millers' discrimination in pricing policies for the purchase of grain. Leaders of the group included J. E. and Z. C. Plummer, John G. Coy, Peter Anderson, and Joseph Murray. The farmers built the Harmony Mill, which had the capacity to process six hundred 100-pound sacks of flour each day. The Harmony Mill, across the street from the Lindell Mill, quickly ran into problems through mismanagement, and by 1901 the mill was closed and in litigation with creditors. In 1906, the Sanborn Insurance Map describes the building as a "vacant old mill." The Harmony Mill building was restored and remodeled in 1995 and is used today for office space. A third mill was located near the Greeley and Salt Lake railroad tracks to

Greeley just outside of Fort Collins. It was owned and operated by J. M. Hoffman. A fourth, the Interocean Mill, also added to Fort Collins' flour capacity. The first Weld County flour mill was built in Greeley in 1873 by S. S. Kennedy and Company. It used the trademark Snowflake, and the flour was milled especially for high-altitude baking. The mill, called the Model Flour Mill, used a special process for Weld County's hard, dryland wheat and marketed its flour nationally.[14]

Farther east on the plains of Colorado, mills were also built at Lamar, Holyoke, and Wray. New settlers homesteaded the dry plains soils using irrigation water from the Platte, Republican, and Arkansas rivers.

In 1891 the Wray Milling Company constructed its mill. Officers of the company were L. M. Butts, J. W. Fulton, and J. W. Pickle. Later a fourth interest was sold to H. H. Mason. The millrace started on the Republican River and was dug to allow a fall of one foot per mile. J. W. Pickle was general manager in charge of construction of the mill. Machinery for it was purchased from Barnard and Lees Company of Indianapolis. The building's basement and foundations were of stone from the nearby hills, and the rest was lumber purchased from Mankato, Kansas. About forty men, including farmers, raised the mill in three to four days. The waterwheel turned on a wooden shaft designed by Pickle.

The mill ground three grades of flour: Patented, Straight Cream, and XXXX. Flour was placed in fifty-pound bags and shipped as far as Denver. Bran, buckwheat flour, and shorts—a by-product of wheat processing that consists of germ, bran, and coarse meal—were also produced and sold. Carload lots of feed grain were shipped to Akron and Yuma. Farmers often brought two bushel sacks of wheat, about sixty pounds, to be exchanged for thirty-two pounds of flour, ten pounds of bran, or eight pounds of shorts. Pickle sold his interest in the mill to Butts and Fulton in 1893, who, in turn, sold to Mr. Stickley and Richard Beaver in 1896. The mill later was sold to the Shannon Grain Company.[15]

Holyoke chartered a Farmer's Cooperative in 1920 and bought the Holyoke Equity Merchantile Company, which included a flour mill. Flour was milled there until 1936, using the brand names Tip-Top and Holyoke's Best.[16] Brighton had the Marvel Flour Mill, located on Main Street southwest of the railroad tracks. Like many of Brighton's landmarks, this building was torn down.[17]

In later years, after the Colorado Central Railroad completed its rail line between Longmont and Cheyenne, flour mills were built along the grade in the towns of Loveland, Berthoud, and Longmont. The Big Thompson Milling and Elevator Company built a new mill in Loveland in 1891 that produced flour under the brand names Silver Dollar and Loveland Patent.[18]

Longmont would ultimately have seven mills. As the population of the area swelled with people who had expertise in farming, much more grain became available,

Longmont had three flour mills, including this one, the Farmers' Coop Mill. Farmers often banded together to try to get better prices for their wheat than offered by Colorado Milling and Elevator, which also had a large mill in Longmont. Courtesy Denver Public Library, Western History Collection, X-10261.

and that supply increased the demand for mills. Many farming communities had a mill so that grain didn't need to be transported long distances. The relationship between demand for local milling at small volumes, transportation and storage costs of grain, and more efficient milling at larger and better-capitalized mills continues to the present. It was a complex relationship colored by egos of well-financed mill and elevator operators, who could buy grain from farmers at harvest when prices were lowest, store the grain, and resell when prices rose.

As transportation costs diminished, farmers could go elsewhere for better prices, and mill operators could likewise bring grain from longer distances to larger, more efficient mills. Farmers resented the difficulty of capitalizing storage elevators built in their area. Grain elevator operators sometimes earned more profit from the storage of wheat than the farmers made growing it. Consequently, the farmers banded together in the form of cooperative organizations to build and operate both elevators and mills. Sometimes the strategy worked, as in Longmont and Denver, but sometimes it didn't, as at the Harmony Mill in Fort Collins. Every town close to a wheat field wanted its own flour mill. J. K. Mullen took advantage of this local pride to expand his Colorado

The Eaton Milling & Elevator Co.

WHOLESALE

FLOUR, GRAIN, FEED AND POTATOES

Graham and Corn Meal.

OUR SPECIALTIES.

Silver Coin Flour, Gold Dust Flour

Gold Coin Flour

G. H. DENIO - - Manager.

EATON, COLO.

The little town of Eaton, north of Greeley, also had its own flour mill, selling Silver Coin, Gold Coin, and Gold Dust flour, as advertised in the *Weld County Directory*. The mill ground other grains besides wheat, as clearly stated in the ad. Courtesy Greeley Museum.

Milling and Elevator into those towns, and he was smart enough to name the mills after the towns: Alamosa Flour Mill, Pueblo Flour Mill, Lamar Flour Mill, etc. The advertisements for flour also reflected this local flavor with the term "Pride" in the names: Loveland Pride, Arvada Pride, and Pride of Colorado.

No article about flour milling in Colorado would be complete without a discussion of Mullen. He absolutely dominated the industry in the state from his Denver base. John Kernan Mullen, a young Irish immigrant, had left school at age fourteen to work in a flour mill in his hometown of Oriskany, New York, and eventually headed a multimillion-dollar milling empire. He came to Colorado in 1871, having managed mills in both New York and Kansas. His timing was less than perfect. In the early 1870s, wheat production could not keep up with the demand of overabundant grain elevators

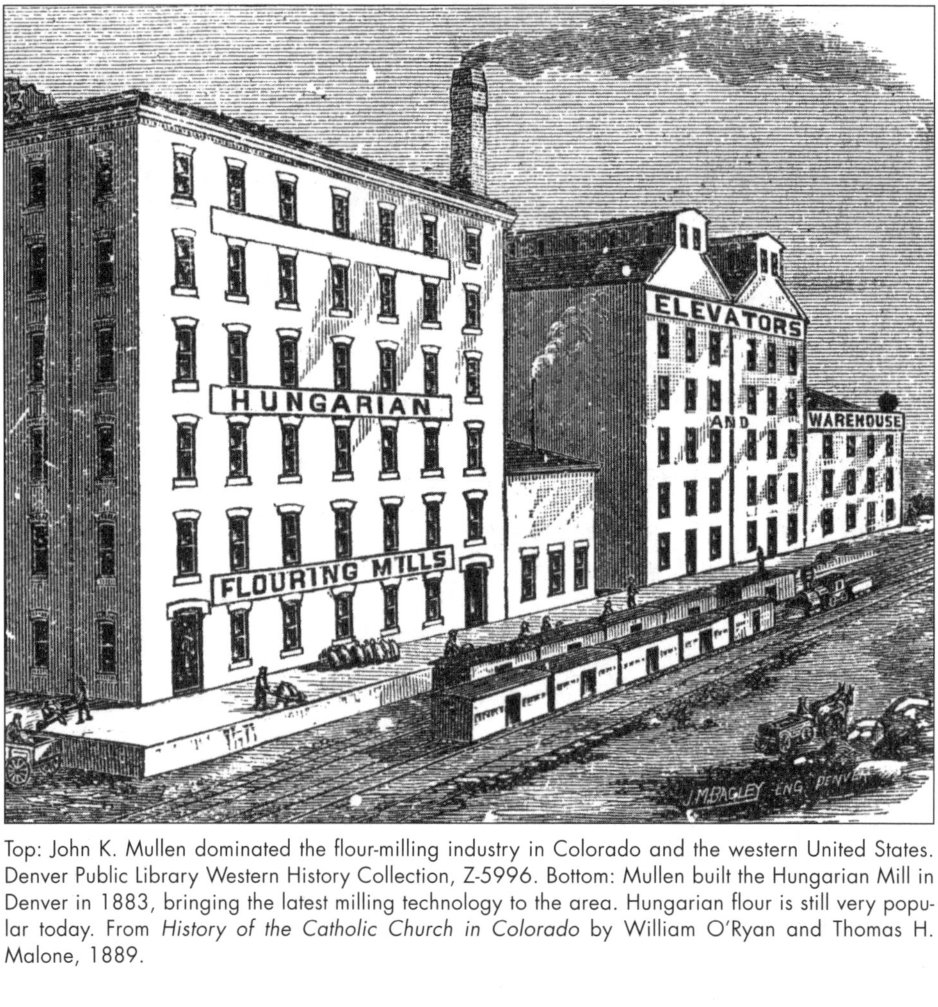

Top: John K. Mullen dominated the flour-milling industry in Colorado and the western United States. Denver Public Library Western History Collection, Z-5996. Bottom: Mullen built the Hungarian Mill in Denver in 1883, bringing the latest milling technology to the area. Hungarian flour is still very popular today. From *History of the Catholic Church in Colorado* by William O'Ryan and Thomas H. Malone, 1889.

and new mills. No one was hiring. He did, however, finally start work in west Denver for the Merchant Mills in exchange for room and board. He rose quickly to mill manager and, in 1875, quit to become part owner of another Denver mill. By 1880, he was the acknowledged leader of the industry. Mullen's Colorado Grain Elevator and Hungarian Flour companies owned wheat fields, grain elevators, and flour mills throughout the Rockies.

Mullen consistently was at the forefront of milling technology. He was the first to bring to Denver the Hungarian roller process of gradual reduction of wheat to flour. In 1881–1882 he renovated his Excelsior Mill, modifying it to use the new process and building a big new mill called the Hungarian Milling and Elevator Company.

This change in the process occurred in the eastern United States in the early 1870s. It was different enough from the old process to be granted a U.S. patent, and the flour was advertised as "patented" flour: Minneapolis Patented, Buffalo Patented, or Colorado Patented. The new process increased the amount of bread that could be made from a pound of wheat. To the old steps of cleaning, grinding, and sifting were added two more: purification and regrinding. The earlier process attempted to cut and grind the wheat in one step with the stone burrs very close together. All bran, middlings, and undesirable pieces were removed in the later sifting step. The new process, with stones slightly apart or at lower pressure, cracked the outer shell or bran, then screened or purified the bran and middlings and reground them. The purifier was a group of moving sieves with a strong air blast that blew away the lighter bran and allowed the middlings to pass through. They could then be reground. The old process sought to minimize the middlings, the new process to maximize and regrind them.

With the new system, it was discovered that using rollers to crack the wheat worked better than grinding stones. This change was first developed in Central Europe, where the wheat was similar to the harder wheat being grown in the U.S. Midwest. The rollers—originally granite, then porcelain, and eventually chilled cast iron—gradually cracked and smashed the wheat to flour in decreasing steps, lowering the heat that built up in the roller and discoloring the flour. The rollers took far less power to crack and smash the grain, and the whole process was continuous, with wheat passing through the various reduction rollers and emerging as flour at the end. Rollers were easier to control and maintain. A mill's stone grooves were redressed every three to four days, requiring that the mill be shut down, but rollers could run for months before needing maintenance. Also, since the process was done in steps, wheat of many different grades could be marketed to the public. In Hungary, eleven grades were sold, although the American consumer preferred no more than four or five. The new flour was called Hungarian Flour, and the process soon was recognized as superior. Hungarian flour became highly desirable and is still popular today.[19]

Mullen also led the industry's consolidation phase as smaller, less efficient mills went out of business in the age-old profit-margin squeeze. The Colorado Milling and

The Berthoud Museum has this old set of millstones from one of the Berthoud flour mills. The steel bands help hold the stones together during the milling process. The stone on the right turns with the shaft passing through the stationary stone on the left. Author's collection, 2006.

Elevator Company (CM&E) purchased many of the mills, selling flour under common trade names, buying grain from more distant sources, building new modern mills in wheat-producing areas of the western states, and generally making the milling operation more efficient. The CM&E was the organization most despised and mistrusted by the state's farmers, leading them to organize cooperatives for grain elevators and competing mills almost always having the word Farmers in their name. By 1889 the CM&E owned four mills in Denver, plus mills in Golden, Longmont, Greeley, and Fort Collins. It also owned grain elevators in Erie and Berthoud.

Mullen earned millions of dollars milling flour in Colorado. He also gave a large portion of it back to his adopted state and city. He was a generous benefactor to the Catholic Church, to a home for the aged, and to a home for young wayward boys that would become Mullen High School. In many ways, Mullen epitomizes the pioneer who came west to find not only gold in the streams around the foot of Pikes Peak but also the opportunity to better oneself through hard work, vision, luck, and skill.

Notes

[1] William M. Thayer, *Marvels of the New West* (Norwich, CT: The Henry Bill Publishing Co., 1890), 235–236.

[2] Janet LeCompte, *Pueblo, Hardscrabble, and Greenhorn* (Norman: University of Oklahoma Press, 1978), 143–145.

[3] Connell, 96.

[4] *Rocky Mountain News*, October 8, 1860.

[5] LeCompte, 256–258.

[6] Connell, 133.

[7] A. A. Hayes, *New Colorado and the Santa Fe Trail* (London: C. Kegan Paul & Co., 1881), 29.

[8] *From Maces Holes to Beulah* (Beulah, CO: Beulah Historical Society, 1979), 74–76.

[9] Phyllis Smith, *From Settlement to City* (Boulder, CO: Pruett Publishing, 1981), 152.

[10] Barker, "Over the Shoulder," *Boulder Daily Camera, Focus*, 1970.

[11] Smith, 152.

[12] Anne Dyne, *Pioneer Voices of Boulder County* .

[13] *Fort Collins Express*, January 1, 1887.

[14] Carol Rein Shwayder, *Weld County Old and New* (Greeley, CO: Unicorn Ventures, 1983), A43.

[15] Charles Pickle, "History of the Wray Flour Mill," manuscript (Denver Public Library, Western History Collection).

[16] *West Yuma County Colorado* (Yuma, CO: Centennial Book Committee, 1985).

[17] *History of Brighton, Colorado and the Surrounding Area, 1887–1987* (Curtis Media Corp., 1987), 40.

[18] Jessen, *Railroads of Northern Colorado*, 168.

[19] William Convery, *Pride of the Rockies* (Boulder: University Press of Colorado, 2000)

CHAPTER 2

Breweries

D. C. Oakes' guidebook list did not include a barrel of beer for the trip from his home along the Missouri River. It included, instead, fifty pounds of coffee and eight pounds of tea. The weight difference between dry coffee and tea ingredients and the much heavier barrels of beer made the drinking of beer on the trip prohibitive. The six gallons of brandy he did include probably was used for more than "medicinal" purposes. On the trail to the Pikes Peak region, Oakes could have sipped a few suds at Dobytown, the nearby "town" used by Fort Kearney's soldiers to get some rest and relaxation.

But even before 1859, beer was brewed from wheat at the well-known whiskey distillery outside of Taos, according to Lewis Garrard in his book about the Taos Trail in 1847. This establishment furnished both beer and whiskey to the trappers, traders, and settlers in what would become southern Colorado. Garrard also mentions hops and grapes being grown by William Bent at his farm along the Purgatory River.[1]

After the initial gold rush to the Pikes Peak region, there was a strong demand for beer in the new territory, but there was virtually no supply. Full kegs were heavy and expensive to transport across the prairie. Therefore, it is not surprising that an entrepreneur would anticipate this demand for beer. In Colorado that person was John P. Good.

Good brought a wagon full of hops to the Pikes Peak gold region in 1859. Upon reaching Denver, he sold the hops to Fred Z. Salomon, agent for the J. B. Doyle Mercantile Company. Good headed back east for more brewery supplies, and over the next eight years he made sixteen trips to the supply towns of Leavenworth and Saint Josephs, bringing a variety of merchandise, including hops and barley seeds, for the local farmers.

Salomon partnered with Charles Tasher to turn the cartload of hops into beer from Denver's first brewery, the Rocky Mountain Brewery. Four months later, Tasher

Top: The area's first brewery, the Rocky Mountain Brewery, was located in Denver, west of the Platte River. At the time of this drawing, it was owned by Salomon, Endlich, and Good. A single horse is shown turning a wheel to supply the necessary power. Courtesy Colorado Historical Society, 10038107. Left: John P. Good fathered the brewing industry in the region by bringing brewing supplies instead of mining equipment. He would own breweries in Denver and other Colorado towns, including Denver's first, the Rocky Mountain Brewery.

left for Central City, and Salomon brought Good and Charles Endlich in as partners. Four years later Good was the sole owner of the Rocky Mountain Brewery, even though he continued to make the long trip back east for supplies.[2]

John P. Good would remain in the center of the competitive brewery wars in Colorado Territory. He was born in Alsace-Lorraine in 1835, immigrated to the United States in 1854, and went west with the Pikes Peak gold seekers in 1859. After being accused of favoring one particular Denver barkeeper, Good stated in an 1866 advertisement in the *Rocky Mountain News,* his business practice of selling beer at low prices to all saloon owners. He hired Phillip Zang as manager of the Rocky Mountain Brewery in 1869 while he expanded his own holdings into the developing Leadville area. There he built a brewery, invested in railroads to the area, and expanded his Denver real estate, building the Good Block at Sixteenth and Larimer streets. He sold the Rocky Mountain

Brewery to Zang in 1871. In 1900, Good foreclosed on the owner of Denver's Milwaukee Brewery, renamed it Tivoli, and a year later consolidated it with the Union Brewery. He continued as one of Colorado's leading capitalists until his death in 1918.[3]

In the mid-nineteenth century a major social change occurred in the brewing and drinking of beer. Prior to that time, beer had been a domestic drink, the major drink of all—men, women, and children. People drank beer because drinking water made them sick. No one knew why, but when water was processed into beer, the liquid was safe to drink. We now know that the boiling of water, part of the brewing process, kills microbes that carry diseases. Because beer was a domestic process, it fell under the jurisdiction of the woman of the household. Most brewers in colonial America and in England were women—alewives. This was no longer true once large numbers of Germans immigrated to America, bringing their male-dominated beer traditions and a desire to commercialize the process.

The brewing process as practiced by Good and his Colorado counterparts in the 1860s varied little from that of most brewmasters elsewhere: the grain was soaked in warm water for several days until it germinated. How long the

Prohibition was a difficult time for breweries. Most closed and never reopened. Those that survived sold "near beer," which was nonalcoholic beer and malt extract. Coors was no exception, as shown in this advertisement. Courtesy Coors Brewing Company.

sprout was allowed to grow varied from brewmaster to brewmaster. Nature turned the starch of the grain to maltose, a natural sugar. The sprouted grain was then dried over an open fire, but in later years, in a kiln. The dried malt was ground fine in a malt mill, which was similar to other grain mills. This process, called malting, yields a powder called malt, the same ingredient used in malted milk. During Prohibition, most breweries marketed and sold malted milk or bulk malt. The malt could be roasted for a longer or shorter period to impart different amounts of color to the finished product.

Once in powdered form, the malt was added to hot water in a container called a mash tun, where it steeped for one to two hours. Maltose leached from the mash into the hot liquid, making a sweet mixture called wort (pronounced wert). Different mashing times and temperatures slightly change the flavor of the beer to come. The wort was transferred to a brew kettle, where it was boiled for up to two hours. This kettle was usually made of copper, which conducts heat evenly. Boiling effectively killed any unwanted bacteria or yeast that might spoil the brew.

Up until the mid-nineteenth century, boiling of the wort in the brew kettle was always done over an open fire, with the brewmaster testing the temperature of the kettle by touching it. Although brewmasters were very good at this, maintaining consistent temperatures from batch to batch was not guaranteed. With the advent of steam power, the open fire was soon replaced. Uniform heating of the kettle became a matter of proper kettle design and control of steam temperature.[4]

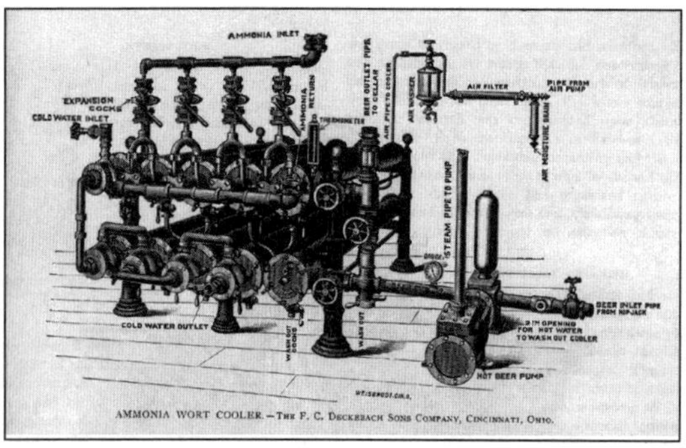

Drawing of an 1890s heat exchanger for cooling wort during the brewing process. From a catalog by the F. C. Deckebach Sons Co.

Hops were added in varying amounts at this step to counteract the sweetness of the brew. More hops steeped for a longer time made the beer more bitter. To produce a stronger-tasting beer, hops might be boiled for up to thirty minutes. Other ingredients were sometimes added at this point. Cereal grains such as corn or rice were added to lighten the finished product. It is illegal to add anything but hops to the wort in Germany and still call the finished brew *bier*.

After brewing, the wort was cooled and strained to remove the hop leaves and other residue. This was done in big flat pans in olden times, but as refrigeration equipment became available, a variety of cooling methods using chilled liquids were employed.

The next step in the brewing process was transfer of the wort to a fermenting tank and cooling it to the desired temperature—cooler for lager, warmer for ales. When the right temperature was reached, the proper yeast was added or "pitched." Fermentation lasted from a couple of days to two weeks, until the yeast had consumed the sugar, turning it into alcohol. The more sugar that was consumed, the higher the alcohol content. At this point the wort was considered beer.

Two types of brewers' yeast were used, depending upon the kind of beer desired. Ales used *Saccharomyces cerevisiae*, and lagers used *Saccharomyces uvarum.* The lager yeast prefers fermentation at cool temperatures: 38 to 50 degrees F. The ale yeast prefers warmer temperatures: 60 to 72 degrees F. Lager yeast ferments on the bottom of the wort, ale yeast on top.[5] A good lager required brewers to chill the fermentation tanks to below 50 degrees F. Before mechanical refrigeration, this meant that every brewery had ice-storing capability, and hence the size of the icehouse or the ice pond was an important statistic in describing the brewery. Breweries led the way in bringing modern refrigeration methods and equipment to the nation.

The beer was allowed to age in an airtight tank, where it continued to ferment, adding natural carbonation. Aging could take weeks to months and might be done in wooden containers with wood chips added that clarified the beer and imparted a pleasant taste, such as "beech wood aged."

Each part of the process affected the color, taste, or odor of the final product. Brewers used these differences to market their beer as the finest, best-tasting brew in the whole world or at least in the small part of the world that was their local market.[6]

Other German immigrants also adopted the Colorado Territory as their new fatherland and started businesses and breweries. Moritz Sigi built a brewery in Auraria on the site of what would become the Tivoli in 1866. Phillip Zang bought the Rocky Mountain Brewery and renamed it after himself in 1871. Adolph Coors arrived in 1873 and with venture capital from Jacob Schueler started the Schueler and Coors Brewery in Golden. Frank Weisenhorn and Charles Voegtle established a brewery in Boulder in 1875, although one had been there in the mid-1860s, built and operated none too successfully by William Cook. Weisenhorn's Boulder City Brewery became the Crystal Springs Brewery in 1897. It burned down in 1921.[7] Charles Fischer built and operated breweries on the Western Slope at Silverton, Gunnison, Lake City, and Howardsville.

Henry Schneider started a brewery in Trinidad in 1873, one of only five that survived after Prohibition. It closed its doors during World War II only to open under different ownership, and after several ownership changes finally closed permanently in 1957.

Along with the change from female to male domination of the brewing process in the mid-nineteenth century, women organized a movement against the drinking of all alcoholic beverages, as excessive drinking by their men was causing stress in the family unit and in society as a whole. The temperance movement was born in this country when the state of Maine passed a law prohibiting the sale of alcoholic drinks in 1846. Prohibition laws were passed state by state, with Colorado shutting down the sale and manufacture of alcohol in 1915. Finally, the federal government passed the Eighteenth Amendment to the Constitution, eliminating all sales of liquor in 1920. All breweries stopped making beer and most went out of business. The Prohibition laws were repealed in 1933 with the passage of the Twenty-first Amendment to the Constitution.

In Colorado, less well-known people started small breweries in almost every permanent or semipermanent settlement. It did not take much: large pans, open fires, water, hops, yeast, and barley. Paul Lindstrom in Empire, along the Berthoud Pass road, built a brewery to supply beer to miners and loggers in the Empire Valley. His wife traveled to Denver by covered wagon twice a year to obtain barley and hops. The brewery had a heated, perforated floor to dry and sprout the barley and a waterpowered malt

Top: The Zang brewing company, the largest in Denver at the time of this advertisement in the *Colorado Illustrated Business Directory*, had a capacity of one hundred thousand barrels of beer per year. It replaced the Rocky Mountain Brewery in 1859. Above: The Boulder Brewery was located about where the current library is near Ninth and Arapaho streets. In 1897 the original owners sold it, and it was renamed the Crystal Springs Brewery. Courtesy Carnegie Branch Library for Local History, Boulder Historical Society Collection.

Left: The Silverton Brewery, c. 1891, owned by Charles Fischer, supposedly had a beer tap on an outside wall for use by thirsty locals, possibly from the hot, smoky, smelter in the background. Courtesy Denver Public Library, Western History Collection, X-1739. Below: Tivoli was one of the breweries that survived Prohibition, brewing Tivoli beer from its Denver location until 1969. Only Walters' brewery in Pueblo and Coors' brewery in Golden lasted longer. Courtesy Colorado Historical Society, X9229.

mill to grind malt near gold and silver mills grinding ore. Lindstrom's son-in-law, Joseph Guanella, helped manage the operation, which was listed as Guanella's Brewery in the 1879 *Colorado Business Directory*.[8]

To make barrels of the brew required more in the way of capital. The brewery at Rosita in the Wet Mountain Valley, operated by T. D. Townsend, had a capacity of twenty barrels a day, each barrel holding thirty-two gallons of beer. He brewed only twice a week in 1881. His brewery is described in the 1881 Baskins' *History of the Arkansas River Valley*.

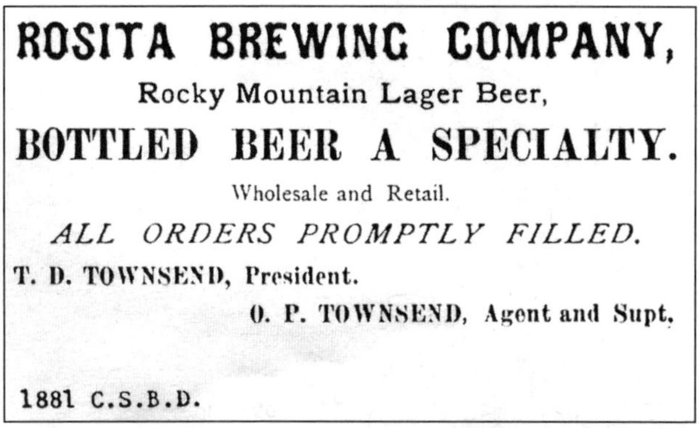

Top: The Townsend brothers placed this advertisement in the 1881 *Colorado Business Directory*. Rosita had a brewery and a bottling plant, supplying suds to the citizens of the Wet Mountain Valley. Bottom: This drawing of the brewery in Aspen depicts not only the brewery but also the ice pond and the icehouse that were used to maintain a supply of ice to keep the wort and beer cool during the brewing process. From *One Hundred Years of Brewing* by H.S Rich.

> This company was established in Rosita with a capital of $1500, in 1874, has grown to be one of the largest manufacturing enterprises of the county, it being one of the largest breweries in the state. The establishment consists of a three-story concrete building, 40x60 feet, with iron roof and capacious cellar, besides a large granary, engine-house, boiler house, large vats for freezing ice and an ice-house capable of holding 200 tons, bottling-house, etc. Recently a new boiler, 30 horsepower has been added. The brewery has a capacity of twenty barrels at a brew, which could be made daily, but, at present, only two brews (forty barrels) are made per week. The quality of the beer is excellent, equaling the best Milwaukee beer, the climate and water being favorable to the manufacture of an extra article. This beer was shipped in large quantities to Leadville and Saguache County, until recent home competition in these places has taken away the profit. The establishment is worth $70,000.[9]

Baskins' historical series on Colorado's counties were "vanity articles," often telling exaggerated stories and facts. The above is a good example. The brewery at Rosita may well have been one of the largest manufacturing enterprises in the county, but it was not even close to being the largest brewery in the state. Even its seven-day maximum capacity of 140 barrels could not compare to the Zang Brewery's output of two hundred barrels a week actually sold (ten thousand barrels a year). Even Gaw's Brewery in Leadville, probably the "home competition" alluded to in the article that has "taken away the profit," produced 120 barrels a day in 1881. Installation of a new boiler is an indication that the brew kettle was probably heated by steam.

Townsend's Rosita Brewery did last, however, from 1874 to 1889, the last year it was listed in the *Colorado Business Directory*. A cloudburst wiped out long segments of the Rio Grande's narrow-gauge railroad up Grape Creek to nearby Westcliffe, causing abandonment of the line in 1889. This probably was the death knell for the brewery.

Another brewery was established in the Wet Mountain Valley a little later when Carl and Demgan listed a brewery in Westcliffe in the 1894 *Colorado Business Directory*. Four years later Hallanger replaced Demgan, and one year later Fuchs and Wissler purchased the business. Various owners struggled to keep the brewery open, exchanging ownership and brewery names until the Wet Mountain Valley Brewing Company finally closed in 1904 after it moved to nearby Silvercliffe.

On March 11, 1874, the *Golden Transcript* reported:

> Adolph Coors' new Golden Brewery installed a mash tub of sixty barrels capacity and a brew kettle that would hold thirty barrels of wort. His six horsepower Clayton steam-powered pump would push sixty barrels of brew around the new brewery each hour. There was a malt mill, a storeroom for grain, malt and hops and a ninety-barrel water tank. Under the ice house was the fermenting cellar with nineteen fermenting tubs each capable of holding twenty barrels of fermenting beer and a nearby cellar with twenty more of the twenty barrel casks.

The same article states:

> The brewing apparatus was put in motion on the 27th of February and beer may be expected in three weeks from the date of this paper [indicates the brewing cycle took thirty-two days]. The present capacity of the Golden Brewery is one hundred kegs per day, of eight gallons each.[10]

Henry Gaw was another well-known Colorado brewer. He was born in Ireland in 1834 and with his parents immigrated to Montreal, where he began to learn the brewing trade. In 1875 he moved to Idaho Springs and purchased a brewery already in production. He did well there until a fire destroyed the business in late 1877 or early 1878.

Adolph Coors first named his brewery the Golden Brewery after the town he chose to settle in. This modest 1880 structure gives little indication of the size of the future Coors Brewery, which remains on the same site130 years later.

Instead of rebuilding, he took the few undamaged vats, and with capital raised from selling his gold watch he started another brewery in Leadville. By 1880 he was producing 120 kegs of beer a day and when the railroad reached Leadville, he began shipping it all over the state. From Baskins' 1881 *History of the Arkansas River Valley*:

> This is the Pioneer Brewery of Leadville, the ground being broken for it in March 1878. From a very small beginning it has gone on, steadily increasing in size, until it has now attained a capacity of 120 kegs a day. The brewery has all the modern improvements; no establishment in Leadville has greater or better facilities for making the best of beer. The cellars have patent ice floors, and the buildings are heated by steam. Water is obtained from never failing pure springs. The brewery is very convenient and compact; lacking nothing it should have to make it complete. The beer manufactured here has the deserved reputation of being the best made in the mountains. Mr. Gaw has, in connection with his brewery, a large bottling establishment on the Oro Road, furnished with all modern appliances, with facilities for turning out 100 dozen per day. The brewery is situated on the south side of California Gulch, in a spot especially adapted for it. Mr. Gaw was married to Miss Stuppel, of Montreal, in June, 1860, and has a family of four children.[11]

Henry Gaw's Columbine Brewery produced five thousand barrels of beer in 1885 and remained in business until Prohibition shut down all breweries in the state in 1915.

Leadville had other breweries. The astronomical growth of the Cloud City led to Gaw's Brewery and two others in 1880—Feurstein's Brewery and the Leadville Brewery—operated by Alois Kock and John Lister. Vincent Albus moved to the area in 1879 after his brewery in Trinidad closed in 1873. John Good and Jacob Mack were also involved in a Leadville brewery, probably the Leadville Brewery, in 1884.

William Bingel opened a brewery in Del Norte, in southern Colorado, in 1873. He also opened a "lager beer depot" to retail beer in Alamosa on Fifth Street in March 1879, according to an article in the *Rocky Mountain News*. Bingel served as a county commissioner in 1881. The *News* also reports that he had a son, born in 1879:

> From private advices received here the friends of William Bingel, the big brewer of San Juan, are informed by THE NEWS that he has an heir of the male gender, and in consequence his head is bigger than one of his beer vats.[12]

Bingel died in 1891, and the brewery passed into the hands of Eric von Bruddenbrock and, later, Adolph Biesler. Biesler renamed it the San Luis Brewery in 1901. It remained the major producer of beer in the San Luis Valley until Prohibition in 1915. Von Brudderbrock, the brewmaster, was an officer of the Trinidad Brewery, owned by Henry Schneider.

Top: Henry Gaw first purchased a brewery in Idaho Springs but relocated it to Leadville in 1878 after a fire. He was the first brewer in Leadville. From O. L. Baskins's *History of the Arkansas River Valley.* Above: Gaw's Brewery, located on the west side of California Gulch in Leadville, had ice floors for cooling and produced Columbine beer, a favorite of the Leadville miners. From O. L. Baskins's *History of the Arkansas River Valley.*

Henry Schneider started Trinidad's brewery in a small adobe building in 1873. In the 1880s, improvements were made when a brewhouse and cooling cellars were added. Schneider added refrigeration in 1888 and ice-making equipment in 1893. In 1900–1910 the cellars' capacity was increased with the installation of new Pfauder glass-enameled steel chip tanks. This brewery was one of only five in the state to survive Prohibition. Although Schneider died in 1907, it remained in his family's hands with his son, Phillip, operating it until his death in 1925. His sons carried on the family's ownership and management into the 1950s.[13]

The San Luis Brewery.

ADOLPH BIELSER, Manager.

KEG AND BOTTLED BEER. SODA AND SELTZER WATERS.

DEL NORTE, COLO.

1899 Colorado State Business Directory

William Beisler supplied the San Luis Valley with beer from his brewery in Del Norte before Prohibition. The brewery had been built in 1873 by William Bingel but was renamed the San Juan Brewery by Beisler in 1899 when he placed this advertisement in the *Colorado Business Directory*.

The first brewery in Pueblo was built and operated about 1865–1866 and its ownership was passed around like free-flowing beer, with sixteen different owners from its beginnings until 1898. Competition from the larger breweries in Denver was strong. At least one brewery, the City Brewery, was more interested in providing a microbrew for its attached saloon.

But the real story of Pueblo brewing began not in southern Colorado Territory but in west-central Wisconsin. There, in 1874, a German immigrant and his large family settled and began a brewery in the town of Spencer. Johannes Walter had brought his knowledge and experience in making lager beer to his new home and wasted little time building several breweries in the area. Other family members operated breweries nearby in Menasha and Appleton, Wisconsin, and West Bend, Indiana. The younger sons ran out of space and, like most of the younger sons of the nation, headed west for untapped opportunities. Martin Walter settled on Pueblo for his dreams, and in 1898 bought the still-struggling Pueblo Brewery, renaming it after himself and the family breweries in Wisconsin. Backed by family capital, Martin Walter quickly upgraded equipment, adding capacity to its forty-five-barrel daily output. By 1902 he was brewing 170 barrels daily and had added a new fifty-ton icemaker, two new boilers, and a new brewhouse. The Walter Brewery supplied Colorado and adjoining states with beer until 1915 and Colorado's passage of Prohibition. Then, unlike most other breweries, it reopened in 1933 and again marketed and manufactured beer until shutting down in January 1975. In 1944 another brother, Karl Jacob Walter, purchased the Schneider Brewery in Trinidad and operated it for several years.[14]

Top: Henry Schneider and his family operated the brewery in Trinidad from 1873 until the 1950s. It was one of five in the state to survive Prohibition. Courtesy Colorado Historical Society, CHS-A740. Above: Almost every brewery had a cooperage—a shop that made the barrels the beer was in. Coopers are shown here in the shop at the Walters Brewery in Pueblo. Oak staves rest on the cart to the left of the frontmost worker, and metal rings hang from the post above his head. Courtesy Pueblo County Historical Society.

Bottling

In the early days of Colorado brewing, the bottling of beer was contracted out to companies solely in the business of bottling liquids of all kinds. When Adolph Coors first came to Colorado, he operated a bottling plant in Denver. He then sold the operation to help finance his beer-making venture in Golden. There were five beer bottlers in Denver in 1879, but only four breweries. Coors began brewing operations in Golden in 1874, and C. E. Stevens' bottling company opened in 1876. As the breweries grew, it became profitable to integrate, and bottle houses became as permanent a fixture at a brewery as the malt house. Because tax regulations were not changed until much later, each brewery had to place its beer first into a barrel or keg with a tax stamp over the bunghole. If the brewery was going to bottle beer, it had to move the stamped barrel to the bottle house or bottling company and transfer the brew from barrel to bottle.[15]

In 1933, after the repeal of Prohibition, five breweries reopened in Colorado: Tivoli in Denver, Coors in Golden, Walters in Pueblo, Schneider's in Trinidad, and the Telluride Brewery in Telluride. The last year the Telluride Brewery was listed in the *Colorado Business Directory* was 1937, and 1941 was the last year for Schneider's, although it reopened under different ownership until finally closing in 1957. In 1969, Tivoli closed its doors, and Walters quit brewing beer in Pueblo in 1975. This left Coors as the only remaining brewery, until Anheiser-Busch built a huge facility in Windsor in 1991 and, with Coors, propelled Colorado to the top of the rankings for the highest beer production in America during the 1990s.

Just as some people bear a striking resemblance to a grandparent or great-grandparent long deceased, small microbreweries scattered around the state are now brewing small quantities of a variety of beer made very similarly to the way it was done in the old days. These fine-tasting products resemble the beer consumed by our forefathers and -mothers. At present, there are more breweries in the state than there were before Prohibition or even before the twentieth century, as Colorado brewers prolifically re-create these reminders of the past. Cheers!

■ ■ ■

Notes

[1] Lewis H. Garrard, *Wah-To-Yah and the Taos Trail* (Palo Alto, CA: The American West Publishing Company, 1968).

[2] Margaret Coel, Jane Valentine Barker, and Karen Gilleland Gilleland, *The Tivoli: Bavaria in the Rockies* (Denver: Colorado and West, 1985), 6–7.

[3] Ibid., 36.

[4] Stanley Baron, *Brewed in America* (Toronto and Boston: Little, Brown and Co., 1962), 229.

[5] *Microsoft Encarta 2001,* "Beer."

[6] The description of the brewing process, including the information about the yeasts comes from the 2001 Microsoft's Encarta article on beer.

[7] Haenel, *Boulder Business Report*, May 1985.

[8] Louise Harrison, *Empire and Berthoud Pass* (Denver: Big Mountain Press), 104–105.

[9] *History of the Arkansas River Valley* (Chicago: O. L. Baskins and Company, 1880).

[10] *Golden Transcript*, March 11, 1874.

[11] *History of the Arkansas Rivey Valley.*

[12] *Rocky Mountain News*, September 13, 1879, 8.

[13] Mike Hennich, *Brewing in Trinidad, Colorado* (Irving, TX: Ale Publishing Company, 1992).

[14] Robert Collyer, "History of Brewing in Pueblo Colorado: The Walter Brewing Company," *American Breweriana Journal.*

[15] Baron, 245.

CHAPTER 3

Ice

Had D. C. Oakes come up the Santa Fe Trail instead of the Platte River trail to the Pikes Peak region in 1859, he would have stopped and rested at the ruins of Bent's old fort. Oakes would have been surprised to know that thirteen years earlier he could have drunk a cool, ice-filled beverage of his choice, even had he been traveling during the hottest part of the summer.

In July 1846, thirteen years before the Pikes Peak Gold Rush, Susan Magoffin recorded in her diary what it was like to travel along the Santa Fe Trail.[1] She was the wife of Samuel Magoffin, a Santa Fe trader with commerce and politics on his mind. Susan was pregnant and not feeling well as their wagons pulled into Bent's Fort, on the north bank of the Arkansas River in what is now southeastern Colorado. Bent's Fort was the last stop on U.S. soil before the Santa Fe Trail entered Mexican land south of the Arkansas River. Susan described both the journey and Bent's Fort in some detail. But before she reached Bent's, she described the first mirage she had ever seen:

> It is so deceiving to the eye, that the thirsty traveler often breaks from his party with anxious eyes and heart to gain first the long wished luxury, but ere he reaches the brink it vanishes from his sight.[2]

At the fort every possible thing was done to make the lady comfortable: she was given a light, airy room on the top level and, much to her surprise, a glass of good water filled with ice to drink. As Susan describes, in 1846, Bent's Fort had good wells inside its walls as well as Colorado's first icehouse filled with blocks of ice cut from the nearby river during the winter months. Susan would miscarry a few days later at the fort, but cold water with ice in the middle of the Great American Desert left a lasting impression on her.

Although this icehouse was the earliest in the Denver-Auraria area, another was built one year earlier in Montana City, a not-so-permanent camp several miles up the Platte River from Cherry Creek. In 1859 the people of Montana City moved some of their cabins and all of the population downstream, leaving a "gigantic structure" for storing ice with no population to serve. Courtesy Denver Public Library, Western History Collection.

The demand for ice certainly existed in the Colorado gold rush region. Winters were cold and summers were hot. Soon citizens of Colorado communities harvested ice from local ponds and filled small icehouses or basements in commercial buildings. On January 11, 1860, the first icehouse in Auraria was completed.[3] It was located at the end of Larimer Street near the banks of the Platte River (now the site where the Colfax viaduct crosses the Platte River), and was filled with ice in February.[4] By May 30, 1860, the Crystal Lake Ice Company was setting up daily delivery routes for Denver citizens, according to an advertisement in the *Rocky Mountain News Weekly*. In the same paper, the company offered a $100 reward "for the detection of the person or persons that are in the habit of breaking into our ice house on the banks of the lake above town."[5] A strong enough demand for ice, indeed!

In January 1871 at Greeley, Captain Abbott harvested and stored sixteen-inch-thick blocks of ice in a single-wall frame structure insulated with two feet of hay. Hay was a common insulator for icehouses and two feet of it would keep the ice through the spring and summer months. There was no reference or advertisement to sell the ice, but only the conclusion that "no greater insult can be offered to a temperance man than to offer him warm water to drink."[6] In January 1878 seventy-five railcar loads of ice were shipped from Greeley to Kansas City on the Kansas-Pacific Railway.[7]

The mountains offered a longer-lasting supply of ice for harvesting than sites in the Midwest. Because railroads had been built up to mountain mining centers, they were soon used to bring ice to the Front Range population. No better transportation medium was available.

The process for harvesting ice from lakes varied little from that originally developed by Bostonian Nathaniel Wyeth in 1825. Harvesters scraped snow and loose ice debris from the surface of a pond or lake with a scraper that was pulled by horses with special studded horseshoes. Next, parallel grooves twenty-two inches apart were cut into the ice by the iron blades of an ice saw, also horsepowered. These grooves were from eight to ten inches deep, but not all the way through the ice. Continued parallel passes were made across the lake, and then other grooves perpendicular to the initial set were cut using the ice saw. After a large section of the ice surface was cut, special bars were used to break the ice into blocks that could be floated to the icehouse or to a wagon or railcar. The blocks were raised to the proper height in the icehouse by a horsepowered lift and stacked tightly inside. Sawdust or hay was placed between the layers and packed around the entire mass.[8]

Harvested ice always had the potential to become contaminated, as frozen stagnant or already contaminated water was still contaminated once it melted. The ice also could become contaminated by horse manure. One of the

Workers mark, score, cut, and load ice for transport to nearby Greeley by wagon. In 1879 seventy-five railcars of Seeley Lake Ice were shipped to Kansas City. Photo by F. F. Baker. Courtesy City of Greeley Museums, Permanent Collection.

A six-foot-long ice plow in an exhibit at the Longmont Museum. It required a one- or two-horse team for power and a man to keep the plows in the marked grooves with enough pressure on the handles so the plows would continue to cut ice. Author's collection. Courtesy Longmont Museum.

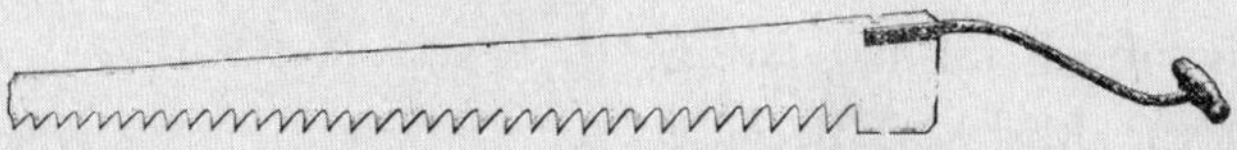

The saw was used to open channels and separate sheets from the field. Farmers and small operators that could not afford ice-plows used saws exclusively to cut ice blocks.

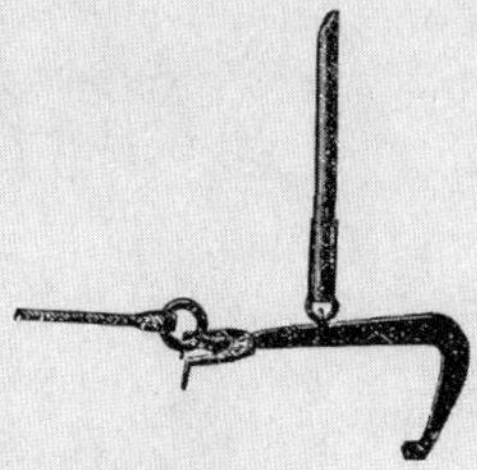

The grapple; used for towing sheets by horses along the channels. It was also used to haul blocks of ice up an inclined plane with horses.

The breaking-off bar was used to detach large sheets of ice from the field. The wide blade was for detaching large sheets. The small blade was for splitting off smaller blocks.

A calking-bar; used to fill grooves in the ice with snow or chips. This prevented flooding and freezing up of the groves.

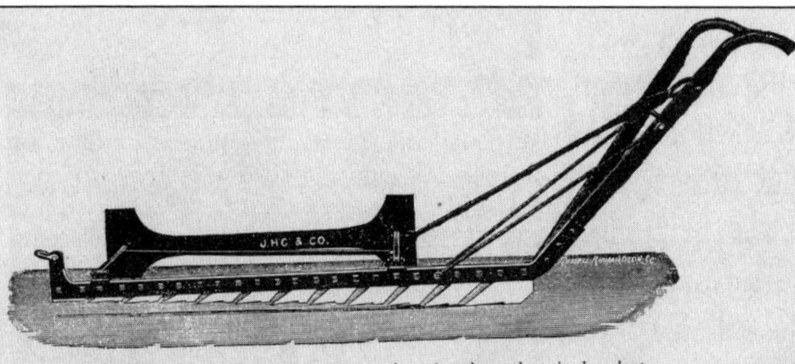

A marker plow with swinging guide. This tool cut ice about three inches deep.

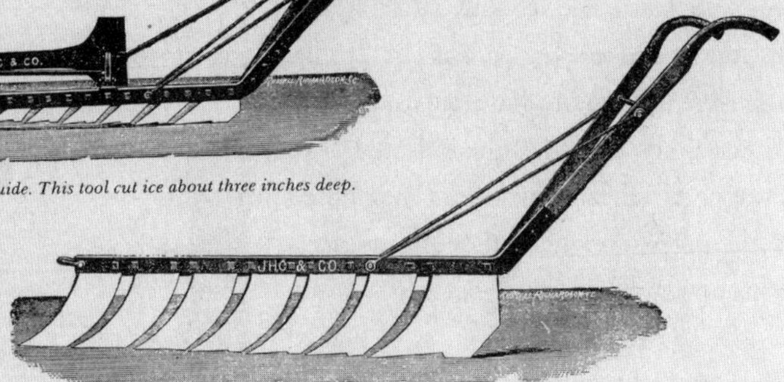

An ice-plow. It followed the marker and cut ice to the depth of 6 to 12 inches.

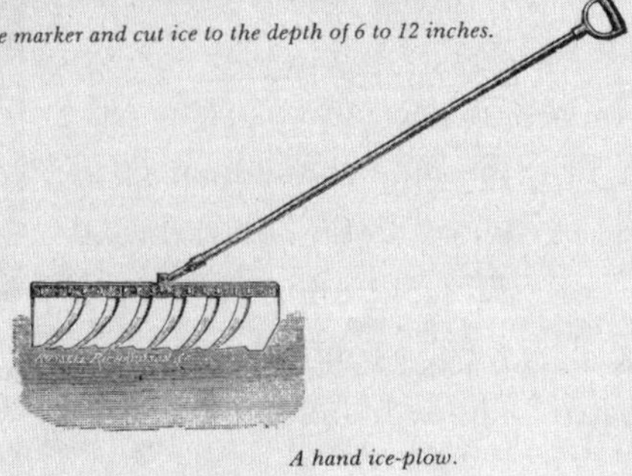

A hand ice-plow.

A bar-chisel; used to loosen and trim cakes.

A house-bar; used to separate smaller cakes from each other.

A splitting-chisel; used to separate ice sheets (floats) into cakes.

A ring-handle chisel; used to cut holes in ice in order to flood the field.

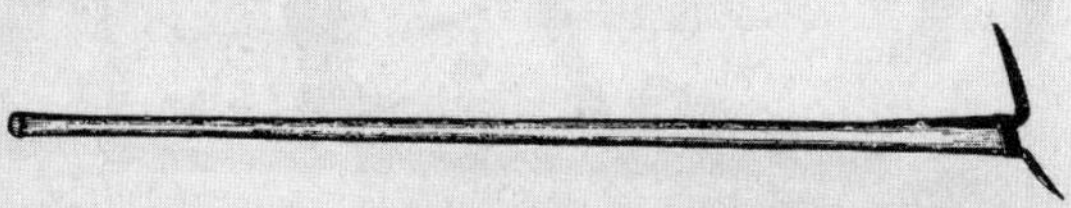

The ice-hook; used to pull or push cakes of ice. Handle sizes ranged from 4to 10 feet long.

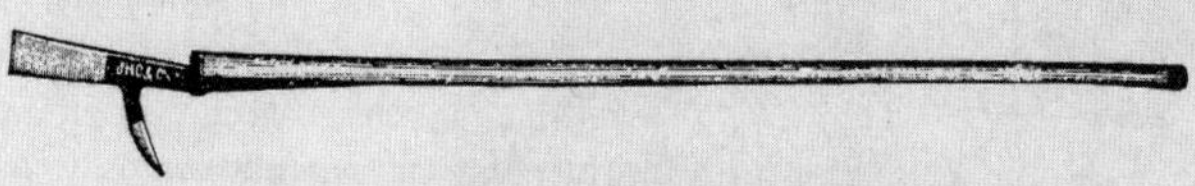

A hook-chisel; used for splitting blocks of ice and getting them secured on the elevator.

The scoop-net; used to clean channels of broken ice.

most hated jobs for ice harvesters was cleaning up manure from the horses pulling the scrapers and cutters.

Icehouses were an integral part of the process. They came in all sizes, depending on the amount of ice required for an entire season. Ice blocks were stacked in orderly piles so only the outside areas of the pile needed insulation. Insulation usually consisted of bales of hay or walls filled with cork. The icehouse generally was located next to the lake from which the ice was harvested or in the town or city where the ice blocks were to be delivered. Three of America's first four presidents had icehouses at their private estates at Mount Vernon, Monticello, and Ashbury.

Top: The icehouse began as a small structure just large enough for the needs of a single family or business. This one could store a five-by-nine-by-eight-foot block of ice—about 360 cubic feet, weighing 3,000 pounds. This icehouse now resides in Greeley's Centennial Village. Author's collection. Left: Icehouses became larger as the demand and the population they served increased. This one in Craig served a small town during the early twentieth century. Courtesy Museum of Northwest Colorado, Craig, 69-24-290 e. Below: This icehouse at Lake George was even larger than the one at Craig, although still of wooden construction. Wooden icehouses were susceptible to fire, and most of them have burned down. This one could hold an estimated five thousand tons of ice harvested at the lake for consumption by the people of Colorado Springs. Courtesy Dan Abbott.

Above: The change from wood to masonry and concrete minimized the risk of loss to fire. This icehouse at Pactolus, west of Pinecliffe, was cinderblock and wood. Author's collection. Right: The Greeley Ice and Storage building and business was considerably larger. It was built of brick and served northeastern Colorado into the 1970s. This business had ice-making equipment, so it did not need to store enough ice to last through the summer. Consequently, there was more space for cold storage than for ice storage. Courtesy City of Greeley Museums, Permanent Collection. Below: This concrete icehouse that belonged to the Denver and Rio Grande Railway was the largest in the state. It had a sixteen-thousand-foot ice dock with a four-story, automatic ice-filling tower that could fill 102 refrigeration railcars at one time. This was one of the major refilling stops on the transcontinental rail lines. Courtesy Colorado Railroad Museum.

Alfred Petersen's lake and icehouse were in Lafayette. Peterson was called "Petey the Iceman." In this photograph he and a neighbor boy are harvesting ice. Courtesy Frank Lilja Family.

In Boulder in 1872, a butcher named Will Sommer hung his beef carcasses in a mammoth icebox instead of in front of his store, as was the usual custom. He also stored butter on racks in the icebox.[9] The *Boulder County News* does not mention who provided the ice, but three years later, businessmen Anthony Arnett and his partner Mr. Snyder harvested blocks of ice from Captain Tyler's pond a mile northeast of the city with a new $100 ice cutter and stored the harvest in the basement of their building in downtown Boulder. Three hundred tons were to be used by the town's citizens the next summer.[10]

In 1876 both Arnett & Co. in Boulder and J. C. Adams in Greeley were listed in the *Colorado Business Directory* as ice dealers. In 1877 two dealers in Denver, Vinot and Higgins, listed their business in the directory. By 1900 the directory included ten ice businesses, and there were thirty-seven by 1905. Soon every town had its own ice business, for example "Petey, the Iceman," also known as Alfred Petersen, of Lafayette, who delivered ice to residents of neighboring Louisville and Erie as well as to his hometown of Lafayette.

In the mid-1800s, German immigrants brought the formula for lager beer with them to the United States. The brewing of lager required cooler temperatures than the ales and porters made by the English and Irish. Breweries soon became the largest consumers of ice, often installing their brewing equipment below icehouses and providing delivered ice to the local population as a revenue-generating side business.[11]

Adolph Coors built an icehouse along with his brewery in Golden.[12] The icehouse was sixty-by-forty feet and sixteen feet high. Coors stored fourteen hundred to fifteen hundred tons of ice the first season, but it wasn't until 1878 that he advertised ice to Golden citizens at forty cents per hundred pounds. There was a delivery service by ice wagon, and charges differed depending on the amount delivered each day. Coors continued in the ice business until 1880, when another Golden businessman, A. J. Quaintance, started a city ice service.

The ever-increasing demand for ice eventually brought competition in the form of mechanical refrigeration equipment that would be used to make the blocks of ice at the local icehouse, eliminating the entire harvesting and transporting system from lake to icehouse. Mechanical refrigeration had been known of for years but was not fully understood. However, the development of the steam engine and other industrial devices led to a better understanding of the thermal dynamics of the refrigeration process. More efficient and more reasonably priced equipment became available. Again, breweries led the way by stimulating the demand for equipment that would chill beer as well as make ice.

Ice blocks made by refrigeration could be from artesian well water or even better—from distilled water from steam from the boilers required to power the equipment. An

This 1892 advertisement from the Hercules Iron Works of Aurora, Illinois, illustrates an automated plant for the manufacture of pure ice from distilled water. Nothing but coal and water for the steam boiler is required. Starting from the left, steam from the boiler powers the ammonia compressor that produces enough refrigeration to freeze the cooled steam distillate in the block cans. An automatic handling crane lifted the ice blocks to the storage area, where they were sold to customers. Salt brine was used to transfer heat from the condensed steam to the ammonia refrigerant.

1896 automated ice plant needed coal and water for the boilers inserted in the back end of the plant, while pure ice blocks were automatically manufactured and mechanically manipulated until taken out of the front for sale to the customer or delivery man.

In 1891, refrigeration technology came to Colorado in the form of the first ice refrigeration plant. Colonel Francis K. Sowers of the Colorado Ice and Storage Co. installed his equipment in Denver that year. A reporter for the *Denver Daily News* interviewed Colonel Sowers, and the following article was published June 23, 1890.

About Ice

Colonel Sowers tells what his company will do.

Colonel F. K. Sowers, President of the Colorado Ice and Cold Storage Company, was seen by a reporter for the news last evening in regard to the controversy over the ice combine.

"My opinion of the stand the *Republican* has taken," said the colonel, "is that it is ridiculous. The prices published in their own paper very evidently show that we have no intention whatever of abusing the public, much less robbing them. The prices established by us are certainly 50 to 75 per cent less than last year and in many cases over 100 per cent less as the following price list shows":

1890

5 pounds daily, per month	$3.25
10 pounds daily, per month	$3.75
15 pounds daily, per month	$4.25
20 pounds daily, per month	$4.75
25 pounds daily, per month	$5.25
30 to 75 pounds, per 100 pounds	$0.65
100 to 250 pounds, per 100 pounds	$0.55
300 to 400 pounds, per 100 pounds	$0.50
500 pounds and upward, per 100 pounds	$0.45

1890–91 FAMILY TRADE

10 pounds daily, per month	$2.00
15 pounds daily, per month	$2.25
20 pounds daily, per month	$3.00
25 pounds daily, per month	$3.75
30 pounds daily, per month	$4.50
35 pounds daily, per month	$5.25
40 pounds daily, per month	$6.00
45 pounds daily, per month	$6.75

For the season of 1890, from June 13, general trade:

20 pounds	15 cents
25 pounds	20 cents
30 pounds	25 cents
40 pounds	30 cents
50 to 75 pounds	45 cents per 100
100 to 300 pounds	40 cents per 100
325 to 500 pounds	35 cents per 100
600 to 1000 pounds	30 cents per 100

1,200 to 2 tons each delivery, artesian ice, per ton, $5.50; lake ice, $4.50; 3 to 5 tons each, delivery, artesian ice, $5; lake ice, $4; 6 tons and upwards, artesian ice, $4.75, lake ice $4.

"We intend to treat the public fairly and never by any manner or means charge them exorbitant prices. Such a step would be very foolish on our part. Some people expect us to deliver in 10-pound lots at the price of a ton of coal delivered to one single family, and I wish they would kindly state how much it would cost each family if this ton of coal were divided up into 10-pound lots and so delivered.

"What action did this paper take last summer before we established our works here, when ice was worth more than double what it is today? It looks as it is not worth their while to attack small concerns, but prefers to throw mud at large companies."

"How are you getting along with the reorganization of the new company?"

"We are, indeed, taking everything into consideration, doing well, and we think that by 12 o'clock tonight all the different routes will be thoroughly laid out, and then the distribution will go like clockwork.

"We are making about 140 tons of artesian ice a day, which is sufficient to supply the hotels, restaurants and private families. We have an abundance of lake ice, about 50,000 tons, which we use for the butcher trade and other large refrigerators."

"Is it your intention to put up more machinery?"

"Yes, we hope to do so, and in the course of time nothing but artesian ice will be used."

"Have you anything to say about the proposals of the Board of Health in regard of condemning lake ice?"

"Well, my answer is this: In case the board of health should have the lake ice analyzed and find any proceeding from stagnant ponds injurious to public health we would not try to prevent it from being condemned, for it should be known that the health authorities have condemned all impure ice."

Maddox Ice Company of Denver had two lakes east of Kenosha Pass where they harvested ice. Blocks were loaded into railcars of the Colorado and Southern narrow-gauge line, as shown here. The cars were unloaded at the Maddox icehouses in Denver at Sixth Avenue and the Platte River. Courtesy Earl Maddox.

From this article it is apparent that manufactured ice from artesian water was more expensive than lake ice, and that business combines were already trying to regulate the prices. There was also concern about the risks of using lake ice. Colonel Sowers was correct about the replacement of lake ice with manufactured ice, but he would have been surprised at how long the transformation finally took in Colorado. Both the continued growing demand for ice and the cost difference between lake ice and mechanically made ice supported ice harvesting as a business until after the Second World War.

By 1900 there were six ice manufacturing plants in Colorado. Often a city would take on the responsibility of providing ice for its citizens, as Brighton did by manufacturing it at its electrical power plant, Brighton Ice, Power and Light, which

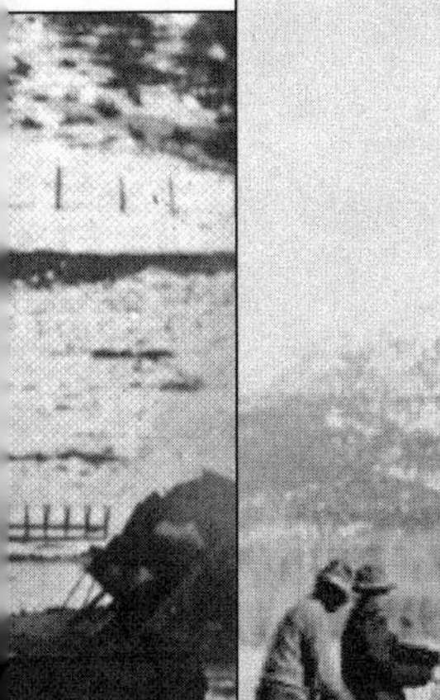

In 1911 two workers and two horses plowed grooves in the ice for the winter harvest. Paonia's icehouse was next to the lake, so transportation was quick and easy. Photo by W.S. Eduards. Denver Public Library, Western History Collection, X-12957.

had an ice-making capacity of four tons per day. A city might also allow the use of its reservoir for ice harvesting, as Idaho Springs did.

In 1803, Thomas Moore, a butter merchant in Maryland, patented an insulated tub that could be cooled by ice for his twenty-mile trip to Georgetown, where he peddled his butter. By using this "refrigerated" tub, he was able to sell his firmer butter to housewives at premium prices.[13]

Iceboxes built following Moore's plan were made by Colorado carpenters. Local start-up businesses began selling iceboxes to middle-class families, as they found that meat and particularly dairy products tasted better, longer. Soon iceboxes were available through catalog stores such as Sears and Roebuck at even lower costs, and for marketing reasons they were called refrigerators. An extra-tall upright Acme refrigerator sold for $10.40 in the 1897 Sears catalog.[14] It wasn't long until most homes had an icebox and were on a route for daily ice delivery.

The segment of the ice industry most familiar to Colorado citizens was delivery. Ice companies organized routes of customers who had agreed to buy their ice. Deliverymen filled horsedrawn ice wagons and followed their own route each day. Home owners and businessmen were given ice cards—diamond-shaped cards with the numbers 25, 50, and 100 in three of the four corners. The fourth corner was usually blank, signifying no

SEE PAGE 2 FOR OUR LIBERAL NO MONEY DOWN OFFER. 65

We Trust You

See Page 2

Fine White Enamel Lined Refrigerator

With Removable Galvanized Ice Chamber
Case is Made of Solid Ash Lumber
Has Sanitary Removable Wire Shelves
HAS PERFECT COLD AIR CIRCULATION

$11.35 TO 21.95

It Will Save You Big Money

WHITE ENAMEL LINED

ABSOLUTELY SANITARY. This high class refrigerator is the last word in sanitary perfection. It is easily cleaned, is positively odorless and the most economical in ice consumption. And still our prices represent but a small fraction over and above the actual cost to manufacture. If you care to have a fine, baked-on, non-chipping WHITE ENAMEL LINED refrigerator of undisputed merit, send us your order for this one and we will send it on approval. It is constructed with an inside casing of odorless lumber, matched and clamped together in a very substantial manner. The outside case is solid ash lumber, splendidly finished golden. The cold air circulation is a great feature of this refrigerator. The air, after passing over the ice, falls directly into the provision chamber from where it is forced up over the ice and is purified, cooled and again falls, thus keeping up a constant circulation.

THIS PRINCIPLE of cold, dry-air circulation works an economy in ice and insures absolute satisfaction in the preserving of foods. This perfect system of cold-air circulation, together with our superior method of insulation, warrants the statement that our refrigerators require less ice for their size than those of any other manufacture in the country. All lift lids are supplied with our patent lid stop. Hinges and locks are all of genuine nickel plated brass and are heavy and thoroughly substantial. Wire shelves in provision chamber and galvanized iron ice chamber are of removable type for cleaning purposes. Is white enamel lined, baked on, and guaranteed not to crack. Look over the list of sizes shown below and decide what capacity refrigerator will best suit your requirements. Each one is a marvel of value for the money.

White Enamel Lined

Is Sanitary and Odorless

Has Removable Drain Pipe and Patent Drip Cup. Also Strong Lid Holders.

Order a Size Large Enough for Your Needs

Number	Height	Width	Depth	Ice Capacity	Size of Ice Chamber	Shipping Weight	Price
7HW765	39½ in.	22½ in.	14½ in.	40 lbs.	15½x 9¾x10 in.	115 lbs.	$11.35
7HW766	41 in.	23¾ in.	15½ in.	50 lbs.	16⅞x10¼x10½ in.	120 lbs.	13.65
7HW767	43 in.	25½ in.	18½ in.	75 lbs.	18¼x13½x11 in.	155 lbs.	15.85
7HW768	45 in.	27¼ in.	19 in.	90 lbs.	20¼x14 x12 in.	175 lbs.	18.75
7HW768½	47 in.	30¾ in.	20 in.	110 lbs.	22½x14½x12½ in.	195 lbs.	21.95

Two Very Exceptional Refrigerator Bargain Offerings

$16.95

Choose This Very Fine Number
Is Expertly Made of Elm Lumber
It Has Double Dead Air Space
Lined With Galvanized Iron
WHITE ENAMEL FINISH INSIDE

THIS REFRIGERATOR is built up to a standard and not down to a price. It has in it the essentials of a good, substantial, serviceable article; yet the price is very reasonable considering its supreme qualities. The workmanship is executed by experts from the cutting of the lumber to the last finishing touches. The illustration will give you a fairly good idea of this fine refrigerator; but we urge you to have it sent on approval, before you come to a final decision as to its worth. Although this picture shows four shelves, the refrigerator that we supply is made with only three wire shelves. One of the features of this article is the double dead air space which is recognized as a perfect and reliable method of producing refrigeration. Don't overlook that fact.

THE LUMBER used is the practical elm well joined at all points. The finish is a rich golden. The interior is carefully lined with galvanized iron, to which is applied a white enamel finish. The latter not only gives the inside of the box a very pleasing appearance, but is a sanitary feature as well. A moist cloth now and then will keep it clean and sweet. This box is odorless—a feature of great importance. Note that there is a large provision chamber on the left, and an ice compartment and small provision chamber, on the right, the sizes of which are given in detail below. The ice chamber will hold 60 lbs., which is sufficient for the needs of the average kitchen. You can make no mistake by sending us your order for this fine refrigerator.

Catalog Number	Hgt. In.	Wth. In.	Dth. In.	Large Provision Chamber	Small Provision Chamber	Ice Chamber	Ice C'p'y lbs.	Ship. Wt. lbs.	Price
7HW764	41	29	17½	11¾x12½x 31 in.	11¾x12½ x10 in.	11¾x12½ x15½ in.	60	155	$16.95

Buy On Credit

No. 7HW764. Has Three Wire Shelves. (Cut Shows Four).

By the late 1880s, half of the annual ice crop was used for home food storage. Hundreds of refrigerator systems competed for the market until the Great Depression. A large number were sold through catalog stores of companies like Hartman Furniture & Carpet and Sears, Roebuck Co., both based in Chicago. This page is from the 1915 Hartman Furniture & Carpet mail order catalog.

delivery. The home owner would turn the card and place it in the window so that the iceman could see how much ice was requested. The iceman would stop his wagon, grab the proper size block with his ice tongs, take it into the home or business, and place it in an icebox.

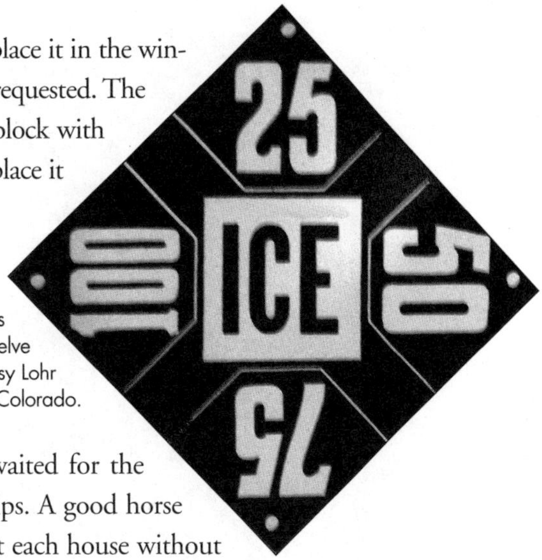

On delivery day, the customer would place the ice card in the window with the appropriate size block facing up. Ice was sold by the pound, so when the number 50 faced up, was a request for a fifty-pound block of ice. The cards were ten to twelve inches square and usually included advertisements. Courtesy Lohr Agricultural Heritage Farm, Longmont, Colorado.

During the summer months, eager children waited for the iceman, hoping for a sliver of ice to cool parched lips. A good horse came to know the route by heart and would stop at each house without direction. Horsedrawn ice wagons of the nineteenth century were replaced by small delivery trucks by the end of World War I.

The ice business was always highly competitive in Denver, where entrepreneurs could enter the market by manufacturing ice or delivering only to residential customers, depending on the amount of capital they wished to invest. Independent delivery people went to customers on other companies' routes and tried to fill orders, hence steal-

The citizens of Longmont took their ice delivery from the St. Vrain Ice Company. Ice was harvested at a pond near the St. Vrain River. Courtesy Longmont Historical Museum.

Top: Sleek vans replaced bulky trucks, as shown in this photograph at the Convention of Ice Dealers in Greeley in 1935. The delivery business was rapidly changing with the advent of mechanical refrigerators. Courtesy City of Greeley Museums, Permanent Collection. Left: The automotive revolution in the United States influenced the ice-harvesting and -delivery business. Gasoline powered saws replaced horse-pulled ice plows, and the delivery truck replaced the two-horse wagon. Maddox Ice was one of the largest and longest-lived ice businesses in Denver. Courtesy Earl Maddox.

ing customers. To try to prevent this, one ice company asked its customers to leave different numbers of empty milk bottles on the porch to signify the amount of ice desired. This company often reran its routes to satisfy customers who had forgotten to put the card or the bottles in place before the earlier deliveryman arrived. This attention to customer service served Maddox Ice well, as it was in business from 1904 to 1992.[15]

Once again, technology fundamentally changed the way business was done. Refrigeration equipment became smaller and more efficient. Soon small refrigeration systems could be placed inside the icebox itself, eliminating the need for ice block delivery.

Market niches grew in importance as companies like Denver's Espy Ice focused on the demand of the railroads, building an icehouse next to the railroad with facilities to fill refrigeration cars. Espy also had icehouses along the tracks of the Denver and Salt

Lake Railroad at Tolland and at Trappers near Yampa. The Denver and Rio Grande Railroad had icehouses all along its routes at Gunnison, on Marshall Pass, at Miniturn, Montrose, Grand Junction, and elsewhere. The Atchison, Topeka and Santa Fe had icehouses along tracks all the way to California, including the railyards at La Junta.

Near the tracks of the Colorado Midland Railway in central Colorado, an entrepreneur named George Frost bought land at the eastern end of Elevenmile Canyon, flooded a meadow there, and called the body of water Lake George, after himself. He built a series of large icehouses and went into the ice business. Even after the Colorado Midland failed and abandoned its grades through South Park and beyond, the train continued to service the ice business at Lake George for many years. Frost had also built a beautiful residence near the lake, which he sold to a Michigan corporation that turned it into a hotel. It burned to the ground in 1922.

The railroads became one of the largest ice consumers because ice was needed to cool refrigeration boxcars and preserve perishable foodstuffs being shipped from farm to market. It wasn't too much of a stretch from Thomas Moore's 1803 ice tub to a larger tub with wheels for transporting larger quantities of perishables.

In June 1851 a patent was issued for a refrigerated railcar with bulkheads for ice in each end and louvers for the movement of cool air from the ice to the transported goods. The cars were built of wood for insulation, and ice was loaded through hatches in the roof. Another popular design had a bulkhead that ran across the entire ceiling of the car, with louvers to control the flow of cool air down to the load below. Meltwater was then drained away from the perishable items.

Surprisingly, the railroads resisted development of the refrigerated boxcar, or "reefer" as it was known, since it allowed for the shipment of processed perishables rather than the whole item. Butchered carcasses of beef and lamb weigh about half of the whole live animal, hence railroads could not charge as much for the shipment of carcasses to population centers from the western cattle and sheep ranches. They charged, instead, for the usable part of the carcass. Thus reefers were owned and used by private companies, far more than by the railroads, until the railroads realized that the concept would also be profitable for them. In 1880, private meatpackers and brewers owned and operated an estimated one thousand reefers, while only 310 were owned by the railroads. In 1890, 15,000 reefers were privately owned, compared with 8,570 by the railroads. In 1900, private firms owned 54,000, while the railroads had increased their total to 14,500.

Each railroad had ice stations and terminals where the refrigeration cars were refilled with ice.[16] Often the stations were at natural ponds where the ice was harvested. The 1914 *Journal of American Railway Bridge and Building Association* detailed the many methods of building icehouses along with the railroads' general strategy for preventing food from perishing during transportation.

This editorial cartoon appeared in the September 14, 1919, *Rocky Mountain News*. Lake ice left from the previous warm winter was in poor condition, and ice manufacturers were having difficulty keeping up. Ice was in short supply and customers were paying high prices for the little they could get. The small, independent distributors often could not furnish ice to their customers at all, leading the customers to try to buy ice from others or directly from larger manufacturers. The *News* attempted for a week to get the district attorney to prosecute, but to no avail.

Colorado Ice and Storage manufactured ice in their large plant under the Colfax viaduct and sold it to other distributors, independent dealers, and commercial businesses such as meat markets, groceries, and restaurants. Warm winters when lake ice was not available for the annual harvest were particularly challenging, as the independent dealers were forced to pay much higher prices for ice and had to pass the cost along to customers. In the warm winter of 1919, the pricing and availability of ice caused enough of a furor in Denver that the local papers called for an investigation for price fixing and fraud.

The mechanical refrigerator lessened the demand for delivered ice, squeezing out smaller dealers until only the largest, most efficient, or best sales businesses survived into the 1950s, '60s, and '70s.

Surprisingly, ice is still manufactured and sold in larger quantities than ever before in Denver, and in Colorado in general. The biggest company, Reddy Ice, has plants around the country, including one in Denver. Ice is manufactured and packaged without being touched or handled by a person. This bagged ice is shipped to thousands of grocery stores, convenience stores, and gas stations to be purchased by the general public from refrigerated cases that display it. Ice is still needed for some commercial applications and by the transportation industry. Concrete suppliers still use large blocks of ice in their mobile cement trucks to slow curing of the concrete, which allows the cement to remain in the truck for a longer period of time, expanding their delivery areas. And finally, ice sculptures have become a minor consumer of clear blocks of ice.

National companies ship ice from plants to locations of highest demand, minimizing capital expenditures for seasonal requirements. Truck transportation is inexpensive enough to make it impossible to compete on a local level in the smaller towns of the state. There are no more ice plants in Greeley, Gunnison, or Craig. Lake ice was harvested in Littleton in the 1990s as a historic preservation event, but as a commercial venture it is a thing of the past.

■ ■ ■

Notes

[1] Susan Shelby Magoffin, *Down the Santa Fe Trail and into Mexico: The Diary of Susan S. Magoffin, 1846–1847* (Lincoln: University of Nebraska Press, 1982).

[2] Ibid.

[3] *Rocky Mountain News Weekly*, January 11, 1860.

[4] Ibid., February 8 1860.

[5] *Rocky Mountain News Weekly*, May 30, 1860.

[6] *Greeley Tribune*, January 25, 1871.

[7] John Dugan, *Greeley and Weld County: A Pictorial History* (Norfolk, VA: Doning Co., 1986), 25.

[8] J. C. Jones, *America's Icemen: An Illustrative History of the United States Natural Ice Industry, 1665–1925* (Humble, TX: Jobeco Books, 1984).

[9] *Boulder County News*, June 14, 1872.

[10] *Boulder County News*, January 1, 1875.

[11] Oscar Edward Anderson, *Refrigeration in America: A History of a New Technology and Its Impact* (Princeton: Princeton University Press, 1953), 55.

[12] *Golden Transcript*, March 11, 1874.

[13] The Ice Industry of America.

[14] Sears Roebuck Catalog, 1897, 104–105.

[15] Author's interview with Earl Maddox, 2005.

[16] Anderson, 47–52.

C H A P T E R 4

Millinery and Dressmaking

D. C. Oakes brought his wife, Olive, to the Pikes Peak region in the fall of 1860, and the following spring she wrote to her sister, Minera D. Wing, back home in Iowa:

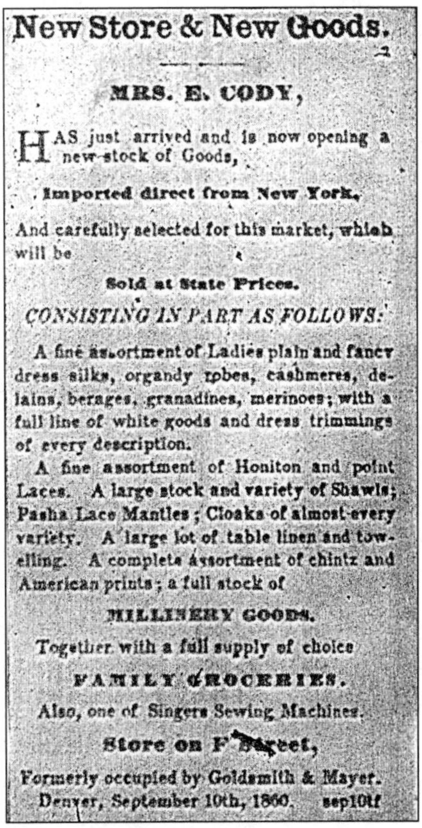

> Our cousin Cody from Weston Mo. is out here keeping store, the business is done in his wife's name; she keeps (a) milliner and dressmakers establishment, all kinds of fancy dress goods. I have not seen them yet, but I am going to their store one of these days.[1]

"Cousin Cody" was, in fact, William Cody, the uncle of the famous Buffalo Bill Cody. His wife, Elisabeth, ran a milliner's and dressmaking shop in Denver on F Street. In later years, both Buffalo Bill and Kit Carson were frequent guests of the Oakeses when D. C. was the Indian agent for the western region, including Colorado. But Olive's visits with her cousin William and his wife, Elisabeth, in their shop on F Street took place many years before.

Elisabeth certainly was not the first milliner and dressmaker in the Denver area. Miss A. E. Carpenter advertised the opening of her shop on March 23, 1860.[2] In 1860 there were not many women in the new territory, but there were enough to justify two very important business activities: women's dressmaking and hatmaking. In Colorado the number of dress shops and millinery stores grew steadily, following the opening of Miss Carpenter's shop. In the *Denver Directory* of 1866 there were three, and Mrs. A. R. Palmer had the good business sense and enough spare capital to advertise her wares in the local newspaper.[3] By 1871 there were 20 dressmakers and milliners in Colorado, and by 1900 the number had grown to 180. This compares with 60,887 in all of the states in 1860.[4]

MRS. A. R. PALMER'S
Millinery and
Dress Making Establishment,
Larimer Street,
Opposite the Rocky Monntain News Office

Thankful for the past generous patronage, Mrs. P. hopes to merit a continuance of the same. A large and well selected stock of goods have just been received, making, in addition to the stock on hand, the most complete and elegant assortment in the city. Among the articles offered are choice

Laces, Dress Goods,
Superior Black Dress Silks,
Fine Linens,
Balmoral Skirts, Hosiery, Gloves, and Head Ornaments of all kinds. Also—Howe & Steven's Family Dye Colors.

Mrs. PALMER'S goods having arrived late, will be sold very low, to make room for a large spring stock. dec5dtf

This industry was a unique one run by women and strictly for women. It relied on the Victorian mores of dress, creating a strong demand for product, and it was limited by the same mores concerning women's role in any venture outside the home.

The most important person influencing dressmaking and ladies' hats in England, colonial America, and the emerging West was Queen Victoria. Her ascension to the throne of England in 1819 ushered in the Victorian era when women of means wore complex dresses created from myriad materials: silks, velvet, linen, and wools trimmed with ribbons, feathers, and yards of lace.

Each dress was an individual creation planned and fabricated by a professional dressmaker and her staff, if she had one, usually one or two apprentices, and a journeywoman trimmer or fitter. Dressmakers and milliners were almost always female, and their businesses used the apprentice system for more than one hundred years to train younger women in the complexities of the trade.

In the mid-nineteenth century, girls entering the trade would be bound over to a *modiste* or madam for years of training, beginning with typical apprentice work of errands and chores, then perhaps learning to sew easy straight stitches or block out cheap material for hats or dresses. As their skills increased, the girls would be allowed more difficult sewing on more expensive material or working on more difficult cutting and stitching, and eventually became full-fledged seamstresses and dressmakers. This trade takes a high degree of skill. Trimmers and finishers using the most expensive materials would expertly and artistically complete dresses and hats. Cutters and fitters were also higher in the hierarchy, as the shaping of the materials was one of the most important and difficult parts of the process in both millinery and dressmaking.

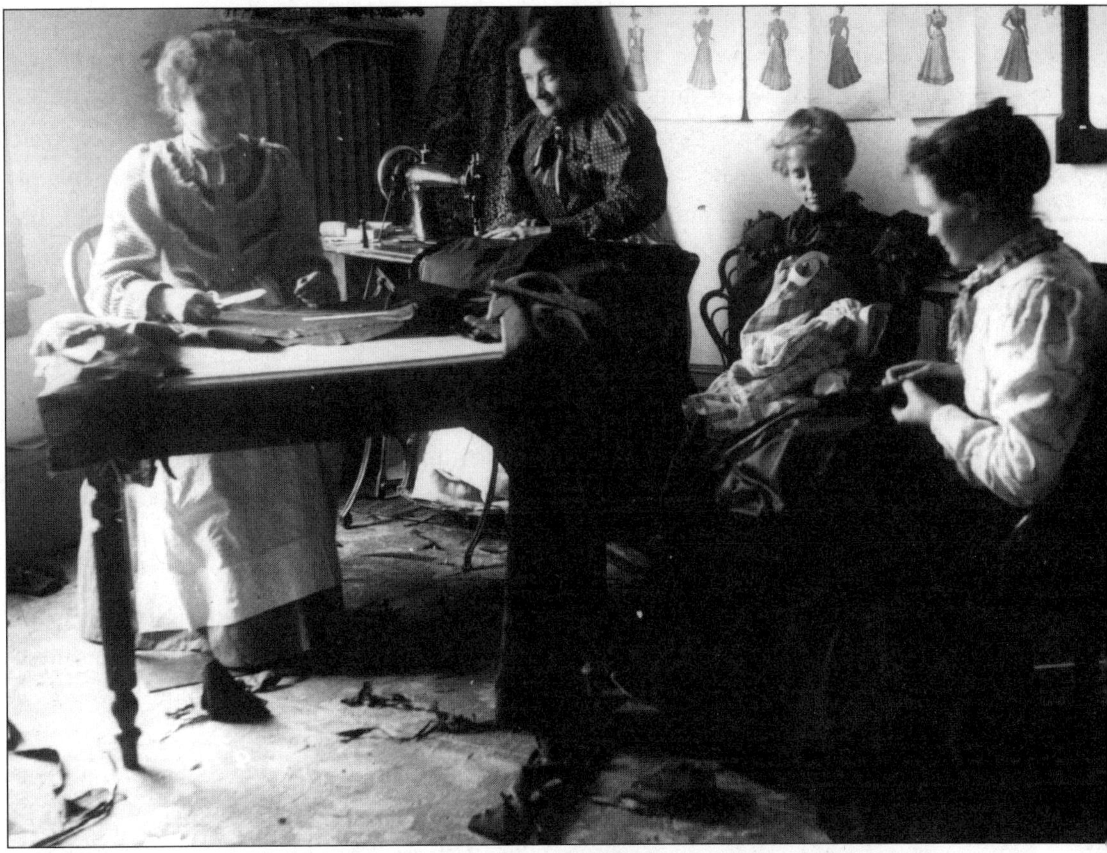

This dressmaking shop in Boulder in 1913 is typical. Pictures from the latest fashion magazines hang from the wall above a treadle-powered sewing machine. The seamstresses at right are handstitching, while the women at left carefully cut material. Courtesy Carnegie Branch Library for Local History, Boulder Historical Society Collection.

Although there are many fictional accounts of poor treatment of girls by greedy shop owners in both the millinery and dressmaking industries, the relationship between the high and low ends of the apprentice hierarchy probably was little different from that in any profession, female or male. Human nature being what it is, there were undoubtedly both good and greedy madams. However, these professions and only a few others allowed female advancement toward financial independence during this period.

The apprenticeship system slowly disintegrated in the United States during the late nineteenth and early twentieth centuries because of the rapid growth of the western frontier. Although pioneer women who could take care of themselves were admired as they helped tame the frontier, female financial independence was not a high priority in the Victorian scheme of things. It was highly frowned upon, and independent businesswomen were often accused of using their legal businesses as fronts for houses of prostitution. That there never seemed to be any men inside did not deter wagging tongues or repair disputed reputations.

Female shop owners were also discriminated against in other ways. Operating a small business was a difficult proposition for all entrepreneurs, and women faced additional obstacles.[5] Credit was extremely difficult for a woman to obtain from male-dominated wholesalers, bankers, and material vendors. Credit investigators such as the Dunn Company often would refer to a female owner as "respectable but without any independent means of her own." U.S. laws made it very difficult for a woman to own her own land or assets, and generally women were not given any training in the handling of business financial procedures, as it was assumed that a proper Victorian lady would quickly marry and settle down to raise a family and manage the home for the male head of the household. If a woman did acquire property or a business, she could quickly lose it by entering into a marriage contract, as the new husband became instant owner of her chattel and real estate, with a few exceptions. (The Spanish legal traditions of the Southwest, including southern Colorado, were more lenient toward a woman's right to own real estate.)

On the other hand, a well-respected or well-to-do husband or father as partner offered easier access to credit and usually some education or training in business-related financial dealings. About 15 percent of dressmaking and milliner shops were managed by husband-and-wife teams, with the wife in charge of the day-to-day operations and the workforce, and the husband handling the finances and purchases. Olive Oakes specifically mentioned her male cousin, Cody, as keeper of the Denver shop, which was in his wife's name. The ad claims the business had a large and diverse quantity of goods on hand, which implies capital requirements to purchase and transport the stock to Denver directly from the East.

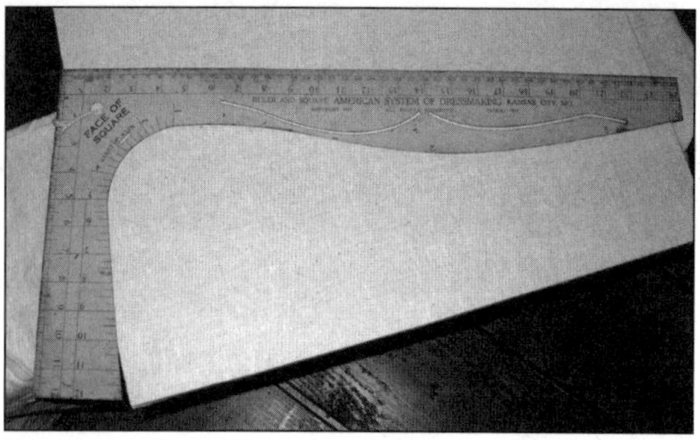

This dressmaker's T-square and ruler were used by dress shops to properly size and cut patterns and material. Dressmaking was a complex and highly skilled occupation, and the dressmaker possessed an aptitude in mathematics. Author's collection. Courtesy Loveland Historical Museum.

As for the tools of the trade, the first needles—the most important of tools—were made of bone. By the mid-nineteenth century, needles were made of steel, and the dressmaker could boast of a set of different sizes to aid in handstitching her creations. Metal pins were expensive and in short supply. Sewing machines were beginning to come on the market, and Elisabeth Cody had a Singer machine in stock, probably the first in Denver, that was for sale at her shop.[6]

A series of patents had been issued for sewing machines starting in 1755, but Isaac Singer combined the necessary entrepreneurial skills of raising capital, aggressive marketing, and ruthlessness with someone else's technology (he lost the court battle

A Victorian play on words shows a western sense of humor. This five-person shop busily tends to business. Photo by W. W. Cecil. Courtesy Colorado Historical Society, CHS-C2.

with Elias Howe over Howe's sewing machine patent) to bring the machine to market by the mid-1850s.

Dressmakers of the period used measuring rules to aid in precisely cutting the materials. These tools were produced in curves (the French curve), straights, squares, and ells and are much prized by collectors today.[7]

But the process was little changed prior to Colorado's development. A woman would go to her dressmaker's shop, or have the dressmaker come to her if she was sufficiently well-off to command this level of servitude. The two would discuss the dress as to its style, materials, and completion date. Together they would look at fashion prints or catalogs for current dress or hat styles. Patternmakers and others in the industry sold monthly magazines and mailed them all over the world, and to any frontier settlement that had mail delivery, to eager subscribers longingly observing the fashions in Paris, New York, or London.

The customer might have the first of many fittings at that time or make arrangements for the first fitting or measurement. She was contracting for a unique dress, custom designed and fabricated to her specifications and physique. She might rely entirely upon her dressmaker's professional judgment, but it was much more likely that the dress would be designed by committee: the dressmaker, customer, and possibly a confidante, such as the customer's mother, sister, or friend.

The first fitting would consist of covering the customer with rolls of paper or bolts of inexpensive material to "fit" the inner most layer by measuring, marking, and cutting to match her shape. Fitting was one of the primary factors used to judge a dressmaker's level of professionalism. As one might expect, this initial fitting was often a difficult task, as a proper fit was as much a qualitative judgment by a finicky customer as an actual physical match.

Bt the mid-nineteenth century, needles were made of steel.

There might be as many as ten fittings as different layers of the garment were added to the base layer. The parties viewed the fittings differently, and the relationship between them was, in general, far more complex than customer-salesperson meetings today. Since the dressmaker or milliner was acting as a fashion consultant, she would be expected to know what the opposite sex was interested in leading to a more personal relationship with the customer, especially concerning her husband or beaux.

The millinery shop in Loveland passed seamlessly through several local women's hands. Located on Fourth Street between Cleveland and the railroad tracks, it was owned by Miss Farham in 1886, Miss Rickard in 1887, and Mrs. Leedham in 1889. That year, Leedham sold it to Miss Hannah Huggy, the twenty-four-year-old daughter of Henry Huggy, a local footwear salesman who had once owned shoe and boot stores in Denver. Miss Huggy operated the store for two years until she married William C. Vorreiter. The Vorreiters moved to Silvercliffe, and the store reverted back to Miss Farham. It's possible that Farham actually owned the building and business and leased it to the other women. The Vorreiters spent ten years in Silvercliffe until returning to Loveland, where they leased a dry goods and millinery store.[8]

Westward expansion and migration of America's population had two opposite effects on the apprentice system so prevalent in Europe and England. New settlements were constantly springing to life only one or two days ride from yesterday's "new town," continually creating a demand for skilled labor in any and all disciplines. If only one man had any experience as a blacksmith, he could hang up a sign and be in business. Consequently, it was difficult to keep apprentices in service for the required length of time during which they were to learn their trade. Young men who were short on experience but long on wanderlust simply disappeared, moving west to become the owner of a new shop on the new frontier. Perhaps they didn't know the trade as well as they might, but the westward flow of society created instant opportunity for thousands of people. This was certainly true for young women in the dressmaking and millinery business. By moving west into small villages and mining towns, a woman with some experience in sewing could become a seamstress and the town's dressmaker or milliner, running a one-person business from her home or from a small room in the village. She might be supplementing her family's income or simply supporting herself.

It was difficult to keep apprentices in service for the required length of time.

In Colorado's larger population centers, the one-room mercantile store soon grew into larger establishments with merchandise divided into departments to better aid the customer in finding what they desired. Department stores created by men such as David May, William C. Daniels, and J. J. Joslin soon dominated the marketplace, a concept that has continued to the present day. Daniels and Fisher and the Golden Eagle were especially successful in the millinery and dressmaking areas, with large staffs of milliners and seamstresses creating custom and semicustom designs for their clients. The 1899 Daniels and Fisher's catalog contained a section of new dresses designed by the Butterick Company of New York City, which Butterick wrote especially for that store.

Ebenezer Butterick started the Butterick Pattern Company in 1863, making patterns for boy's and men's clothing first, and women's clothing three years later.[9] The idea of proportional patterns was revolutionary—that the same dress could be fitted to different customers by requiring only one or two measurements. Butterick would design a dress and sell the paper pattern in several sizes, eliminating a major part of the work necessary to create a custom dress. This was especially important to women in rural areas of the country, like Colorado, as they could select a dress, receive its paper pattern by mail, and sew their own more cheaply than by hiring a professional dressmaker. Less-qualified workers who had good sewing skills but who lacked creativity could also use patterns to compete in the marketplace. And in large department stores like Daniels and Fisher in Denver, customers could choose a dress based on a printed picture of the product instead of rough sketches done by a dressmaker.

Fashion magazines and national pattern makers distributed the latest fashions in hats and dresses by U.S. mail. This March 1897 advertisment from *Standard Designer*, a New York–based magazine, is typical.

Proportional patterns also eliminated most, but not all, of the fittings that were traditionally required with custom dressmaking. But this also eliminated the person-to-person interchange necessary for a perfect fit and the constant communication that might keep a particularly well-off but hard-to-please customer happy enough to return for repeat business.

National pattern companies such as Butterick did a booming business across the country and helped disperse fashion concepts to all by publishing monthly magazines and catalogs with the latest styles, conveniently available as patterns.

The hatmaking profession was very much like dressmaking, with apprentices coming up through the trade in a similar fashion. The business aspects were slightly different, however, as hats and bonnets needed fewer trimmings, with the emphasis placed on the seemingly infinite selection of materials available. This required the shop owner to stock supplies of "fancy goods" for a custom-made hat that might not be used for months. Stocks of goods required the wholesaler to advance credit to the shopkeeper, and as stated earlier, female shopkeepers had difficulties obtaining credit. The success of these ventures, then, was based not only upon sound business practices and financial backing but also on the artistic creativity of the owner or highest-level trimmer or fitter, as well as on the interpersonal skills used to satisfy her customers.

She could ride, but could she breathe? From *Standard Designer* magazine, March 1897.

Westward migration in America affected not only the apprenticeship system, but also the financial system's attitude toward credit. As more and more small-business people, both male and female, owned their own shops, competition for their business caused credit restrictions to ease. By the early twentieth century, credit was more freely given to women dressmakers and milliners based on the strength of their business rather than on their gender.

Millinery and dress shops were well spread out among the population. The fitting process dictated that dress shops be close to where customers lived. Obviously, larger urban areas such as Denver, Leadville, Pueblo, and Colorado Springs had the most shops, but the transportation system of railroads and freight wagons brought millinery and dressmaking materials and dress catalogs to every town in the state.

Four Victorian-era women sit near the lake at Denver's City Park. Their choice of fashionable hats bodes well for Denver's millinery industry. Charles S. Lillybridge Collection. Courtesy Colorado Historical Society, CHS-L1454.

The demand for ready-to-wear garments that were easily available at much lower cost changed fashion. Looser-fitting dresses were better suited to factory fabrication, and soon only the most affluent customers patronized dress shops and millinery stores for custom creations, while department stores offered both custom and factory clothing. The Forrest A. Heath Clothing Factory in Denver offered ready-to-wear clothing throughout the Rocky Mountain states.

Larger retail stores such as Denver Dry Goods, Golden Eagle, and Daniels and Fisher used many dressmakers and milliners in various departments whom their customers could visit. These stores were often training grounds for unskilled workers trying to enter the trade.[10]

One such apprentice was Kate Ferretti, who was born in Denver in 1891, the second child of immigrants Henry and Louisa Malnati from Lombardi, Italy. Henry, a stonemason, came to Colorado to work on the State Capitol Building. The family loved the mountains, the area reminding them of their home in Italy. When Kate was

The dressmaker's shop gradually changed from a service business to a retail outlet of dresses and hats manufactured by larger, more efficient businesses. This is Mrs. Peyton's Ladies Finery in Cañon City. Courtesy Denver Public Library, Western History Collection, X-7595.

first born, her name was Henrietta, but her older brother, Carl, told her first teacher her name was Kate when he escorted her to the first day of school. Kate she would remain.

Kate started in the millinery trade at Denver's Golden Eagle store at age thirteen. She was not bound over to a modiste; when her older brother started working there, she hung around the store, and was drawn to the millinery department. Eventually the department manager asked Kate if she wanted to learn how to make hats. Of course, she did! After two years, she transferred to the Denver Dry Goods store, where she earned $5 more per week. That Kate initiated the transfer, asked for, and received a substantial raise indicates there was a healthy demand for skilled hatmakers as well as a free-market system that was in good working order for laborers. Kate did the same thing two years later, crossing the street to Madam Mulroy's shop, The Bon Marche, one of the most exclusive millinery shops in Denver, where she received an additional $5 per week. There she met and made hats for Denver's high society, including the famous Molly Brown. Kate married

Colorado had a few clothing manufacturers. The Heath Clothing factory in Denver had industrial sewing machines, which replaced the treadle-powered ones used by the dress and hat shops decades earlier. Courtesy Denver Public Library, Western History Collection, X-24027.

Giocomo Ferretti on April 10, 1917, completing the transformation of Henrietta Malnati to Kate Ferretti.

When Madam Mulroy closed The Bon Marche, Kate Ferretti became the preferred milliner for Denver's wealthiest women. She traveled twice a year to Paris, bringing back materials and, more importantly, designs for her western clientele, all on credit. Women from Utah, Texas, and New Mexico traveled to Denver for her creations. Kate set up shop at her home at 4245 Tejon Street in North Denver and was so in demand that she had her customers send their chauffeured cars from the Capitol Hill district to North Denver to pick up their hats. She was a monthly visitor to the Bonfils Mansion at Eighth Avenue and Wadsworth, mostly to work with F. G.

Bonfils's older daughter and heir, May. The personal relationship between milliner and wealthy customer was still strong well into the twentieth century.

During most of this time, Kate had at least three full-time workers. Her daughter, Ann, came to work with her, eventually taking over the business in the 1970s. Kate's two sons also helped by managing the finances and other overhead tasks, a typical division of labor by gender.[11]

Kate Ferretti remade this hat in 1974 to match one she had originally created for one of her better-known customers, Molly Brown. It resides at the Molly Brown House in Denver. Author's collection.

Like the dressmaking industry, the millinery business also changed. Ready-to-wear base hat forms and then complete hats were shipped from factories in the East. And as fashions changed, the hat lost its allure and hairstyles became more important.

Only three millinery shops and three dress shops were reported in Colorado by the 1930 census. Daniels and Fisher and David May of the May Company had won the states competitive battle for the women's fashion business, just as Macy's and other department stores had throughout the eastern United States. Nonetheless, there was still enough demand for women's hats in the 1970s to support an exclusive, top end millinery shop in Denver, and today's women can still have a custom-made gown designed and sewn to their exacting specifications.

■ ■ ■

Notes

[1] D. C. Oakes, letters and manuscripts from 1859 to 1885. Denver, Colorado Historical Society, Hart Library.

[2] *Rocky Mountain News*, March 24, 1860, 3.

[3] *Rocky Mountain News*, December 5, 1866.

[4] United States Census, 1860.

[5] Wendy Gamber, *The Female Economy* (Urbana and Chicago: University of Illinois Press, 1997).

[6] *Rocky Mountain News*, Cody ad, September 10, 1860.

[7] Claudia Kidwell, *Cutting a Fashionable Fit* (Washington, DC: Smithsonian Institute Press, 1979), 25–75.

[8] Loveland–Big Thompson Centennial, 132–133, 140–143, 146.

[9] "History of Butterick," http://www.butterick.com.

[10] *Golden Eagle Catalog*, Denver Public Library Western History Manuscripts.

[11] Oral history interview of Kate Ferretti.

CHAPTER 5

Carnations

D. C. Oakes and the Fifty-Niners weren't too particular about the "presentation" of the dinner table when they were on their way to the Pikes Peak gold region. Flower gardens and floral arrangements would have to wait for the civilizing influence of women after they arrived.

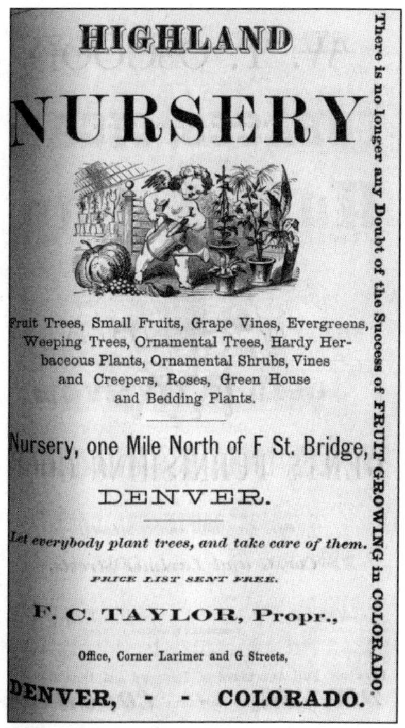

By June 1863, seed companies in the eastern United States were advertising both vegetable and flower seeds in their catalogs to Denver's "Seedsmen, Florists and Nurserymen."[1] You could buy flowerpots from Golden City Pottery in 1867[2] and specialty roses from E. D. Marion's Capital Nursery greenhouse at the east end of F Street in 1868.[3] (F Street was renamed Fifteenth Street in 1873.)

In the 1871 *Rocky Mountain Business Directory*, F. C. Taylor placed a prominent advertisement for plants of all kinds, including roses and greenhouse and bedding plants from his Highland Nursery at the other end of F Street, one mile north of the F Street bridge.[4]

The following article appeared in the *Rocky Mountain News Weekly* in 1873:

> The greater interest which our people are manifesting in the cultivation of flowers is manifested by the prosperous condition of our greenhouses and nurseries. In Highland Mr. Marion has a fine collection of plants, and ample arrangements for their cultivation. Mr. Opitz, on California Street, is doubling his hot-house, and greatly enlarging his facilities for growing

> flowers, vines, etc. The "Bellevue Gardens" of Mr. Rushmore & Son, are being improved and a large greenhouse being erected. Mr. R had followed gardening in New York state and in Virginia, but he informs us that flowers grow finer in this soil—with water—and bloom more richly than in any other he ever saw. The existence of the greenhouses and their evident growing prosperity is an evidence that our people are turning their attention in a larger degree to horticulture. There is a visible increase in flower gardens, while house plants are now to be found more frequently in our homes. The fact betokens a very proper direction for the public taste to take, and continued growth is to be desired.[5]

Marion evidently had moved from one end of F Street to the other and purchased the Highland Nursery from Taylor.

By 1883 the Capital Nursery, at the east end of F Street, was owned by the Mauff family and renamed the Capitol Hill Nursery. That year a water tap, which stretched a full block from Twelfth to Thirteenth streets along Logan Street, was installed to help fill the growing requirement for water at the greenhouse. It would remain a greenhouse or floral shop to the present, and is now called Ardelt's Victorian Gardens.

Greenhouses proliferated in all Colorado settlements, as wives and mothers created a market for some of the prettier things in life. Nurseries provided trees, shrubs, and plants for the home and garden, as well as cut flowers for special occasions such as weddings and funerals. E. C. Kimbell's greenhouse was next to his home in Colorado Springs in 1875.[6] H. M. Sammis was supplying flowers and plants in Longmont in 1880,[7] T. A. Kerr supplied flowers to the Durango-Silverton area,[8] and the Western Slope Greenhouse supplied Montrose in 1899.[9] The South Denver Floral Company tried to expand its market by advertising in northern Colorado towns like Greeley and Boulder, as shown in this ad.[10]

From the *Greeley Tribune*, April 13, 1893.

Elitch Gardens originated as a greenhouse to grow vegetables and flowers for the tables at John and Mary Elitch's restaurant—the Tortoni—in downtown Denver. John had been an actor in California before coming to Denver. The couple soon expanded their gardens at Thirty-eighth and Tennyson into a family gathering area to watch theater and stroll among the gardens. Rides were added through the years, and Mary and her second husband opened a flower shop on the grounds to sell flowers to the folks who came to enjoy the gardens.

It was only natural for Mary Elitch to go into the flower retail business and later into the wholesale side of the industry. This truck delivered flowers to customers from both the retail outlet that was downtown at Fifteenth and Stout streets and the greenhouses at Elitch's Gardens. Courtesy Betty Lynne Hall Collection.

The multitude of bright, sunny days and good virgin soil of the state were ideal for the industry and by 1900 there were four hundred thousand square feet of greenhouses.[11] Greenhouse owners produced vegetables for off-season consumption, with local restaurants as steady customers. Outdoor plants for gardens were and are still a good supply of revenue, but it was the cut flower industry that bloomed in this unlikely region and made Colorado, for a time, the carnation capital of the United States.

The carnation, *Dianthus caryophyllus*, is native to southern Europe and blooms during the warm summer months in its wild state. It has been used for hundreds of years as a decorative cut flower because of its ability to retain its beauty after being harvested. It was grown and used profusely in England, where it was preferred by the royalty for decoration during special occasions. Indeed, the legend of its name is that it came from the term "coronation flower," because it was used abundantly during the coronations of the British royalty.

The greenhouse at Robbins Floral Company in Longmont teems with carnations that are almost ready to be cut. Strings were run above the trays to hold the stalks upright. Courtesy Longmont Museum.

Carnations were first reported in the Colorado newspapers in 1898 in Glenwood Springs, where Hayes Greenhouse exhibited a "fine blooming Marguerite Carnation" at a Glenwood fair.[12] A year later in Greeley, Searing's greenhouse grew carnations for its early citizens.[13] Colorado's well-known and -advertised annual three hundred days of sunshine and its greenhouse technology suited the carnation. The bright sunlight of the day and the cool temperatures of the night helped produce large-bloomed flowers with hardened stems and calyx, enabling the stems to grow long and still support large flowers.

There were only a few varieties of carnations before the turn of the century: the Marguerite; Day Break Pink; Laddie, another pink; Red Spectrum, a red bloom; Carthage; and several others.

Carnations are not grown from seeds but from cuttings. The cut stem pieces were set in soil outside in May or June and then transplanted in August or September inside the greenhouse. They bloomed after two years. Timing was critical; an early frost could destroy the entire crop, so a grower needed to get the plants inside the greenhouse before the freeze. But once inside, the heat of late summer days could just as quickly kill them. During such hot days, early Denver greenhouse workers would throw dust and manure from the city streets on top of the glass roof and hose it down to provide shade for the plants inside. At maturity, the plants were about a foot tall with three to five blooms per stem. Later hybridization would increase the count to ten to sixteen blooms per plant.

Greenhouses had to be heated during the winter nights to keep the plants from freezing. There were two major ways of doing this. The first used hot water that heated the space through pipes. The water was heated in boilers, and the system was similar to that being used to heat homes during this time. The second method used

Top: Daniels and Fisher had a large department of floral products in their downtown Denver store. A horsedrawn delivery wagon, which is not being used, sits outside among the farm's chickens and turkeys, proving the farm raised more than just flowers. Courtesy Denver Public Library, Western History Collection, X-22813. Above: The Robbins Flower Shop had two different kinds of delivery trucks, shown in this photo outside its Longmont business. Courtesy Longmont Museum.

heated air that flowed under the space. A firebox was placed at one end of a narrow but long greenhouse, and the chimney at the other. A tunnel below the benches carried the flue gas and heat from the firebox to the chimney, heating the bench space. This was called a flue-type greenhouse.

The business of selling flowers in this period followed the practices of other local businesses, consisting of small shops at the greenhouse for drop-in customers or an office or small showroom downtown where customers could order flowers, shrubs, or other plants. Some shops delivered to customers' homes, using horse-drawn delivery wagons heated in the winter by a small charcoal stove that kept plants from freezing.[14] Delivery trucks replaced the wagons in the 1920s.

The Daniels and Fisher floral department sold more than just flowers. Courtesy Denver Public Library, Western History Collection, X-22865.

Retail outlets evolved to become lovely flower shops full of blooms that would attract customers willing to spend their money on the "finer things in life." The women of Denver's red light district were steady customers, as the perception of culture and refinement was important to their clientele.

Some growers realized that expanding the market for their product would be good for business, and they looked outside the Rocky Mountain area for customers. One of the first to ship outside the state was John E. Johnson, founder of Pikes Peak Floral Company in Colorado Springs, who shipped flowers and arrangements to Utah, Kansas, and Texas. Greenhouse workers and nursery operators could not grow carnations in the southern states because the temperatures were too high during the summer months. With the growth of the population centers of Houston, Austin, and Dallas, Johnson found an expanding market. He had vertically integrated his business, producing the flowers in multiple greenhouses in the Colorado Springs area, wholesaling to other florists in state and out, and operating a retail business in Colorado Springs for local trade. Although Pikes Peak Floral Company no longer has shops in Colorado, there are outlets still in Texas and Tennessee.

New technology caught the fancy of Denver businessman John Valentine, who opened Park Floral Company in east Denver in 1879. He used the telegraph to get flower orders from out-of-state florists; cut, arranged, and packed them the next day, and shipped them by rail to arrive three or four days after being ordered—an unheard-of accomplishment at the time. Refrigerated railcars and ice-pack containers for the flowers helped lengthen their life. (A 1959 Colorado State University thesis compares ice-pack and moist-pack methods of shipping flowers.[15]) Customers in New Orleans could order carnations for a wedding or party on Monday or Tuesday and have the flowers in high-quality condition for the weekend festivities. This was the beginning of FTD (Florist Telegraph Delivery), a nationwide florist network still in place today, although the dots and dashes of the telegraph have been replaced by the digital data of computers that show photographs of styles and arrangements available with single-click ordering. The telegraph concept also was modified to allow customers in one part of the country to order flowers by wire, to be delivered to family or friends at another location by a florist nearby. The flowers were from the deliverer's stock, thus ensuring freshness and eliminating the cost of transportation. Valentine, along with W. Penn of Boston, coined the phrase "Say it with flowers," an advertising slogan that is still used today.[16]

Prior to 1909, sales of flowers and plants had been made either at the greenhouse or at a small store downtown where people might shop at the same time as they attended to other errands. The small downtown shops had become elegant storefronts with beautiful arrangements that would catch the eye of potential customers. With increased production but specialization of the greenhouses with a range (a greenhouse

Top: Park Floral greenhouses were located at Petersburg (later Sheridan). McClure photographed the tower and greenhouses in the 1930s. Courtesy Denver Public Library, Western History Collection, MCC-4168. Above: Park Floral Company was one of the largest retail and wholesale dealers in Denver. Its shop was located on East Colfax, as shown in this photograph by Lewis McClure. Courtesy Denver Public Library, Western History Collection, MCC-4165.

or close grouping of greenhouses under a single owner) arose the need for a wholesale house to quickly distribute different products to both local and out-of-state florists, particularly the latter. Instead of a florist in Missouri trying to find a greenhouse in Colorado that raised carnations and another that raised roses or asters, the Missouri florist could contact a wholesaler and place an entire order. The wholesaler would gather the required flowers and ship them directly to the florist or to that florist's customer. Nathan Benson, who immigrated from Sweden, started Denver Wholesale Florists in August 1909. He had previously operated a greenhouse at Hampton and Santa Fe specializing in carnations. He believed that an expanded, out-of-state market would welcome the large-bloomed and hardy flower, and a wholesale arrangement with other growers was the best way to capitalize on the opportunity. In 1909, Benson, W. C. Walter, Emil Gauber, Fred Hall, Benjamin Bolt, Lyle Waterbury, and C. F. Maler incorporated as the Denver Wholesale Florists.[17]

In the world of carnation growers and plant hybridizers a mutant plant did not carry a negative connotation.

DWF, along with Pikes Peak Floral and Park Floral, introduced more and more of the nation to the Colorado carnation. Local growers won national prizes and recognition for high-quality and beautiful new varieties of carnations, and Nathan demanded a high-quality and standard-graded product, enhancing the state's reputation as a provider of quality floral products, particularly carnations.

In 1938, Park Hill Floral Company and Elitch's joined up with several other local florists to start the Park-Elitch wholesale house, capitalizing on the two well-known names to sell floral products out of state and compete with other wholesale houses in the area. Growers aligned themselves with one wholesale house or another, sometimes as partners, sometimes by contract. Disputes often arose between the two as the wholesalers purchased flowers from the growers at a negotiated price, depending on grade and quality. Growers would move to another wholesaler to get a better price for their product and back again as the years passed; as more growers entered production, some banded together to form even more wholesale houses.

In the world of carnation growers and plant hybridizers a mutant plant did not carry a negative connotation. Growers were always on the lookout for a new variety that could be marketed before their competition could react. In 1946 probably the most profitable mutant carnation was found in a New England greenhouse. The Willam Sim was a scarlet red carnation that put other reds to shame and produced up to twelve blossoms on a long, strong stem in the first year. This almost doubled the growers' output and profit. Within five years, no one grew any reds but William Sims. It was thirty-five percent of the entire Colorado crop in 1950, worth $2 million annually to local growers. The blooms lasted ten to fourteen days, even after being shipped two thousand miles by plane.

Two years later, the William Sims grown throughout the country mutated again, with a white flower growing among the sea of reds not only in Colorado greenhouses but also in others across the nation. The white Sim had the same characteristics as the red one, and very quickly growers were producing white Sims and discarding the other whites. In Colorado in 1950, white Sims were twenty-five percent of the entire Colorado market, worth $1.5 million annually.

In 1950, Ray and Harold Crowley of Denver spotted a beautiful pink carnation in the sea of white Sims they were growing. A grower's discovery of a different-colored carnation was equivalent to a miner's discovery of a gold nugget in his pan of sand. The Crowleys realized it could be a national best-seller and grew two hundred fifty thousand stems from that one plant, selling them as fast as they could. The trick was to proliferate the cuttings as quickly as possible, sell the blooms to the retail public, and sell the stems and pieces to their competitors before they could plant the stems themselves.

Because of the high quality of Colorado carnations, sellers in the state had problems with their wholesale customers. Out-of-state wholesalers would buy Colorado carnations and then tag them as grown in their own ranges. Colorado sellers devised a plan to permanently attach a copyrighted plastic seal to the stem of two carnations out of the dozen, advertising to the final customer where these beautiful flowers had been grown.

After World War II, more and more freight was carried by the airlines, a transportation method that favored the cut-flower industry. In 1954 a standing order of two hundred Colorado carnations was prepared, packed, and delivered each Wednesday from the wholesalers of Denver to the White House in Washington, D.C. A deliveryman would drive the flowers to Stapleton Airport, where they would be placed on a nonstop United Airlines flight to the nation's capital. The flowers were displayed throughout the White House each week by Denver native and favorite daughter, Mamie Doud Eisenhower.[18] Standing weekly orders of flowers, or daily orders, were very common. The Santa Fe Railroad had a standing daily order for three dozen yellow carnations of a specific shade for the Turquoise Room diners on their transcontinental Super Chief trains. St. Patrick's Day was a difficult time for carnation sellers. Carnations had been hybridized in many colors, but they refused to grow in shades of green and blue. To satisfy their Irish customers growers had to resort to dipping whites into buckets of water that was dyed green or blue. Overnight, the carnations would slurp up the water and their petals changed to the colors desired.

With the use of air freight, flowers could be ordered by wire or phone and delivered the next day. This allowed other less hardy flowers to be included in the product mix and hence increased the flexibility of Denver's wholesalers. However, this was a mixed blessing to Colorado growers and sellers, as it also allowed increased competition from California, where growers had always been able to produce carnations at a slightly lower cost per bloom, and eventually from growers outside the country, particularly in Central and South America. Lower labor costs in those countries more than offset the increased transportation cost of shipping into the United States.

The cost of producing carnation blooms was always an important marker. California ranges had a ready, expanding market on the West Coast, but as transportation improved they began to take business away from Colorado growers. California greenhouses did not need to be heated, an important advantage as the cost of heating fuel increased in the Rocky Mountain region. Colorado growers continually tried different fuels to lower their heating costs, from cheaper coal to fuel oil to natural gas. The oil embargo in 1973 and resulting increase in oil prices was one of the underlying reasons for the collapse of the industry in the 1970s and 1980s. Production peaked in Colorado in 1974, when 147 growers had 7,402,374 square feet of greenhouses.[19]

Carnations and other cut flowers could also be raised much more cheaply overseas, and with the use of air cargo, all of the national producers were at a competitive disadvantage. Customers care less about where the flowers are grown than about how much they cost. Cut flowers are still grown in the state today, but the major out-of-state market is gone. The carnations (and roses) you buy at your local Colorado grocery store do not come from Colorado greenhouses but from South American growers, who benefit from very low labor costs and the Andean Free Trade Agreement. The U.S. government signed this agreement to allow farmers in Colombia, Bolivia, Ecuador, and Peru to grow something besides cocaine to sell to the U.S. market, and thus killed Colorado's carnation industry. Most of the state's greenhouses raise bedding plants and potted flowers for today's market.

■ ■ ■

Notes

[1] *Denver Weekly Commonwealth*, June 18, 1863, 4.

[2] *Rocky Mountain News Weekly*, June 19, 1867, 3.

[3] Colorado Transcript, June 17, 1868, 3.

[4] *Rocky Mountain Business Directory*, 1871.

[5] *Rocky Mountain News Weekly*, October 22, 1873, 1.

[6] *Colorado Springs Gazette*, January 16, 1875, 3.

[7] *Boulder News and Courier*, June 4, 1880, 2.

[8] *Durango Democrat*, October 14, 1902, 1.

[9] *Telluride Journal*, May 27, 1899.

[10] *Greeley Tribune*, April 13, 1893, 7.

[11] Dick Kingman, *A History—Colorado Flower Growers and Its People* (Denver: Colorado Greenhouse Growers Association, 1986), 11.

[12] *Glenwood Post*, June 11, 1898, 3.

[13] *Greeley Tribune*, May 25, 1899, 1.

[14] Kingman, 13.

[15] Heinzelman, *A Comparison of Two Methods of Selecting and Packing Cut Carnations.*

[16] Kingman, 14.

[17] Ibid., 17.

[18] *Saturday Evening Post.*

[19] Kingman, 83.

CHAPTER 6

Mining Precious Metals

After 1848, Americans had watched and listened to the incredible stories of instant wealth coming out of the California goldfields. Never mind that very few Forty-Niners actually struck it rich. "If only I had gone," they thought.

By 1857, hard times and a debilitating recession affected the entire country. In 1858–1859 the restless population was offered another opportunity to strike gold, and tens of thousands headed to the eastern slopes of the Rockies—a considerably easier trip than traveling to the California goldfields. The Pikes Peak gold strikes were based on even less-credible evidence that there was gold than were those in California, but it didn't matter. The Fifty-Niners became only the latest in history to hunt for and mine precious metals, and it was based more on faith than on fact.

D. C. Oakes had arrived in the Pikes Peak area in October 1858 to see for himself if the reports were true. After watching Green Russell and his party pan for gold in the sands of the Platte River, Oakes returned to his home in Pacific City, Iowa, and with Luke Tierney published a guidebook for going west. In the book, Oakes listed the following equipment for a party of four who wanted to mine gold in the Pikes Peak region: four steel picks, four steel shovels, four axes, four new gold pans, three augers, a one-inch chisel, one handsaw, one drawing knife, and one twelve-inch file.

Based on the experiences of the California miners and the discovery of gold in the gravels of the South Platte the year earlier, the Pikes Peak Fifty-Niners expected to find most of the gold in placer deposits in the plentiful streams along and within the Rocky Mountains. However, Oakes also purchased a steam sawmill along with his

Every gold seeker carried a gold pan to see if gold was present. If it wasn't, he moved on to the next likely looking spot. From *The Metallurgy of Silver, Gold and Mercury in the United States* by Thomas Egleston.

The cradle or rocker would handle five to ten times as much gravel and sand as a gold pan, but the process was the same. The miner agitated the mass with water to allow the gold to sink to the bottom. Everything else was washed away. From *The Metallurgy of Silver, Gold and Mercury in the United States* by Thomas Egleston.

A long tom, or "tom" for short, used the force of water to wash the lighter gravels and sands away from the heavier gold. A tom could handle even more than a cradle or rocker and was the main production tool of the placer miner. From *The Metallurgy of Silver, Gold and Mercury in the United States* by Thomas Egleston.

They did it the same way in 1556 when George Bauer published *De Re Metallica* in Latin. The book and its woodblock illustrations would guide miners worldwide for the next two hundred years.

mining equipment and headed back toward the Front Range on March 10, 1859. If he couldn't find gold, he would supply lumber to the other miners.

Those early miners would search streambeds for "color" by using a gold pan. Panning entailed placing gravel and dirt in the pan and using water from the stream to wash away everything except the gold. This worked only because of the higher weight of gold. Panning gold was hard work. In order to wash more dirt and gravel, miners used rockers, "long toms," and sluice boxes, which all were based on the same principle as the gold pan—water flowing over the gravel fast enough to wash away the lighter material. The long toms and sluice boxes usually had layers of cloth in the bottom so the gold would become entrapped in the fibers, to be removed or "cleaned up" at the end of the day. Even the ancient Greeks used this sluicing concept, by using a sheep's fleece to catch the gold. Perhaps the image of a golden fleece is different to us than it was to them.

The Pikes Peak gold seeker placed a cotton or wool cloth in the bottom of his tom to trap the gold pieces. In 1556, gold seekers used a sheep's fleece. In the lower left corner of the illustration, two argonauts are running water through a fleece to catch any gold running out of the spring or creek.

It was not long before most free or placer gold had been removed from the surface so that miners were forced to follow the veins of paying ore down into the mountains, which made mining much more difficult. In California, miners looked for the mother lode; in Colorado the lodes were much more dispersed thanks to the geologic folding and faulting that caused the veins to pinch out or simply disappear. Places like Summitville and Cripple Creek were volcanic cores that spread the heavy metals out over huge areas, requiring special techniques to recover very small amounts of precious metal from low-grade ores. And there's a reason they are called the Rocky Mountains: picks and shovels were replaced by hammers and drills with blasting powder inserted in the drilled holes to reduce hard rock to rubble at the faces of shafts or for a stope or vein. Miners would follow a vein of high-grade ore any where it led. If it went up at an angle, the resulting shaft was called a stope. Precious metal mining was known as hardrock mining, as opposed to coal mining.

Free gold was still the object of the search; quartz veins were considered ideal, as free gold often resided among the quartz crystals. Miners dug quartz ore, ground or milled it in Spanish *arrastras* or pulverized it in stamping mills brought west by entrepreneurs, and then washed the resultant particles by hand or sluice box. Mercury was used to help separate the fine gold, a process known as amalgamation.

Often sluices were built in and under the stamps so that washing became a continuous operation that complemented the pulverizing of quartz ore. Quartz mines like the Horsfal at Gold Hill and the Gregory and Bobtail mines in Central City were the major producers during the early 1860s. An impressive $27.2 million worth of gold, $330,000 of silver, and $40,000 worth of copper were taken from the Pikes Peak gold region in the years prior to 1870.[1]

Top: An *arrastra* was a contraption of Spanish origin used to crush ore. The burro or horse (or slave) would pull the arm around a pit. The arm was attached to a big rock, and as it was dragged, it would crush anything placed in the pit. This *arrastra* was in the Colorado mill town of Dumont above Idaho Springs. Courtesy Denver Public Library, Western History Collection, X-60013. Top right: Another way to crush ore was to stamp it. Agricola illustrates how it was done in the sixteenth century. The stamps are powered by a waterwheel. The wheelbarrow looks a little strange, but the process remains the same 450 years later. From *De Re Metallic*. Above: In 1879 this stamp mill was probably steam-powered, with the crushed ore washed out from under the stamp's feet (called mortars) and into a sluice of mercury-coated copper. Gold was captured by the mercury and was later separated. From *Colorado: Its Gold and Silver Mines* by Frank Fossett.

As miners dug farther into mountain veins, the ores became difficult to identify and even harder to process. The precious metals seemed locked in the rock and would not come free as before. Mines failed as less and less gold and silver were recovered from the mills. The first gold rush to the area ended, and many of the Fifty-Niners returned home discouraged and broke. Most mine and mill operators knew there was still gold and silver in the mines, but the so-called refractory ores defied all efforts to separate out the precious metals.

Finally in 1868 a mining professor from Boston named Nathaniel Hill developed a process that concentrated the valuable Gilpin County gold and silver into what was termed a "matte" of copper sulfide. This matte was shipped all the way to Swansea, Wales, where a refining process finished the separation of the gold and silver from the copper sulfide. Hill's technique was called the Swansea process, and his mill and furnaces, built in Blackhawk near the Gregory diggings, rekindled gold fever and a second gold rush in that area.[2]

During the 1860s and '70s this is how the mining process could be described:

> Colorado miners would hand drill holes into the face of rock presently being worked. One miner working alone would hold a piece of drill steel with a chisel end and strike it with a 4 lb. hammer called a single jack. Between blows he would twist the drill steel in the hole presenting a slightly different tool angle to the rock in the bottom of the hole. When the hole became too deep for his drill rod, he exchanged it for a longer one, until his hole was to the proper depth. Not so surprisingly, this was called "single jacking."
>
> Often miners would work together with one holding and turning the drill steel and the other striking it with an 8 or 10 lb. hammer using both hands. This was called "double jacking." The miners used different patterns of drilled holes in the rock face depending on what depth and direction of the blast was required. After the pattern was finished the holes were carefully packed with blasting powder and fuses inserted in such a manner as to properly time the blast in each hole. The area was evacuated and the charges set off. Miners very carefully counted the number of explosions as a smaller number of explosions than holes packed with blasting powder meant that when they went back to the face there might yet be some unexploded shot or shots. After the dust had cleared the rubble was "mucked out." The rubble was shoveled into an ore cart and pulled away by hand, mule or windlass. After all the rubble, with or without paying ore, was removed the process was repeated.[3]

The miner was an independent cuss who might move on after a particularly frustrating shift or simply because the "gold looked richer in the next new bonanza camp." He was never paid much, about $3.50 a day; foremen received more and muckers received less. Because of the low pay, he assumed it was his right to do a little high grading to make up for it. "High grading" was the universal term for taking small amounts of extremely valuable ore out for oneself. The mine owners called it stealing and did their best to eliminate it but with little success. The saloon keeper or store owner handled it as easily and as often as gold dust or legal tender.

A mine in the Rocky Mountains was almost always a wet place, so the miner wore boots or ankle-covering brogans to keep his feet dry. He wore baggy trousers of a strong

material over union drawers, and usually only his hips or perhaps a belt of Bickford fuse cord held up his pants. The fuse cord was also used to tie off the trouser legs just above his brogans if he didn't wear boots. He wore a heavy shirt, usually plain in color; he was one of the original blue-collar workers. Under his shirt he wore a short-sleeve or sleeveless undershirt, and if the area where he worked was hot, he quickly removed his outer shirt. Both pants and trousers might have hidden pockets sewn on the inside to aid in his high-grading attempt, as would a false top to his hat. The hat was felt with a midsized brim, and was soaked in resin until it had enough hardness to fend off light blows or rocks falling from above. It was much like the construction hard hats that are mandatory for current construction workers and miners. The hat was no thing of beauty, as its lumps and scrapes were something of a badge of courage and experience. If there was falling water in his work area, the miner would wear an oilskin overcoat to stay dry. A warm, heavy coat was usually kept near the mine entrance to keep him warm outside in the cold Rocky Mountain winters. One could catch one's death of cold out there![4]

Although there were small amounts of silver in the ores dug by the Fifty-Niners, there is no doubt they were searching for gold. But it wasn't until 1870 that the silver deposits at Caribou in Boulder County revealed the importance of silver to the mining community in the Rocky

Top: A tunnel was dug, one hole at a time; in this picture, it was dug one man at a time. A miner using a hammer (usually weighing four pounds) hits a drill bit that he holds and turns after each stroke, a technique called single jacking. From *The Mining Camps Speak* by Beth and Bill Sagstetter. Middle: If one miner held the drill steel and another hit it with the hammer (usually a twelve-pound sledge), it was called double jacking. A pattern of holes would be drilled into the face of the tunnel. The holes were packed with blasting powder or later with dynamite, and the explosion would advance the face a few feet. From *Colorado: Its Gold and Silver Mines* by Frank Fossett. Bottom: Compressed, air-powered drills sped up the drilling process, and hence the speed the tunnel could be dug. Debris from the blasting was removed by hand by miners called muckers. Muckers were at the entry level of the mining workforce, while drillers were higher up the ladder. From *The Mining Camps Speak by* Beth and Bill Sagstetter.

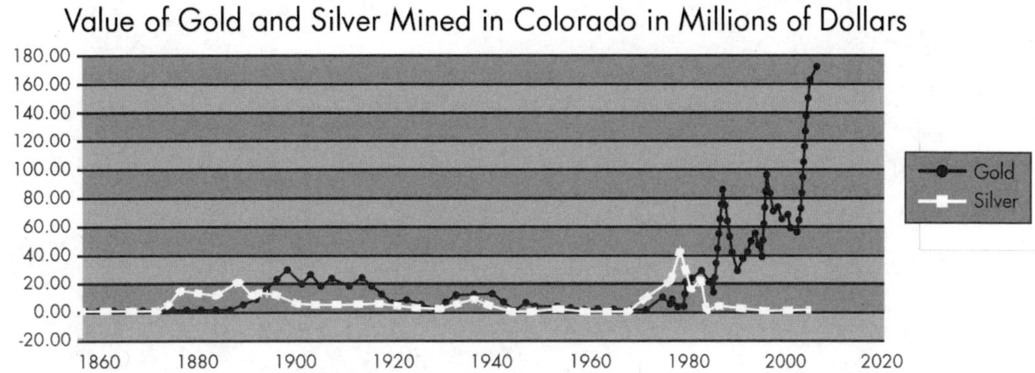

Mountain area. By 1873 there were more dollars' worth of silver mined in the territory than gold, and with the addition of the silver from Georgetown and the Leadville area in the late 1870s, silver became the dominant mined metal in the state. Both were important to the growth and development of Colorado. Silver and gold are the "colors" that represent the University of Colorado. It wasn't until the silver crash of 1893 and the Cripple Creek Gold Rush that gold assumed its dominant position once again.[5]

There are many stories of miners cursing valuable minerals because they did not know what they were. Gold telluride is a good example. It was plentiful in the Rockies, but unexpected. Even after it was identified, no one could reduce it to gold bullion. Its successful separation caused another boom in regions around Boulder and in the San Juans. Salina, Wall Street, Sunshine, Magnolia and of course Telluride were all telluride camps.

In Leadville, miners looked for gold for almost twenty years along California Gulch near the headwaters of the Arkansas River, naming their little settlement Oro City after the metal they sought. Most of the work centered at the placer claims along the gulch. Then a metallurgist named A. B. Wood and his partner, William Stevens, identified the black, heavy, iron-stained sand that clogged the miners' sluice boxes as a carbonate of lead that happened to contain a very high percentage of silver. They bought up a number of claims abandoned by the gold seekers, and their success in 1877–1878 created the silver boom at Leadville. By 1880, $11 million worth of silver was taken from the Leadville area. The town's population grew from 200 in 1878 to about 30,000 in 1881. The 1880 census for Lake County was 23,562, with 14,820 in Leadville itself. By 1890 the county population had already dwindled to 14,663 as the itchy-footed miner moved on to other promising camps like Aspen, the San Juans, or the Black Hills.

Other methods for finding placer gold in California were employed in Colorado. Hydraulic mining was used in the Breckenridge area to search for gold among the gravels of Swan River and French Gulch. Water from mountain

Top: As placer mining became less profitable, it was replaced by hydraulic mining in areas like Lincoln City near Breckenridge. In general, however, the country proved to be unsuitable for hydraulic mining. *Colorado: Its Gold and Silver Mines* by Frank Fossett. Above: The penstock was the top of the hydraulic mining water pipe. This illustration shows how the water was diverted into a flume and then dropped from the head box into the penstock. If no hydraulic mining was occurring, the water flowed back into the stream. From *The Metallurgy of Silver, Gold and Mercury by Thomas Egleston.*

streams was piped down the valleys to the areas to be mined, then was shot at high pressure through nozzles similar to those used by firefighters today, to wash the dirt and gravel down through sluices, where the gold would be trapped and saved. Ditches and flumes were used to bring water to old, dry streambeds or to move the entire creek in order to placer-mine the streambed down to bedrock. Placer mining was

Oro City was the settlement close to where Leadville would be. The miners, supplied by Horace Tabor and his wife Augusta, placered for gold for seventeen years before two miners identified the heavy black sand that clogged their sluice boxes. The sand had large amounts of lead and silver. From *Pencil Sketches of Colorado* by Alfred E. Mathews, 1866.

destructive to the environment; areas that were placer-mined more than a century ago still bear scars from the force and power of water.

Gold dredging was another way to placer large amounts of stream gravel, and was done in and around Breckenridge, near Twin Lakes northwest of Craig, at Hahns Peak north of Durango, and at Russell on the western side of La Veta Pass. A dredge was essentially a boat with a bucket digger on the front and a conveyor on the back, and floated on its own pond, dredging its bottom and sides continuously. Some dredges replaced the buckets with a separate dragline shovel to load the placer gravel into the boat. The dredged material was conveyed to a large, continuous ball mill that crushed the gravel and allowed it to drop out of the bottom of the tube into "tragles"—sluices that separated the gold in the same manner as a long tom or sluice box, the only difference being the size. The dredge might have five thousand square feet of riffles across which the crushed gravel was washed. Waste rock, dirt, and boulders were removed by the back conveyors and piled behind the dredge. Dredging in Colorado continued into the 1950s as the equipment grew in size and capacity.

During the late 1800s, steam-driven, compressed-air drilling machinery replaced the miner's single-jack and double-jack hammers. These air-driven hammers could drill holes in the rock face many times faster than by hand. Early models, called widow makers, created large quantities of rock dust that collected in miners' lungs, causing silicosis and death. Silicosis has been common among miners for hundreds of years. J. George Leyner of Colorado solved the problem with his patented air and water drill.

Leyner came west in his mother's womb as she and her husband, Peter, settled in the lower region of Left Hand Canyon, north of Boulder, farming and selling produce to the miners of Gold Hill and Four Mile Canyon. George was born August 20, 1860, in the canyon, the first white baby born in what would become Boulder County.[6] Although the family moved the farm farther east into the Canfield area, George was always interested in mining. The 1880 census listed him as a nineteen-year-old stable feed manager in Boulder County, but he spent much time watching miners and mining himself in the silver mines of Silver Plume and Georgetown.

His first effort at improving the air drill used spurts of compressed air to clean the drilled holes of dirt and grit. However, he found the best method was injecting water into the holes during the drilling, which not only cleaned out the dirt and debris but also cooled

Top: Forty years after the original Colorado gold rush, a dredge was hauled in to work the gravels panned by the Fifty-Niners on their way to Central City and Idaho Springs. A man and two women watch the proceedings in 1904. The ponds remain on 44th Avenue just west of McIntyre Street in Golden. A stone historical marker indicated the settlement of Arapahoe City. Courtesy Denver Public Library, Western History Collection, X-60126. Middle: Dredges looked out of place in Colorado, with the nearest body of water for big boats being thousands of miles away. They didn't travel very far each day, as they essentially took their pond with them. This small dredge was located at Blevins Placer on Lay Creek in Routt County. Courtesy U.S. Geological Society. Bottom: A large dredge works the gravels in Summit County. Huge amounts of sand and gravel were processed through a dredge. The more efficient a dredge was, the more marginal the area that could be mined. Courtesy U.S. Geological Society.

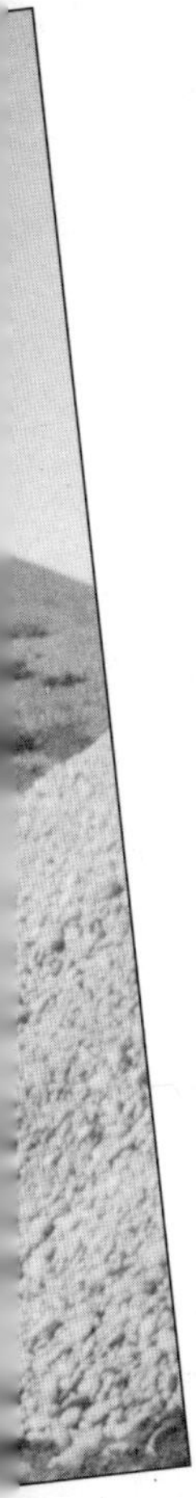

Left: Bucket after bucket of sand and gravel went from the bottom of the pond into a ball mill in the boat. The bucket conveyor was the business end of a dredge. This dredge worked South Park gravels near Fairplay. Courtesy U.S. Geological Society. Above: The Fairplay dredge works its pond. The buckets are on the left side, with the long conveyor on the right depositing the processed ores far behind the boat. Courtesy U.S. Geological Society.

the drill bit, adding life to the drill steel. By reducing rock dust in the air it also added years to the life of the miners, reducing the chances of death from silicosis. Early air-drilling equipment had one compressed air hose; later models had two hoses, one for compressed air and one for water.

Leyner's invention of the water-cooled air drill and subsequent patents in other mining equipment spawned the Leyner Machine and Equipment Company, located in the McPhee Building in Denver. In 1905 he moved the business to Littleton. Leyner's drill and air compressors were recognized throughout the world. In 1911 he sold his company to the Ingersoll-Rand Corporation of New York. Leyner married Fannie B. Batterson on September 16, 1884, in Boulder, and they lived along the Front Range until his death in 1920 from injuries suffered in a car accident near his home in Littleton.[7]

Steam power also made the job of raising ore from the shafts easier, so manually operated or horsepowered windlasses were replaced with those powered by steam engines. Later, steam engines turned new electrical generators supplying electricity to the mines. Steam power had another advantage in that it was a source of revenue for

The Leyner manufacturing plant was located in Littleton along the present-day railroad tracks. George Leyner eventually sold the company to Ingersoll-Rand, which would remain in the Denver area for many years. Courtesy Denver Public Library, Western History Collection, MCC-4219. Photo by McClure.

railroads. They could fill their empty ore cars with coal for the mine's boilers for the return trip from the Front Range cities where the smelters were located.

One of the major problems faced by any mine owner was water. As his mine progressed deeper into the mountain, more water would drain into the shafts and tunnels. Steam-powered pumps were constantly used to dewater the mines, but as the shafts grew deeper, pumps could not keep up, and finally the mine owner could go no farther, even though the paying vein might very well continue.

Tunnels were used to drain such mines. Owners would drill a tunnel from lower down the mountain under their property, then dig a shaft down to the tunnel so that all the water would drain from the mine. The tunnel could also be employed to remove the ores from the mine, using gravity much more effectively and saving the expense of hoisting the ores to the upper surface. The Yak Tunnel was used in Leadville, as was the Newhouse Tunnel under Central City and the Roosevelt and Carlton beneath Cripple Creek. The Newhouse Tunnel, four miles long, was used not only to drain the mines of Central City but also to transport Central City ore to the Argo Mill in Idaho Springs, where it was processed. It took seventeen years for Samuel Newhouse to dig his tunnel, which, along with the Argo Mill in Idaho Springs, opened in 1913. The mill had the latest in milling technology, and in its lifetime processed $100 million in gold. The tailings dump along the northern edge of Idaho Springs is mostly ore from mines in Central City. Since the tunnel was an integral part of the mill, it was also called the Argo Tunnel.

Other equipment also increased the efficiency of the miner. A mucker ore car had a bucket on the front that scooped the rubble from the face of the mine and dumped it into itself or into another ore car behind, thus minimizing hand shoveling of the

Top left: If a miner needed a hoist but had no steam power, he could buy this horse whim from a local mining supply house. A pole attached to the top pivot joined the horse to the hoist, called a whim. The horse went around and around, and the steel cable wrapped around the hoist supplying the hoisting power. From the Mine and Smelter Supply Catalog of 1902. Top right: The Mine and Smelter Supply Company sold six different sizes of the portable Atlas steam boiler and engine in 1902. Bottom: Another source of power for mine work was compressed air, which powered air drills that were used to drill blasting holes. This air compressor manufactured by the Cincinnati Compressor Company was sold by the Mine and Smelter Supply in ten different sizes.

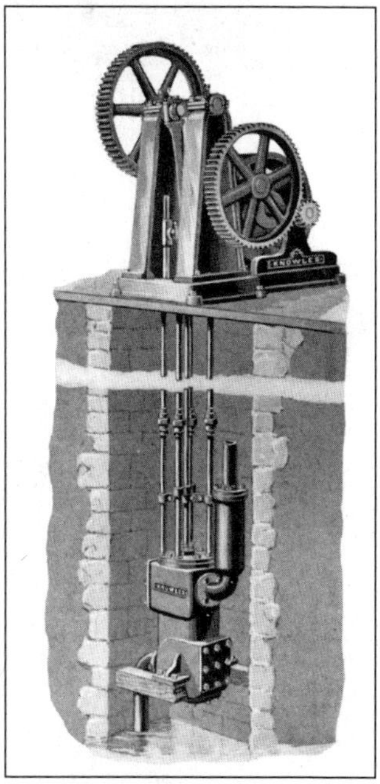

Right: Water had been a problem in mines from antiquity. The miners of the sixteenth century dealt with water using a bucket belt powered by a waterwheel, as shown in this illustration from *De Re Metallic*. Far right: Colorado miners used sump pumps, probably steam driven but possibly powered by an electrical motor when they became available. From the 1902 Mine and Smelter Supply catalog.

The hardest job in mining was mucking. This mucker car helped the miner by scooping blasted debris from the floor and dumping it into itself. This miner has filled the scoop and is moving it back over itself to the car behind. Photo by Bob Zellers. Courtesy Colorado Historical Society, CHS.X5474.

ore. Conveyors and other mechanical means of moving the ore also saved labor. Electric-powered locomotives replaced mules—they could move more ore tonnage on less hay.

As electricity was better understood and electric motors more available, they replaced the steam engine as the main power source in mines. A steam-powered generator or hydroelectric generator might generate electricity, but windlasses, elevators, and mine locomotives became electric powered.

These transformations also occurred with ore processing. Donkey-powered *arrastras* soon gave way to water-powered stamp mills, which were then replaced by steam-driven mills, crushers, rollers, and shakers. Electricity then replaced steam in the mill, as it was easier and cheaper to distribute electricity through wires than steam through

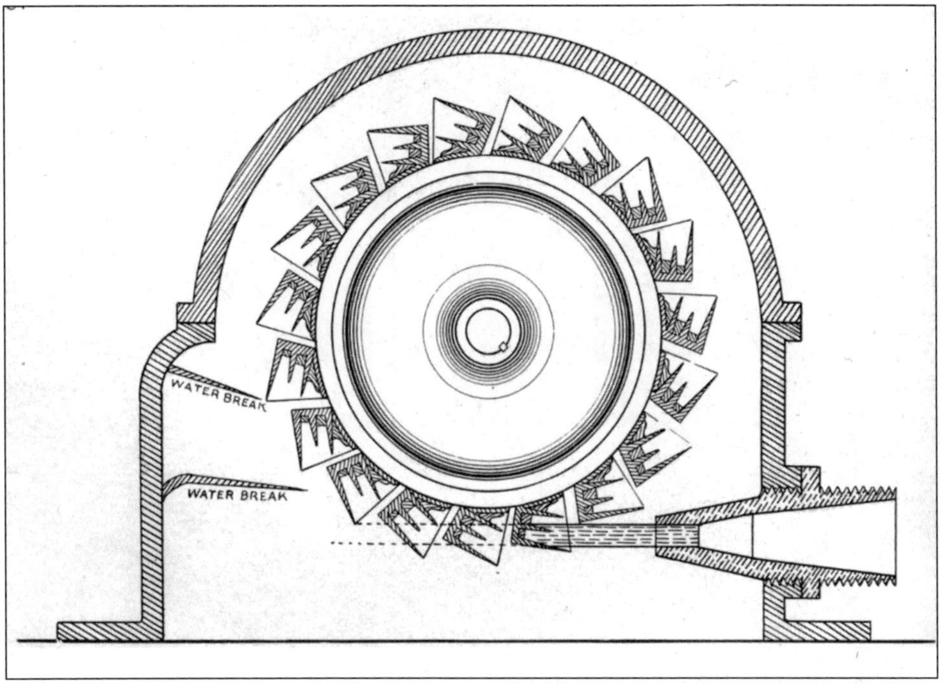

Waterwheels used for power changed during the second half of the nineteenth century from paddle-type affairs to water turbines with much greater efficiency. Mine and Smelter sold the popular De Remer wheel in seventeen different sizes from 0.06 hp to 249 hp. Water was delivered through a pipe to the right-hand bottom of the wheel. The nozzle directed the flow directly onto the shaped cups.

pipes. Gravity was always designed into the mill operation to most easily transport ore through each process.

In general, a mill was a processing site that separated a desirable metal or alloy from its ore by mechanical means, without using heat. The first mills were simple rock-crushing devices that allowed for the separation of gold from the quartz or other formations that contained it. The resulting dry powder was either panned or sluiced. Sometimes it was mixed with mercury (quicksilver), which absorbed the gold and silver into an amalgam that would yield the valuable metals at a later stage.

A stamp mill was a mill built around the use of stamps powered by water, steam, or later by electricity, although early models were also donkey- or mule-powered. Usually they came as batteries of five built as a set. Each stamp was a column or post with a replaceable iron or steel shoe on the business end. This shoe weighed six hundred to one thousand pounds, depending upon the rated size of the stamps. A camshaft crossed the pillars at the top, lifting each stamp as the shaft was turned by the power source. Then the shoe dropped on the ore that had been fed into the stamp's mortars, matching iron dies to the shoes. These mortars provided a solid surface on which the ore was pulverized. The mortar had screens on the sides that allowed finer ore to escape into a waiting collection trough while containing the coarser material, which fell back

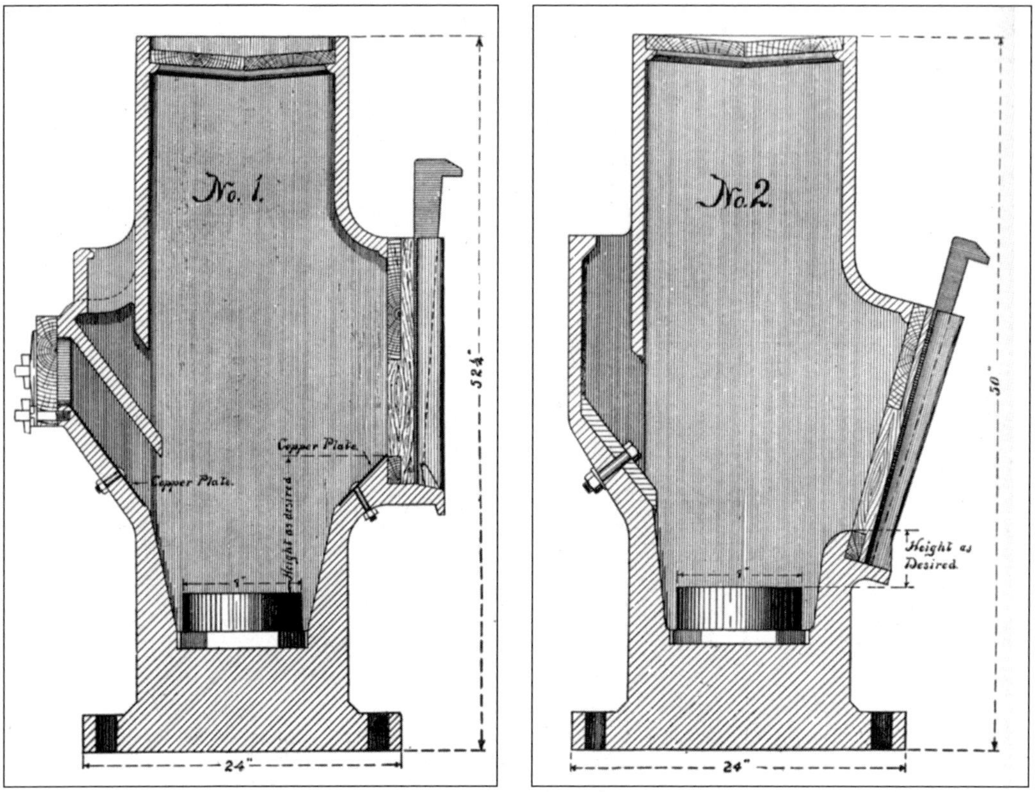

The mortar that the ore was crushed on was not just a flat surface but also contained a chute directing new ore (the left entryway) and a screen covering the opening the crushed ore escaped from (the right side). This opening had a screen across it that allowed finer ore to pass but kept coarser ore in the mortar for the next stroke. From the 1902 Mine and Smelter Supply catalog.

onto the mortar die for the next blow. New material was added through a small chute carefully monitored by a mill man to keep the proper amount of material flowing in: Too much might jam the shoes; too little would allow the shoe to hammer directly on the mortar, possibly fracturing one or the other. The finely stamped material was dry before 1875, but later the mills switched to wet stamping and included water and quicksilver in the mortars, which integrated and sped up the amalgamation process.

A small, independent mill might do custom work for nearby independent miners. The mill might have a single battery of three or five stamps turned by water power or a mule. A larger mill could have ten or more batteries, with the entire process integrated and placed at the entrance of the mine, all owned by the same operator or mining group. The stamp mill was a simple but reliable method of reducing ore to the required powder form for the processing about to occur. Stamp mills were used in Colorado into the 1940s. Hundreds of abandoned mills remain in the state, slowly rotting away. The iron parts of many mills were scavenged for scrap during World War II.

Separation tables called vanners were built to take advantage of the specific weights of different metals, silica, and waste dirt. They usually were set at a slight incline and would shake vigorously enough to move crushed ore across grooves or riffles in the table. Various specific weighted compounds would end up coming off the table in different grooves, hence separating them. Probably the best and most commonly used separation table was the Wilfley table.

The Wilfley table, a series of angular riffles, longitudinally along the surface but having a definite angled ending at the lower end, trapped minerals in the riffles, allowing the lighter gangue and silica waste to be washed over to the bottom edge of the table. The table was tipped along both axes with the ores crushed to the consistency of sand fed onto the table at its highest corner. The entire table was shaken lengthwise, and water was allowed to flow evenly across the shorter side from top to bottom. The consistent mechanical action, the flow of water, and the combination of smooth surface and riffles at the tail of the table separated not only the waste from the valuable minerals but also each type of mineral, something that had not been done before. Most other tables and vanners could separate compounds with large differences in specific gravities, but the Wilfley table was able to separate those that had nearly equal specific gravities. Hence Wilfley was able to separate the difficult-to-process sulfides from more valuable gold and silver compounds. He was even able to

Mine and Smelter sold many Wilfley tables throughout the world. Figure 241 from its 1912 catalog shows a potential customer what to expect.

separate zinc sulfide from iron or copper sulfide that often carried gold and silver. Zinc sulfide inhibited the smelting process of the ores thus making the entire ore body less valuable. The Wilfley table was patented September 28, 1897, by Arthur Redman Wilfley, a miner in the Ten Mile District of Colorado.[8]

Arthur Wilfley came to Leadville with his family in 1879 at the age of eighteen. His father, a Mexican War veteran, had freighted a steam-powered sawmill over the plains, intending to sell lumber to the miners as well as join them in searching for mineral treasures. They soon moved over Fremont Pass to where rich strikes of silver had sparked the birth of Kokomo, Recen, and Robinson. Young Arthur had a good technical mind that he used to secure a job as an assistant to the U.S. surveyor in Kokomo. and then became deputy surveyor. Wilfley astutely and diligently purchased mining claims in the area and became successful as a miner, mine operator, and, with the success of his table, inventor and businessman. He manufactured the first eight tables in his Kokomo shops before moving the operation into Denver, where he was able to find expanding markets as well as better supplies of labor and materials.

Between 1910 and 1924, Wilfley also developed centrifugal pumps for pumping slurries, slimes, and acid solutions, a very important contribution to the mining industry. He and his two sons, who graduated as mining engineers from the Colorado School of Mines, turned the patented pumps into an internationally recognized business that lasted into the twenty-first century.

Water was almost always used to wash and remove unwanted material. According to one mining legend, one washerwoman noticed that valuable metals seemed to adhere to the soap bubbles she used to wash greasy miners' clothes. The principle was adapted to milling by coating the crushed ores with a light oil and then washing them in a sudsy foam and lifting the metals out. They could be rewashed and dried later in the process. The Argo Mill in Idaho Springs used this flotation separation[9] process as one of its separation steps.

Another technique was lixiviation, a process that removed chemical compounds or pure gold or silver by dissolving them in chemical baths. The objective was to remove unwanted compounds, thereby concentrating the precious metals, or removing the precious metal in its salt state, such as was done with silver chloride. The silver or gold was then precipitated out of the substance to yield pure bullion.

In the silver camps of Colorado, refractory ores rich in metal sulfides were rough-crushed and then roasted in the presence of salt to cause any silver present to associate with the chlorine in the salt and form silver chloride, which was then dissolved in warm water. The remaining tailings were removed to the tailings dump while silver in the vats was precipitated out of the silver chloride with copper and iron.[10] It worked well when the ores were of a consistent nature with-

This 1879 illustration shows vats of soupy ore with recipes of chemicals designed to leach out the paying precious metals. The center shaft was rotated slowly to agitate the ores.

out small amounts of other elements such as antimony or bismuth. Mills that used this process were called lixiviation mills, some located in Aspen, Leadville, Lake City, Denver, and Golden.

Cyanide extraction of gold became popular at the beginning of the twentieth century, and there were several plants in the Cripple Creek area. One of them, the Golden Cycle Mill in Colorado Springs, lasted well into the twentieth century. Because of its efficiency and ease of use, the cyanide process soon replaced all other milling methods for gold extraction. It is still the major method used in the recovery of gold from ores. In fact it was so efficient that it was used to reprocess the tailings of earlier smelters and mills throughout the West.

A weak solution (less than 0.5 percent) of potassium cyanide or calcium cyanide was used to dissolve gold directly from the ore. Ores were crushed to the fineness of very fine sand and run through standard amalgamation and water separation to remove the coarse metals. The remaining mass was placed in vats of a weak cyanide solution that dissolved the gold directly. The process took days. After the precious metals were placed in solution, it was necessary to drain the solution from the tailings and then remove the precious metals from it. This was accomplished in either of two ways: carbon attachment or precipitation using zinc. Cyanide extraction is still in use today, although it receives a lot of criticism because of the environmental damage caused by the cyanide tailings or by spills during the process itself.[11]

By 1913, when Samuel Newhouse built his state-of-the-art mill in Idaho Springs at the mouth of the Newhouse Tunnel, he could use all these processes on the complex ores of Gilpin and Clear Creek counties. The mill had a rated capacity of 150 tons per twelve-hour shift and ran twenty-four hours a day. Ore from Central City came through the tunnel only fifty yards from the ore bins of the mill. The Colorado and Southern Railroad had sidings between the mill and the creek and brought in other Clear Creek County ores. After assaying to reach agreement on the worth of ores from individual mines, they were dumped into bins by a rotating ore car dumper that held three cars at a time, turned them upside down to empty them, and then allowed the empties to be returned to the tracks for another load. Rock crushers or a ball mill reduced the ore to pebble size or smaller.

After crushing, ore was sent to the stamp mill battery; the four sets of five running batteries made verbal communication impossible. The ore was classified on the basis of fine sand size, and larger pieces were sent back to the stamps for another round. Ore was then sent over the amalgamation tables, where free gold or silver would attach itself to mercury, in the fashion used by the ancients. This amalgamation would be roasted to drive off the mercury, leaving the precious metals for further separation. The Argo used the flotation method of separation on the remaining ore and then, finally, sent it through the cyanide process. The tailings at the Argo still assay out at 0.15 ounce of gold per ton, showing that even the best processes could not get all the value from the rock. The Argo Mill also removed copper, lead, and zinc from the ores, each adding value to the final bottom line.

Gold and silver usually came out of hard rock. All processes included breaking the rock into smaller pieces, and the rock crusher was the first step. The Blake crusher was a popular brand, and Mine and Smelter sold five different sizes. The owner supplied whatever power was available. From Mine and Smelter Supply 1902 catalog.

In 1943 four miners were blasting a wall at the Central City end of the tunnel and accidentally entered into an abandoned mine area that had filled with water. The resulting flood killed all four miners and shut down the tunnel. Without ores from Gilpin County, the mill closed and never reopened.

Precious Metal Smelters

In Colorado, smelters were plants that used heat to cause the major chemical separations of precious metals or compounds from their ores. The furnaces were designed to heat the entire load of ore, flux, and fuel to a sufficient temperature to melt both metals and rock. Other compounds, called fluxes, such as limestone and iron, were added to help the chemical conversions. As the chemical reactions became better understood, smelters grew more efficient. Well-capitalized companies placed milling and smelting equipment together to eliminate extra handling of ore, a costly part of the operation. Smelters might have only one kind of furnace for smelting of the specific ore in the area it served, but because of the multitude and complexities of the ores mined in Colorado, most had several types of furnaces. The gold-bearing ores of Gilpin and Clear Creek counties were smelted in reverberatory furnaces using Dr. Hill's Swansea process, described as follows:

1. Piles of ore were placed under log fires and stirred and roasted for days. This process used heat and fire to oxidize the refractory sulfide ores, mimicking nature's oxidation but doing so in days instead of centuries.
2. The roasted ores and fluxes were smelted in a reverberatory furnace that used wood or coal as a heat source to melt the entire mass.
3. The slag or iron silica and other waste were skimmed off the top.
4. The matte of mostly copper sulfide, containing what gold and silver was in the ores, was removed and cooled.
5. The matte was shipped to Wales for final separation of the gold, silver, and copper. Later, refining was done in Boston, and later yet, refineries were set up in Colorado close to the smelters. Hill's company opened similar smelters in Alma and near Georgetown.[12]

The reverberatory furnace was so named because of the way the furnace reflected the heat of the fire in the firebox back onto the mass being melted. The firebox was at one end and the flue at the other. The low-curving brick ceiling reflected the heat as it passed across the ores. Fuel could be wood or coal. In Blackhawk, wood was used and was cut from the nearby mountains until it became scarce. The smelter was sued in federal court for destruction of the forests. Clearing of the forests around Central City was one of the major reasons why Professor Hill moved his smelter to Denver, where a plentiful supply of coal was available from both the southern and northern Colorado coalfields.

The first step of the new Swansea process was to roast the ore in large piles, as shown in this 1874 illustration by Frenzeny and Tavernier for *Harpers Weekly*. The objective was to drive off sulfides or change their chemical bonds to make them easier to process.

The heart of the Swansea process was the reverberatory furnace that concentrated the gold, copper, silver, and lead into a copper matte that was then sent to Swansea, in Wales, for further refining. This furnace was in the Argo Mill in Denver. Hill built the Argo to replace his first mill in Blackhawk. Photo by C. H. Hanington. Courtesy Denver Public Library, Western History Collection, X-61407.

Ores from other parts of the state required different smelting processes. Lake City, Leadville, Rico, and Aspen had ores rich in silver but also lead carbonate and other compounds that could be more easily separated in the reducing atmosphere of a coke or charcoal blast furnace. Large numbers of coke ovens and charcoal kilns supplied the fuel, and the local hills provided the fluxes and ores, enabling the carbonate ores of Leadville to be reduced to silver-laden lead bullion.[13] Roasting furnaces or calcining furnaces were usually present to speed the oxidation of the refractory ores that might be mixed with the others before further processing.

Though the reverberatory furnace was a low, wide, horizontal affair, the blast furnace was a slender, vertical-shaft chimney some thirty to fifty feet high. A blast furnace was loaded with a charge of crushed ore, fluxes, and fuel—either coke or charcoal—that was shoveled into the top of the furnace and on top of the melting mass. Blowers supplied a strong draft at the bottom of the shaft at the melting zone. As the charge progressed down the shaft, the free carbon of the fuels turned to carbon monoxide and then carbon dioxide as it picked up freed oxygen from the carbonate and sulfate

Left: They were called blast furnaces because additional air had to be blasted into the hearth area. This air increased the temperature of the furnace, so even ores containing iron could be melted. In 1556, miners used hand bellows to supply the air. The other fellow is agitating the mass in the shaft to be sure all the ore is heated evenly. From *De Re Metallic*. Below: By 1880 the blast furnace had steam-powered air pumps providing air to eight tuyeres (bottom section). Ore, fuel, and fluxes were added through the rectangular opening on the second floor. Slag was removed from the top of the melt on the hearth and bullion from the bottom. From *U.S. Geological Society 1885 Monograph of Leadville*.

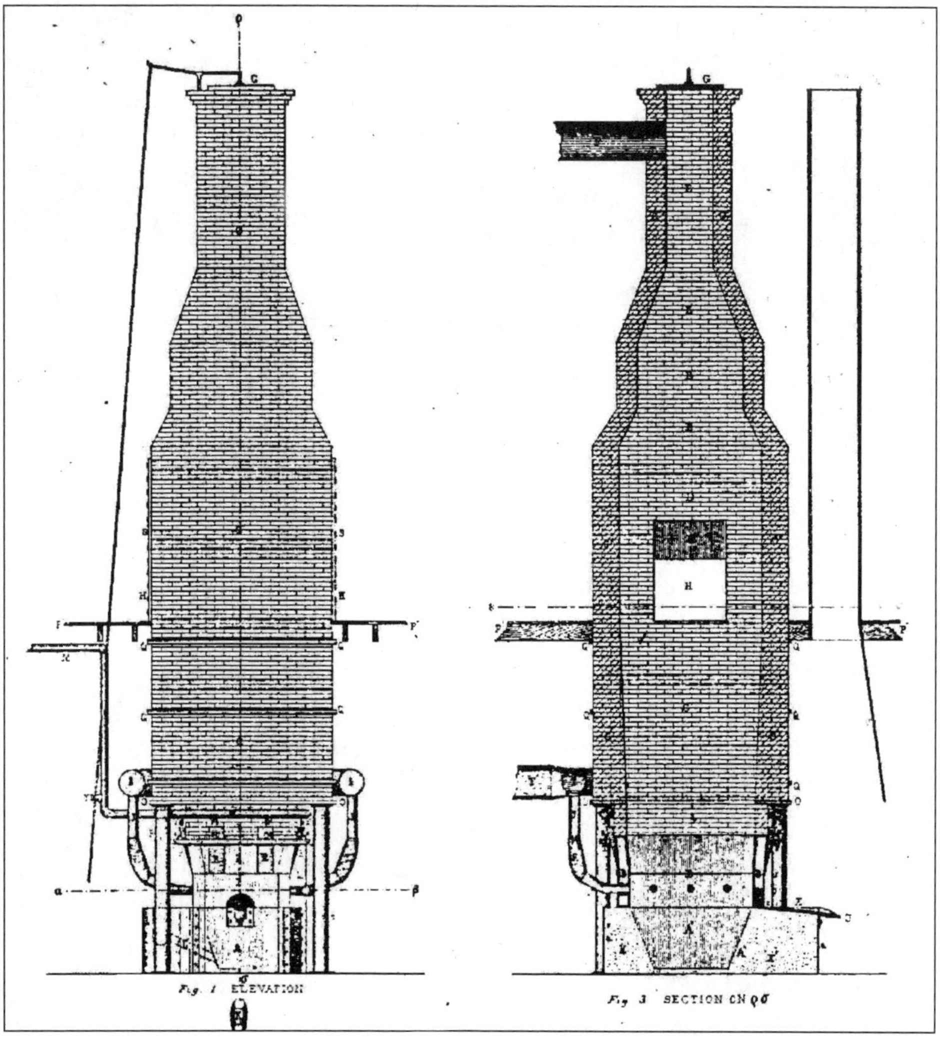

By the early twentieth century, new blast furnaces looked like this one, which was built in Salida. A man leans against a support at the bottom of the furnace, which has sixteen tuyeres to supply air. This is the hearth only; the stack begins with the bricks at the top of the photograph. The trough is for the removal of the slag. Courtesy Denver Public Library, Western History Collection, X-61391.

ores as well as from the draft. This is called a reducing atmosphere. The charge gradually heated up as it sank lower into the hotter zones. As it heated, the lead oxides became pure molten lead and the other metals alloyed with it as they reached their alloying temperatures. The silica material, along with the iron compounds that did not reach their melt points and other material, floated on top of the melted metal bullion and was periodically tapped out of the furnace at the hearth as slag. Some of the precious metals that did not decompose properly also remained with the slag.

As the process improved, smelters reran their own slag back through the furnaces to recover it. The process was never perfect, and all slag has a small percentage of precious metals. Slag was often used as road material, and for this reason the citizens of Leadville claimed that their streets were paved with silver and gold. The bullion itself was poured into molds and taken to a refinery where the gold and silver were separated out. Ninety-five percent of the bullion bars were lead, the other five percent being copper, silver, and gold. The smoke from the stacks contained a large percentage of sulfuric acid and was corrosive. Smelter owners often lived in different locations from where their smelters were.

Top: Different-sized furnaces needed different-sized slag containers. This midsized furnace (probably at Kokomo) used slag buckets much like wheelbarrows to hold the molten slag from the furnace. It was emptied outside on the slag pile, either molten or solid. Photo by Harry H. Buckwalter. Courtesy Colorado Historical Society, CHS.B402. Middle: The Grant Smelter in Denver was larger. It used a tram to transport the slag from furnace to slag pile. Photo by Harry H. Buckwalter. Courtesy Colorado Historical Society, CHS.B1503. Above: The Globe Smelter was even bigger. It used locomotives to pull train-sized slag buckets to the slag piles. Colorado Fuel and Iron also used train-sized slag cars at the Pueblo steel plant. Photo by Otto Perry. Courtesy Denver Public Library, Western History Collection, OP-11766.

Top: Walter Devereaux was the metallurgist responsible for the smelter at Aspen, shown in this photograph. When the railroads finally reached Aspen, he closed it down because of the competition from larger, more efficient smelters at the other end of the tracks. Courtesy Dan Abbott. Middle: The smelter at Kokomo handled most of the Ten-Mile District ores. It was a midsized smelter served by both the Denver and Rio Grande and the Colorado Southern railroads. Courtesy Denver Public Library, Western History Collection, X-61439. Left: Lake City's smelter was built and operated by the Crooke Brothers. It was located just above the falls of Lake Creek and used charcoal from local kilns for the reducing fuel in its silver-lead blast furnaces. Courtesy Colorado Railroad Museum.

Top: The smelter at St. Johns was the earliest lead-silver blast furnace smelter, built in 1868. Courtesy Denver Public Library, Western History Collection, X-13495. Middle: The American smelter in Pueblo was one of the largest silver smelters in the state. Slag cars of smoking slag are hauled away toward the slag heaps to be dumped. Courtesy Denver Public Library, Western History Collection, Z-5771. Left: Professor Hill's smelter in Blackhawk rekindled the Colorado gold rush in 1868. It used the Swansea process and a reverberatory furnace to concentrate the precious metals enough to make everything profitable. Photo by Arundel C. Hull. Courtesy Denver Public Library, Western History Collection, X-61399.

Easy come, easy go. After Horace Tabor made and lost his fortune in mining, he briefly held a job as a common laborer at a smelter in Leadville. This photograph shows him dumping a bucket of slag at his $3-a-day job. Courtesy Denver Public Library, Western History Collection, X-21989.

Most Pikes Peak gold seekers did not strike it rich. More than half returned to their eastern homes, proclaiming the Pikes Peak Gold Rush a hoax. However, some stayed to supply the miners or for other reasons. A few struck it rich and parlayed their newfound wealth into political power. Nathaniel Hill became one of Colorado's early senators after moving his smelter from Blackhawk to Denver. Central City's Henry Teller also became one of Colorado's most influential senators. Jerome Chaffee, newly wealthy from Leadville's silver, was another U.S. senator. James Grant took time away from his smelter to run the state as governor. By contrast, John Routt, the last appointed territorial governor, took time away from his gubernatorial duties to buy Leadville mines and make a fortune. After he grew wealthy enough to pay attention to politics, he ran for and won back the governorship to become the seventh state governor twelve years later.[14] Doing little while in office earns few enemies. Fredrick Pitkin was a lawyer and mine owner in the San Juan region before winning the gubernatorial race in 1878. Horace Tabor, of Leadville fame, was Pitkin's lieutenant governor. Tabor, originally a storekeeper, grubstaked miners and shared one of the richest strikes in the Leadville area. He lost fame and fortune in the silver crash of 1893, working in a smelter for $3 a day and dying penniless.

Old mills, dilapidated buildings, mine shafts, and ghost towns populate the Colorado mountains, most lost in the overgrowth of the present. But each was built by the hopes of humans to strike it rich, and each bears witness to the tremendous wealth that was removed from the hills. As of 2007, the Cresson open-pit gold mine in Cripple Creek was the only producing mine in Colorado. There are still gold and silver in "them thar hills," and mine operators wait for the price of the metals to increase enough to balance the economic equation of value versus cost that has existed in Colorado since the Fifty-Niners first came to the Pikes Peak region.

■ ■ ■

Notes

[1] Colorado State Bureau of Mines Data.

[2] James Fell, *Ores to Metals* (Lincoln: University of Nebraska Press, 1979), 35.

[3] Otis Young, *Western Mining* (Norman: University of Oklahoma Press, 1970), 182–185.

[4] Ibid., 178.

[5] Colorado State Bureau of Mines Data.

[6] Larkspur Historical Society, 2007 Internet.

[7] *Littleton Independent*, August 6, 1920.

[8] Jay Niebur, *Arthur Redmond Wilfley* (Denver: Western Business History Research Center, Colorado Historical Society, 1982).

[9] Young, 231–233.

[10] Ibid., 274.

[11] Meyerriecks, 154–158.

[12] Thomas Egleston, *The Metallurgy of Silver, Gold and Mercury in the United States,* Vols. 1 and 2 (New York: John Wiley and Sons, 1887), 276–298.

[13] Emmons, 285–290.

[14] Joyce B. Lohse, *First Governor, First Lady: John and Eliza Routt of Colorado* (Palmer Lake, CO: Filter Press, 2002).

CHAPTER 7

Cigars

Even before 1859, when D. C. Oakes loaded up his sawmill in Pacific City, Iowa, and headed for the Pikes Peak gold region, folks in Colorado were rolling small cigars for their own consumption. The northern Mexican societies that included people in the area of the state south of the Arkansas River looked forward to their weekly (or more frequent) fandangos—get-togethers for dancing, drinking, and socializing. Between dances, the locals as well as trappers and Santa Fe traders enjoyed Taos whiskey, locally rolled *cigarillos*, and the company of bare-shouldered *señoras.*[1]

The history of rolled tobacco goes back even further in what is now the state of Colorado. Native Americans grew several species of tobacco; *Nicotiana rustica* seeds have been identified in Ancestral Puebloan ruins[2] dating back well before Columbus's sailors observed the natives of Hispaniola "sucking smoke" through muskets of dried leaves in 1492.[3] The local Utes, Navajos, and Pueblos as well as other North American tribes still grow and use tobacco in their ceremonies.[4] *Nicotiana attenuata* still grows in the Southwest, both domestically and in the wild. The leaves of this tobacco species make poor cigars and are better used in pipes and pots, but Native American sites in the state show evidence of the larger-leafed *Nicotiana rustica,* grown in the East, and *Nicotiana tobacum,* grown in Meso-America. The tribes probably obtained these varieties through raiding parties or by trade.[5]

Although tobacco was never commercially grown in Colorado with any success, its use in the manufacture of cigars certainly was. Almost every town and city had its own shop or shops that handmade cigars to be sold to their neighbors' drugstores, billiard parlors, and saloons. Millions of Colorado cigars were turned out between 1871 and 1950. Before World War II, the cigarette and business competition eliminated local manufacturers in favor of larger national and international concerns.[6]

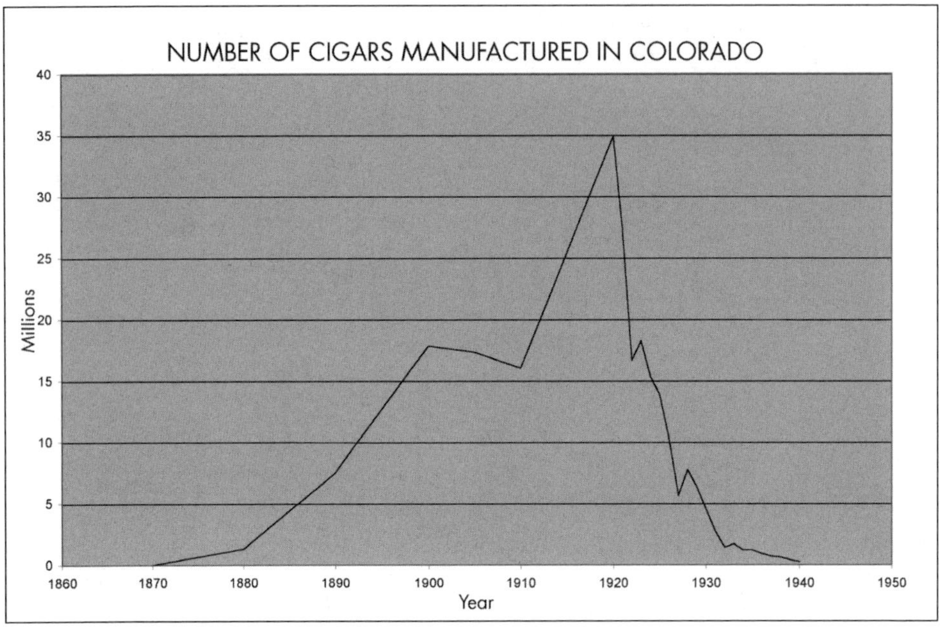

Colorado cigar makers handmade thirty-five million cigars in 1920 before the cigar-rolling machine replaced hand rolling.

In Oakes's time, the demand for cigars had grown in the Pikes Peak gold region, as it had in the rest of the country. The westward-moving Fifty-Niners brought a taste for the increasingly popular cigar, replacing the pipe and "plug" as the most used form of tobacco.

When Oakes's banking friends—the Kountz brothers of Omaha—decided to open a bank in Denver in 1862, they sent Luther, the next-to-youngest brother, to do the job. The Kountzes had been purchasing gold from the miners as early as June 1859 in Denver, and they were confident the new region would profitably support another bank. Luther had been well trained by his two older brothers and kept meticulous records of all the banking transactions, as well as some personal ones. Included were expense records for the

George Kassler was a well-known Denver business that sold books, stationery, insurance, and "segars" from his shop at the corner of F Street and Blake. The segars would have been brought in by wagon from the East. From 1866 *Denver Business Directory*.

purchase of "segars" for himself.[7] In the 1860s this northern European and English spelling was most common, but it soon lost out to the seemingly higher-quality Spanish "cigar" made in Cuba and the Caribbean.

The ninth census states there were no cigar-manufacturing establishments in the Colorado Territory in 1860 or 1870 because of the strict regulation of tobacco by the federal government.[8] The newspapers and business directories of the territory started advertising the retail sale of segars, but it was on December 28, 1870, that cigar manufacturers were first mentioned.

The *Rocky Mountain News* of that date printed an advertisement for John Winker, manufacturer of cigars.[9] Cigar-manufacturing shops grew rapidly as the population increased, as did the popularity of cigar smoking. (Per person usage rose from 26 in 1860 to 754 in 1910.) The Cigar Makers Annual Ball was held in Denver in November 1876.[10] New officers were L. N. Ahrens, Charles Kaltenback, and August Drumm. Membership was twenty-five at the time. Drumm would become a very successful Denver real estate man.

The Rocky Mountain Cigar Company produced cigars at their Salida shop for many years. Political statements about silver were a popular way to sell cigars around the turn of the twentieth century in Colorado. Courtesy of Chuck Tuthill.

By 1882, Fort Collins had its own roller, Charles Lautenbach, who handrolled cigars in his shop in the Vanderwark block of Jefferson Street. The *Fort Collins Courier* of August 10, 1882, reported his arrival. He rolled his cigars only by hand rather than with the wooden mold that was coming into use as a time-saver and method to standardize the shape and size of a cigars.[11] He would later move his factory no. 138 to 210 Linden Street.

Today the Bloom Mansion in Trinidad displays a cigar box for La Trinidad Cigars dated 1883. Trinidad had a lively cigar-making industry, and at least seventeen shops were listed in the city and state directories. In 1892 the King Coal Cigar Factory placed an ad in the T*rinidad Business Directory*.

Local cigar manufacturers, sprang up across the state: A. L. Bowers had a business in Golden in 1877, Charles Kerner had one in Boulder in 1877, and the Gem Cigar Factory was in business in Buena Vista in 1884. By 1888, shops in Aspen, Montrose, Salida, Cañon City, and Leadville advertised in the *Colorado Business Directory*. Others followed in Pueblo, Grand Junction, Lake City, Lamar, Holyoke, Colorado Springs, Sedalia, Telluride, Cripple Creek, Central City, Creede, and

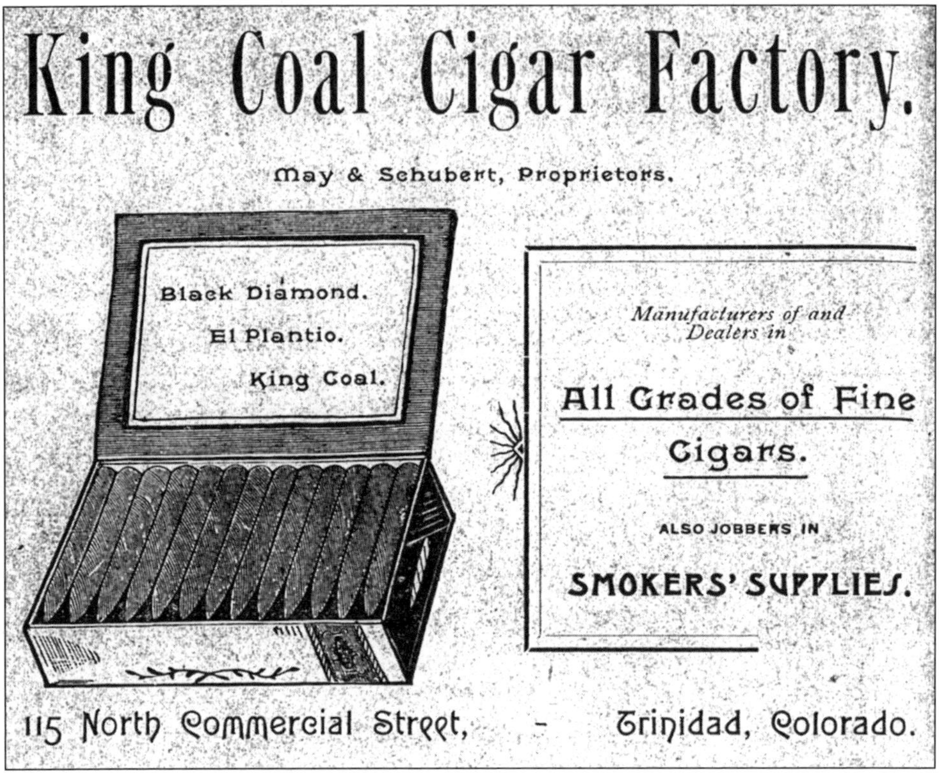

Yampa. The 1904 U.S. census listed 117 cigar-making establishments employing 632 persons statewide, and 56 Denver establishments employed 435 of the 632. Denver shops averaged 7.8 workers per shop, while others in the state averaged 3.2 workers.

Like the majority of early businesses, most cigar manufacturers did not survive, but others provided a living for entire families. A fair number of businesses had "Bros." in their title. The Fette brothers, Albert and Lewis, worked in German-owned shops, including a rooming house and a restaurant, in Denver before starting their own business there in 1893. Albert moved his family to Victor in 1895 to open his own cigar manufacture, then moved again, to Boulder, in 1898. Albert left both the business and his family in Boulder, surfacing as a boarder in Akron, Ohio, on the 1900 census. His wife, Dorothea, managed the cigar business in Boulder with the help of two sons, Lewis and Edwin, until 1922. Lewis died in 1924, Dorothea in 1925, and Edwin in 1926, and all are buried in Boulder's Green Mountain Cemetery.[12] Their shop was taken over by Mrs. Rose Robinson, who kept it open until 1931.

Ed Kreutzer, a well-known Douglas County pioneer, homesteaded land at the top of Jarre Canyon and operated a cigar shop in Sedalia. His wife took the monthly output of their cigars—the Douglas County Belles—into Denver by train and made the rounds to customers. Kreutzer listed his business in the *Colorado Business Directories* from 1882 to 1905. He was one of seven charter members of the Colorado

The Cuban Cigar Company was a midsized factory in Denver with about fifteen cigar makers working the benches. M&O's brand was their main seller. This ad was placed in the Morey Mercantile catalog in 1905.

Cigar Maker's International Union Local 129. His son, William, would become the United States' first forest ranger to patrol the Plum Creek forest where he had grown up.[13]

The union was one of the strongest in the country at the time, and it played an important role in the life of Colorado cigar makers, whether they were members or not. Because of the union, the cigar makers worked an eight-hour day at most, enjoyed great flexibility in their hours, and received fair pay. Denver was considered a good working area for these tradesmen, although the Denver local was financially strained because other union members contracted consumption, which needed to be treated at one of the many sanitariums situated around the Rockies. The Denver local often paid for their treatment if the union members could not. Other locals might send additional funds to help with the treatment of a former member. The union Local 129 was located in Denver in Suite 201 of the Railroad Building.[14]

The BLUE LABEL of the Cigar Makers' International Union is a guarantee that the Cigars are made under Favorable Conditions

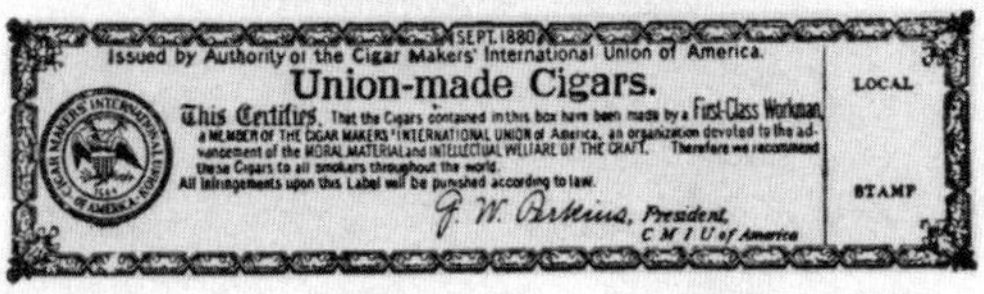

See that this Label is on the Box when you buy a Cigar

CIGAR MAKERS' UNION No. 129

201 Railroad Building - - - - Denver, Colorado

UNION MADE CIGARS

The brands we recommend. The **kind** you will **like.** Guaranteed quality and workmanship at no extra cost to you. We solicit your co-operation in building up a Colorado Industry.

Look for the **Blue Label** on the box.

M. & O.	**Dry Climate**
Mile High	**La Belle**
Columbine	**Principe de Lees**
The Denver	**Capitol City**
Red Band	**Sterling**
Excelsior	**Mark Twain**
Sari	**El Finero**
Ross Pioneers	**Newton**
San Rey	**El Stilo**
V. O. P.	**Little M. & O.**

For Sale at all First-Class Stands

Top: The union label shown above was on a box of Dry Climate cigars. Above: This advertisement of union-made cigars was in the 1905 Morey Mercantile catalog.

Cigar factories and shops had tobacco shipped in by rail from large wholesalers in Chicago, Baltimore, or Philadelphia. Lack of rail transportation was the major reason why cigar manufacturers did not open businesses in Colorado Territory before 1871.

To understand the life of a cigar maker in Denver, let's follow one through a typical day's work circa 1916. William J. Theisen was born in Denver on January 5, 1894. His father was a German immigrant, his mother a U.S. citizen. One of five sons, Bill grew up at 3110 Forest Street on the plains east of City Park. After completing eighth grade, he went to work at a small Denver cigar shop owned by George Schwartzhead (listed as George Schwartz in the Denver directories), first as a deliveryboy, then as an apprentice, and finally as a cigar maker. When Schwartz temporarily shut down his business in 1912, he got a job for Bill at the Cuban Cigar Factory, owner of the Colorado Maid trademark and one of the best-known Denver factories. Four years later, Bill moved to the Solis Factory, the largest shop in the state at the time.[15]

While Bill Theisen was working at his trade, he met Edith Flynt, also of Denver, and married her on June 28, 1916. They settled in a house behind the North Side manual training shops, which are now North High School. The house, now an apartment building, still stands today at 2435 West Dunkeld Place. In 1918, Edith gave birth to their first child, Harold. A daughter, Ethel, would come along in October 1923.

Bill remained with Solis until the company closed in 1924. He worked another year for Schwartz then, who had reopened his little one-man shop at 904 Larimer Street. In 1925, Bill left the trade to work for American Furniture, where he stayed for forty-two years before retiring in 1967. Bill and Edith traveled a great deal in later life. Edith died in 1978, and Bill died in 1991 at the age of ninety-seven. They are buried in Crown Hill Cemetery, Denverites forever. (Information on William Theisen given generously by his family. My thanks to Jeanette Flood, granddaughter and family genealogist.)

Ramon Solis opened his own shop in Denver in 1883. He was born in Spain but was raised in Cuba, where he learned the cigar trade from the best shops and rollers in the world. He immigrated first to New York City but soon came west. The Solis Cigar Company became Denver's largest, producing the well-known Dry Climate cigars. Ramon Solis's mansion, built from cigar profits, still stands at Nineteenth Avenue and Downing Street in Denver. From *Representative Men of Colorado.*

Commercially Grown Tobacco in Colorado

One would think that with all the cigars rolled in the state from 1880 to 1950, Colorado farmers would have grown tobacco to satisfy the demand. Although *Nicotiana rustica*, the domesticated form of tobacco, never grew wild in the state, there were at least three documented efforts to grow tobacco commercially.

The first was by Joseph Doyle on his ranch near the Arkansas River in 1859. Doyle was a successful trader and freighter associated first with the Bent Brothers at Bent's Fort and later with the founders of Pueblo and Hardscrabble. He grew tobacco as well as corn, wheat, melons, and vegetables at his ranch in the Huerfano River Valley southeast of Pueblo.[16] In 1859, Doyle opened general stores in Auraria, Tarryall, Cañon City, and Pueblo, selling far more goods to the incoming Fifty-Niners than he ever did to the cashless Arapaho and Ute tribes. He undoubtedly sold tobacco at his stores, but probably not cigars. In 1888—1890, the agriculturalists at Colorado A&M University grew experimental plots of tobacco in Fort Collins. Cigars made from the tobacco were labeled "vile stuff,"[17] which is probably why tobacco was not raised in the state thereafter.

An article in *Colorado Field and Farm* on June 27, 1903, reported a possible sale of land near Ordway, in the Arkansas River Valley, to a Mexican cigar company to supply tobacco to their factory in Mexico, but no record of the sale exists.[18] And a stubborn Scot in Platteville, who either did not believe the A&M report or never read it, tried again to grow tobacco commercially in 1911. Constantine MacGreagor raised only one crop.[19]

Bill Theisen's experiences, as recorded in an interview in 1979 that he gave to Dr. Patricia Cooper for her book *Once a Cigar Maker*, offer an excellent view of the life of a cigar maker and the cigar-making industry in Colorado during this period.[20]

Bill started his workday by walking half a block from his little home just north of Ashland School in North Denver to Zuni Street. There he caught either the no. 37 or the no. 38 trolley serving northwest Denver over the Sixteenth Street viaduct to the central loop area downtown, where he either walked the four blocks to the Solis factory at 2015 Arapahoe Street or transferred to the no. 66 trolley that traveled north on Stout toward the stockyards, getting him within one block of the factory. The Solis factory, a union shop, opened its doors at 8 A.M.

Bill enjoyed a great deal of flexibility. He might miss the trolley and catch the next, or he might stop for a haircut downtown at the Petrone Brothers Barbershop at 1511 Curtis Street. Antonio and Camillo Petrone were uncles to Bill's good friend Larry Petrone. Larry and his two brothers were also cigar makers. Even if Bill was thirty minutes late to work, there would be no repercussions from his employer because he was paid for the number of cigars he produced, not for the number of hours worked.

Top: Bill Theisen and his fiancée pose for their engagement picture near Dome Rock. Courtesy Theisen family. Above: Bill Theisen ran around with his Cuban cigar-making buddies. They were swimming this summer's day at Manhattan Beach, a popular swimming hole at Sloan Lake. Courtesy Theisen Family.

An average piece rate for cigars in Denver was about $15 per thousand produced. An average cigar maker rolled and turned in about 200 to 250 cigars a day, so he would make between $15 to $20 per week, good wages for the times. In 1913 the Solis Cigar Company employed eighty-six cigar makers at an average weekly salary of $16.38. The Cuban Cigar Company employed forty-four rollers at $17.44 a week.[21] Those who were very fast could produce 400 cigars a day, effectively doubling their weekly wages.[22]

Once in the shop, Bill hung his coat and hat on a hook, put on his apron, and sat down at his station. Albeit a smaller space, it was his personal workplace and reflected his personality as much as do today's cubicles. A cigar maker's bench was about four feet wide by three feet deep. Makers usually sat in rows facing other rows of makers, their benches butted together, allowing conversation while they worked. Although the labor was precise, delicate handwork, it required little mental skill or effort. Cigar makers could listen to books read while they worked to help with the tedium of the day, as was done in the Tampa

Bill and some of the Cuban Cigar Company's employees pose behind the factory with their boss, who stands on the left. Courtesy Theisen family.

and Havana areas, or they might talk about the European war and whether the United States should get involved.

Each bench contained a cutting board, about twelve by fifteen inches, on which the cigar maker cut his or her tobacco and rolled the cigar to its finished size and shape. A trimming mechanism sometimes was attached to one edge. Making a cigar required a sensitive touch. The board was a personal object and was not touched without permission, because with years of use it would become worn in all the proper places.

The cutting blade he used was also personalized. Cuban and Latin rollers preferred the traditional *cheveta*—a thin, steel blade two inches wide by four or five inches long, with a curved cutting edge used to precisely cut tobacco leaves in shapes necessary to roll and wrap at least ten different sizes and lengths of cigars. Belgians and Germans might use other knives or blades shaped as they wished.

Bill received his directions from the foreman of a large shop, or from the owner of a small one. He was told which type and how many of a particular cigar he would be making that day. The owner or manager determined what his workers would produce, depending upon the orders received or expected. Each shop made at least three

Top: The Solis Cigar Factory in Denver, 1914. Courtesy Theisen family. Above: The interior of the Cuban Cigar Factory, 1913. Courtesy Theisen Family.

Top: C. F. Tansy owned and operated Colorado Cigar Factory No. 608, located across from the courthouse on Pearl Street in Boulder. It was a small shop of four cigar makers and support staff, shown here outside the shop. Courtesy Carnegie Branch Library for Local History, Boulder Historical Society Collection. Left: The four rollers pose at work inside Tansy's factory in front of the office staff. Courtesy Carnegie Branch Library for Local History, Boulder Historical Society Collection.

The Boulder Hand Made brand was rolled in Boulder by the Sanitary Cigar Company. Courtesy Rick Sinner.

different brands, and some larger shops produced up to ten different brands. In the United States in 1909, there were 350,000 different brands of cigars.[23] Haulcie Roberts's one-man shop in Fort Collins sold four: Little Chums, Great Divide, Town Boost, and the most expensive, Autocrat.[24] Solis's Cigar Factory brand sold seven, and also made private-label cigars that were special-ordered for railroad companies, large hotels, or individual retail cigar shops, although the custom trade was based in Wisconsin and Pennsylvania. Baby Doe cigars from the Colorado Cigar Company were actually rolled by Factory 534 from the First District of Wisconsin.

When Bill needed tobacco, he went to the stock area, where the amount and type of tobacco were written on his card and precisely monitored. Three different types of tobacco leaves were available for him to use. The largest proportion was used in fillers, the leaf that made up the bulk of the cigar. Actually, there usually were two or more brands of fillers, and adjusting the percentage of one or the other

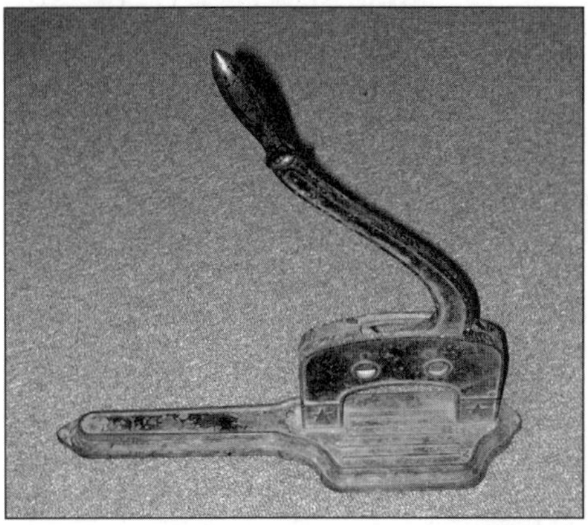

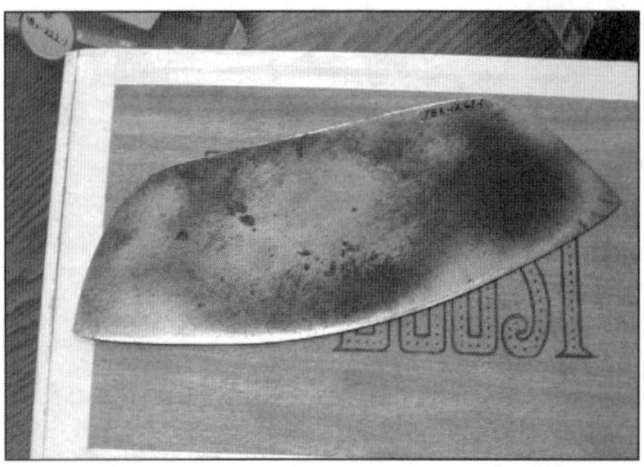

Upper left: A cigar maker would rough-cut tobacco leaves to length with this tobacco cutter. Courtesy Fort Collins History Museum. Above left: Every roller owned a hand knife for precise leaf cutting. This one, a *cheveta*, was preferred by Cuban and other Latin American cigar makers. Courtesy Fort Collins History Museum. Above right: Tobacco leaves were cut on a cutting board. This one has a length cutter attached to the front to precisely cut a cigar to the proper length. Courtesy Fort Collins History Museum.

An advertising version of a bunch maker's work table complete with board, knife, mold, buncher, and small press. It is unlikely that many bunch makers ever got to work at such a clean and modern work space. Miller DuBrul and Peters Manufacturing Company, *Catalogue,* 1895, Tobacco Collection, Extractive Industries, Museum of American History, Smithsonian Institution, Washington, D.C.

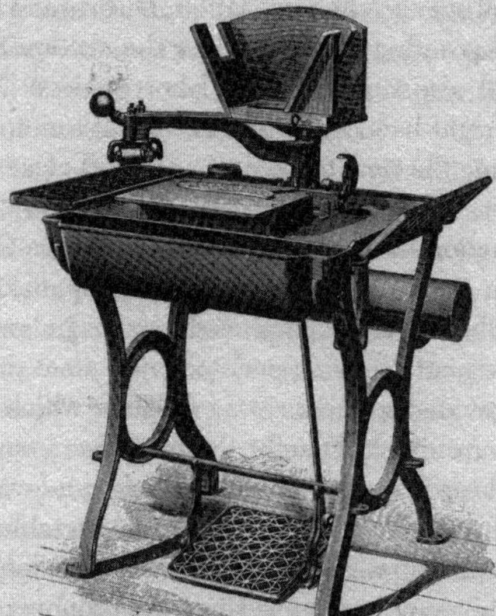

Suction table, Miller DuBrul and Peters Manufacturing Company, *Catalogue,* 1895, Tobacco Collection, Extractive Industries, Museum of American History, Smithsonian Institution, Washington, D.C.

These labels are registered at the Colorado Archives. Denver and Rio Grande private labels were probably rolled by one of the larger factories, although the D&RG purchasing agent would have solicited quotes from more than one.

Well-known local personalities were common themes for the trademarks of local cigars. Left: A Colorado Springs cigar maker would have used Colorado Springs's founder William Palmer's likeness to sell his wares. Courtesy Chuck Tuthill. Right: Although Baby Doe was a Colorado legend, the cigars were actually rolled in Wisconsin. Courtesy Colorado Historical Society.

would alter the cigar's taste. Bill cut these to the right size with his tobacco cutter and bunched the leaf or leaves together, alternating folds, much like a hand fan that is collapsed and expanded. This allowed the smoke to be drawn through the entire length of the cigar. He had to have an exacting sense of how tight to bunch the filler: Too tight and the cigar would not draw well; too loose and it would burn too hot and too quickly. Bill was reprimanded once for bunching his cigars too tightly. His supervisor asked if he smoked, and when he replied that he did not, he was told he should because then he would know that his cigars did not draw well.[25]

Next, Bill took a second type of tobacco leaf called the binder and wrapped it around the bunched filler, forming a cylinder with tapers at both ends. He would have precut this leaf to the right size and shape with his *cheveta*. After 1890, cigar makers would have placed the cigar at this point in a mold box with nine or nineteen others. The box acted as a shaping press, giving all ten or twenty the same shape and size. The cigars remained in the press for forty-five minutes to an hour. Years earlier, mold boxes were not used, and their use was disdained by journeyman cigar makers.[26]

Everything that happened in the cigar industry was affected by the inflexibility of price. In 1917, Vice President Thomas Marshall said in a speech, "What this country needs is a good five cent cigar." From 1870, eighty percent of all cigars were sold for a nickel. The higher-quality brands could be sold for more, but the largest quantity were purchased by the man on the street at five cents, which was all he could afford. The inevitable cost pressures for owners were led by the increasing cost of labor for cigar makers. The cigar union was an aggressive one, striking often and for almost any reason: working conditions, decreasing the free cigars given to members, the quality of leaf supplied, flexible hours, and of course, the piece rate paid per thousand cigars.

Because owners dared not raise the cigar price, they had to make up for increasing production costs in other ways. This was the driving force behind methods to increase efficiency, such as using mold boxes, which allowed lower-paid, less experienced workers to make cigars.

Mold boxes were used to standardize the size and shape of a particular brand. Mold boxes also made shaping a cigar easier. This box is for ten cigars. Photo by author. Courtesy Longmont Museum.

Gradually, shop owners changed the process from one cigar maker doing every step of the rolling process to dividing the steps so that cheaper labor who used the machinery could do most of it. Cost pressure was also why owners tried to break the union by hiring women, particularly immigrant women, who were willing to work for a lower piece rate.

Although it was not a concern in Colorado, some experienced women did come to the state and roll cigars, and some had their own shops. A picture of the Solis Cigar Factory in Denver in about 1914 shows thirty-two women out of 145 people. In *Colorado Business Directories*, one finds women owners in Boulder, Denver, Florence, La Junta, Pueblo, Monte Vista, and Rocky Ford.

While the cigars were being shaped in the box, Bill rolled more for another box or cut and shaped the third type and the most expensive tobacco, the wrapper. This outer layer had to be perfect, with no holes, tears, or slits. Bill cut it from the leaf to its exact size and shape.

A roller might be given different-sized tobacco leaves to cut for his wrapper. He could only get one from a small leaf and as many as three from a larger one, called "1, 2, or 3 cut" leaves. This was important to a cigar maker, as the larger leaves were faster to use and hence increased output and wages that day. Cigar makers had been known to strike a particular shop if the owner provided only smaller, lower-quality wrappers, not because it affected the quality of the cigar but because it affected their weekly wages.[27]

When Bill removed a partially finished cigar from a molding box, he rolled it in a wrapper, starting at the end to be lit and wrapping toward the end to be drawn. The final step was to tuck in the end of the wrapper and adhere it with a small amount of tasteless and odorless glue or gum. Bill inspected the finished cigar for size, shape, and feel. A good cigar, then as now, was firm but slightly yielding to finger pressure. This routine was repeated about every two minutes on average.[28]

Bill received a different piece rate for different brands, as a large ten- or fifteen-cent high-quality cigar took more time and skill to wrap than a five-cent stogie. If a roller was new to the trade or not very skilled, he might not even be allowed to wrap the higher-quality cigars.

After finishing fifty of a brand, Bill tied them up with a string or ribbon and placed them on the top shelf of his bench with his name or seat number attached. At the end of each shift, the foreman collected the bunches from the shelves, took them to the packers, or placed them in humidors before shipping. Bill was given credit for his bunch, and it was added to his weekly total for payment on Saturday.

Larger shops also had packers, office personnel, inventory people, stock boys, and stemmers—people who removed the center stem from the leaf. The Internal Revenue Service demanded rigid control of tobacco and taxed all finished products. Keeping books for a cigar shop was a high overhead expense.

Cigars were banded and then packed in cigar boxes, an art form of its own, with decorative lithographic depictions of Colorado scenes or personalities such as Senator Tabor or Baby Doe. Pictures of Victorian women were very popular. The box probably was created in Denver, as there were three cigar box manufacturers producing boxes for all the shops in the region.

The federal government required all cigars to be placed in boxes or containers that could be used only once, and they had to bear a tax stamp placed in such a way that the stamp was torn when the box or container was opened. The local union also used the box for its union-made stamp, informing the buyer of the desirability of purchasing a union-made product.

The Cuban Cigar Company's five-cent cigar had a hole drilled in its smoking end, hence the reference to "Hole in the Head." Smokers either bit off the end or snipped it off with a cigar cutter prior. Photo by author. Courtesy Loveland Museum.

At lunch, the shop closed for forty-five minutes or an hour. Some workers, like Bill, brought their own lunch from home and ate at the shop or in a nearby park. Others walked over to a local restaurant or saloon for a wet or dry lunch. In Colorado, before Prohibition in 1914, it was not uncommon for single men to drink a little too much during the lunch hour before returning for the afternoon session. If the drunken fellow decided not to return at all, he earned considerably less that week. If his output or quality of work suffered due to his excessive drinking, he received a layoff notice with his pay at the end of the week from the owner or foreman. Bill Theisen neither drank nor smoked, probably a rarity for cigar makers at the time.

Cigars also were packaged in cans as well as boxes, as shown here. Courtesy Rick Sinner.

If things became boring during the day, Bill or one of his fellow workers might play a practical joke on a new stock boy or on the foreman, if he could get away with it. Many a young worker started his first day or two looking for a left-handed mold box or other nonexistent items for a roller.

Near the end of the day, Bill and his coworkers were notified of the shop closing so that they could finish up their bunch or at least finish even batches of fives or tens before closing. The foreman stored the batches in the humidor overnight. All rollers cleaned up their areas, including all scrap tobacco and cuttings to turn in for the day. (Tobacco was strictly weighed and controlled by the owner for the IRS to ensure that none was taken for illegal uses.) The workers were allowed three free smokes they rolled themselves as part of their benefits. These free cigars were also counted and controlled by the IRS.

The rollers removed their aprons, donned coats and hats, placed the three smokers in their coat pockets if they smoked, and either went home or to the local saloon or billiard parlor. There they smoked their free cigars and drank a beer or two, as did workers of all trades until 1914, when Prohibition limited the sale of alcohol in Colorado. (Closing the saloons also eliminated one of the largest retail outlets for cigars.)

Most cigar makers worked Monday through Friday and on Saturday morning. Saturday was payday, so they came in and rolled a hundred or so cigars, if they had planned to, and collected their wages. Since the pay was usually in cash, the shop owner or manager asked all the workers on Friday how many more cigars they were planning to turn in Friday and Saturday. Cigar makers considered themselves professionals, and to turn in a false number or not meet a promised quota was asking for sanction by their peers as well as for dismissal by the owners. Cigar makers preferred Saturday as payday, because they could take their pay and enjoy the rest of the weekend before starting a new week and another cycle.[29]

Cigar makers probably grew tired of the weekly grind as workers everywhere do, even today. They had several options for variety. If they worked in a union shop, they could quit and go work in a different shop, even in a different city. The union aided these traveling members as they helped join and strengthen the union across the country. Owners also found the arrangement to their benefit, as they often had to

Victorian Women were popular advertising images, as shown by this "Colorado Maid." The play on words was not lost on the customer, as locally "made" products were important to local buyers. Courtesy Colorado State Archives.

send workers home because of business demands, material shortages, or taking inventory. A member was seldom penalized for traveling or quitting and could usually count on getting his bench back when he returned, so long as the business needed rollers to meet the current demand.[30] While he was single, Bill hoboed up to Livingston, Montana, with a couple of other temporarily unemployed cigar makers and then to Seattle, riding the rails "On a Union Card"—the term for showing his card to the railroad workers, who were supposed to throw him off the train. Railroad workmen allowed them to stay, however, since they themselves were strong union men.

All cigar makers had a second option: to start their own one-man or one-woman shop. Those who did were called "buckeyes," and the union was fairly strict about whether or not they could remain a member. As soon as they hired another cigar maker, they had to turn in their card and were removed from the union list. Should the business fail, they could regain their card if they wished. Buckeyes started their own businesses for the same reason people do so today. Although rollers had flexible time, good hours, and benefits, some still wanted the independence and challenge of owning their own shop. Buckeye businesses were notorious for their lack of monetary reward, but makers here as elsewhere still left more stable situations to succeed or fail in their own shops. In general, these businessmen could make good cigars, but they couldn't sell enough of them.

James B. Duke, who monopolized the cigarette and smoking tobacco industry, tried to do the same in the cigar industry but was unsuccessful. Cigarettes are made of finely chopped tobacco rolled in a paper wrapper. This was far easier to do by machine than by fan-folding the filler tobacco in a cigar and wrapping it twice in other tobacco leaves. Duke founded the American Machine and Foundry Corporation (AMF) for the sole purpose of building machinery to make cigars and cigarettes. He was not successful with cigars until 1918–1919. However, other smaller machines, such as the suction table, were used to allow less skilled workers do more of the labor that traditionally had been done by the cigar maker. Small vacuum holes in the table surface held the leaf in place and made the more precise handcutting of the wrappers and binders considerably easier.[31]

During the period 1915–1920, events came to a head, with owners closing strong union shops and moving them to areas without unions but with a plentiful supply of immigrants willing to work at lower rates. They would build their shops using the latest equipment and cheapest nonunion labor.[32] In 1919, AMF was finally successful in producing cigars by machine. One machine could make eight to ten thousand cigars per day, compared with the two hundred or so for a cigar maker. It didn't take long for the larger shops to convert, putting many cigar makers out of work. Because of this flood of unemployed cigar makers no apprentices were trained, and the union shriveled to a ghost of its former self. Bill Theisen quit the bench in 1925 to sell furniture in Denver.

Cigars have been produced by machine for the last eighty years, but recently there has been a revival of handrolled, high-quality cigars. One shop specializing in hand-rolled custom cigars opened in Denver in January 2005.

The Business of a Buckeye

In 1925, Haulcie Roberts bought a cigar shop from Fred Watson in Fort Collins and ran the business into the early 1930s before selling it back to Watson. The Fort Collins Museum holds the remnants of the business in its archives, from the tools—*cheveta*, and board—to the business of doing business. Included are the $500 bond required by the IRS to guarantee payment of the tobacco taxes, company catalogs for cigar bands, and lithographs of cigar box labels. There are also cancelled checks for

Haulcie's $10/month rent for his one-room shop and for tobacco from his St. Louis wholesaler, and to the cigar box supplier in Denver. His ledger for 1925 shows he rolled about thirty-two thousand cigars that year and sold thirty-five thousand, pulling out inventory from the nine thousand cigars he had received when he purchased the business. Roberts's customer list consisted of fifty names, from individuals like E. C. Dake, a wealthy Colorado businessman, to Grandview Grocery, a Fort Collins corner grocery store. He sold to shops as far away as Boulder, and his brand graced the display cases in the nearby towns of LaPorte, Ault, and Loveland. Roberts didn't get rich producing cigars; he made about $25 a month in net in 1925, which was enough to remain in business for about ten years before the Great Depression and national competition finally drove him into farming, an occupation he enjoyed for the next thirty-four years. Haulcie Roberts died in 1985 at the age of eighty-nine.

Cigar-making Costs

(Author's estimate, 2005)

Revenue/Monthly—Sales of 3,500 cigars in lots of 50	$175
Cost of tobacco	
$12.32 per 1,000 cigars	1.23 cents per cigar
Cost of labor	
$15 per 1,000	1.5 cents per cigar
Cost of tax	
$2 per 1,000	0.2 cents per cigar
Cost of box	
10 cents per box of 50	0.2 cents per cigar
Cost of goods sold (1,000 cigars)	$31.30
Cost of goods sold (3,500 cigars)	$109.55
Gross profit (3,500 cigars)	$65.45
Other costs	
Rent	$10 per month
Advertising	$10 per month
Shipping	$10 per month
Interest	$5 per month
Bond equipment	$5 per month

The break-even point occurred at about 1,200 cigars.

■ ■ ■

Notes

[1] LeCompte, 60.

[2] Joseph Winter, *Tobacco Use by Native North Americans* (Norman: University of Oklahoma Press, 2000), 108.

[3] Ibid., 3.

[4] Ibid., 37–39.

[5] Ibid., 21.

[6] Colorado Yearbooks and U.S. Census.

[7] Thomas Noel, *Growing Through History with Colorado: The First 125 Years, 1862–1987* (Denver: Colorado National Banks and the Colorado Studies Center, University of Colorado at Denver, 1987), 6.

[8] Ninth U.S. Census.

[9] *Rocky Mountain News*, December 28, 1870.

[10] Denver Paper Cigar Makers Ball.

[11] *Fort Collins Courier*, August 9, 1882.

[12] Papers in Carnegie Library, Boulder.

[13] Len Shoemaker, *Saga of a Forest Ranger* (Boulder: University Press of Colorado, 1958).

[14] William Theisen, interview by Patricia Cooper for *Once a Cigar Maker* (Urbana and Chicago: University of Illinois Press), August 17, 1979.

[15] Theisen, 1.

[16] LeCompte, 256.

[17] *Colorado Rancher and Farmer*, November 26, 1949.

[18] *Colorado Field and Farm*, June 27, 1903.

[19] *Colorado Field and Farm*, September 9, 1911.

[20] Cooper.

[21] Ibid., 60.

[22] Ibid., 62–63.

[23] Ibid., 12.

[24] Roberts Collection, Fort Collins Museum.

[25] Theisen, 4.

[25] *Fort Collins Courier,* August 9, 1882.

[26] Cooper, 130–132.

[27] Ibid., 150–155.

[28] Ibid., 44–50.

[29] Ibid., 75.

[30] Ibid., 27–29.

[31] Ibid., 271.

CHAPTER 8

Food Canning

D. C. Oakes paid particular attention to food preservation on his trip west from his home in Iowa. He carried dried beef, dried fruit, rice, beans, four gallons of pickles, and four gallons of vinegar. Although Oakes did not mention canned foods in his list, some items in cans were available at the Missouri River supply towns.[1] He was planning on feeding four people for the six-month period he had set aside for the gold rushers—forty-five days to get to the Pikes Peak goldfields, three months to strike it rich, and forty-five days to return home, triumphant and wealthy, before the snows of winter returned and closed down the routes.

Not everyone brought such a complete assortment of provisions with them. In Colorado, many different kinds of food were in great demand. The Fifty-Niners could hunt deer and the plentiful antelope for meat, but fresh vegetables or even dried or preserved vegetables and fruit were hard to find. Some early entrepreneurs quickly realized that good profit from the miners could be made on fresh vegetables and planted crops in the spring and summer. Denver and Auraria grocers had canned fish, oysters, fruit, and some vegetables, both wholesale and retail, by spring of 1860, freighted by ox-powered wagons all the way from the East Coast.[2]

The science of canning foods was in its infancy in the mid-nineteenth century. It had been only fifty years since the first successful preservation of food had been done in glass containers by a Frenchman, Nicholas Appert, who had stuffed all kinds of food products in champagne bottles, sealed them with corks, and heated the bottles to a high enough temperature to kill the bacteria inside. He accomplished this for Napoleon's troops, most of whom were dying from food poisoning rather than from battle wounds.[3]

All food preservation up to this time used glass containers, as it "was matter most impenetrable by air," according to Appert. This changed around 1810, when canisters of tin were used. An 1810 patent for the preserving of "animal, vegetable and other perishable foods in glass, pottery, tin or other metal" was taken by Peter Durand, who is credited with the invention of the tin can, even though the Dutch had put up fish in tins prior to 1800.[4]

The tin can and the art of canning developed together, as both depended upon the other. Glass was too fragile and too costly for the less expensive foods. The first tin cans were cut with scissors from thin tinplate, joints butted together and soldered by hand. A very fast worker could make one hundred cans a day. Most improvements on the tin can came in the method of manufacture, so that hand labor was replaced by machines and the cost of the can decreased. The canning process also changed as methods were developed to increase the temperature to which the food was heated and to decrease the time it took to do so.

The first canning company in the United States began in 1819 in New York when Ezra Daggett and his partner, Thomas Kensett, canned salmon, lobsters, and oysters.[5] In 1820, William Underwood has set up a cannery in Baltimore, canning fish and other meat products.[6] The Underwood name has survived in the canning industry to the present time.

Canning companies developed slowly as not all efforts were successful, and spoiled food does not lend credibility to the process. California's fruit growers had early success at preserving fruits in cans and shipping them to the California gold rush miners in the West. Some East Coast canners in Maine had begun canning corn, beans, and cranberries before 1850. In the early 1860s the first cannery in the central states was successful in Cincinnati, Ohio. As American farmers migrated west into the Ohio and Mississippi river valleys, canning companies followed them. Good results depended upon fresh produce, hence the canners built their factories as close to the harvests as possible.

Improved canning processes allowed for more difficult foods to be packed in cans, and tomatoes and pumpkins were added to this list. Beef, ham, and fowl soon followed fish for meat entrées. Some foods remained preserved in glass, notably liquids such as beer, wine, vinegar, and pickles. Oakes's four gallons of vinegar and four gallons of pickles probably were packed in one-gallon jars. Not surprisingly, pickles and other highly acidic items are still packed in glass today.

Thus by early 1859, Pikes Peak gold seekers had some canned foods as they started their forty-five- to sixty-day trip from the Missouri River supply houses to the "diggings."[7] In 1860, Denver restaurants were advertising oysters and canned and bottled fruits for sale in their establishments.[8]

Gail Borden's condensed milk had been patented only three years before, and he had set up a factory in Connecticut, so cans of condensed milk were available, as were canned fish and a few canned vegetables. However, most did as Oakes had done and brought dried meat, cured bacon, flour, coffee, and dried fruits with them.

Vinegar was an important item for cooking as well as for medicinal purposes and food preservation. A vinegar factory had opened in Denver by May 1, 1861, operated by Henry Schwenk.[9] But the surviving and more famous Colorado vinegar and pickle entrepreneurs were the Kuner brothers.

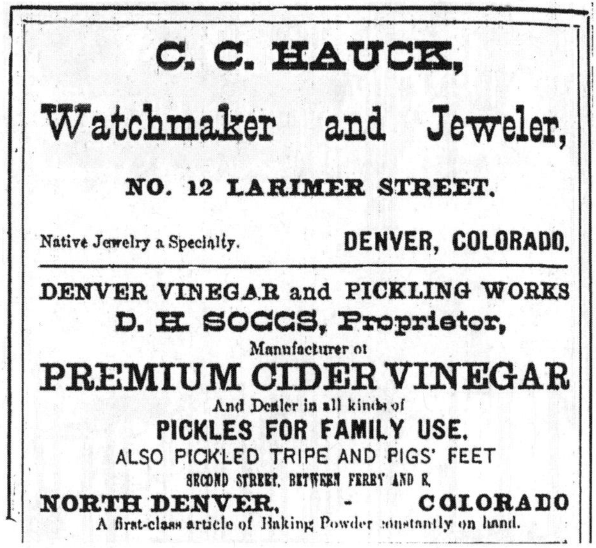

Proprietor D. H. Soggs advertised his vinegar, cider, and pickles in the 1872 *Denver Business Directory*. In 1875 he sold out to J. C. Kuner. When John Kuner's brother Max came to Colorado, he first sought and found employment in his trade—watchmaking—with C. C. Hauck, who had also placed an ad in the 1872 directory.

Although the increased demand for canned goods brought on by the Civil War was beneficial to the canning industry, it wreaked havoc on the country and most of its inhabitants. The Kuner brothers had immigrated from Lindau, an island in Lake Constanz in Bavaria, landing at the port of New Orleans in 1847. They settled in and around Vicksburg, Mississippi, where one brother, John, became a baker and another, Maximilian, remained a watchmaker—a craft he had learned in Bavaria. By the outbreak of the war, both had prospered, with John moving north to Iowa City and then to Marshalltown and Max remaining in Vicksburg as a partner in a local watch shop. The Battle of Vicksburg in 1863 destroyed Max's business and home, but not his business sense, and he seized an opportunity by buying a load of cotton with Confederate money and selling it in New Orleans for Union money, which gave him enough to pay off all his debts and have some left over. He used this capital to invest in a pickle business in St. Louis, in 1864. That company, Gould Pickles, probably sold pickles to the expanding western markets, including the Colorado Territory.

In 1870, John moved to St. Louis, where he, too, went into the pickle business with his son-in-law. John sold his share of the St. Louis business at a loss in 1871 and moved his family and pickle and vinegar vats to Denver to become one of the early food-preserving businesses in the territory. John and his son Randolf started Kuner and Son, located at Tenth and Lawrence streets, in the fall of 1871.[10] Like most start-ups, Kuner and Son was strapped for cash and could not afford a company horse or wagon; John borrowed a wheelbarrow from a friend to make his deliveries of jars of vinegar and pickles. The cucumbers he used were "prime pickles raised in Colorado."[11]

Top: Cabbages were large-volume items for the Kuners Pickle Company. A cabbage line in the factory has two men coring cabbages with core drills, and a line of women stripping outer leaves, cleaning, and chopping the cabbages before canning. Photo by Lewis McClure. Courtesy Denver Public Library, Western History Collection, MCC-4230. Left: Kuner Pickle Company plant in Brighton, January 22, 1910. Photo by Lewis McClure. Courtesy Denver Public Library, Western History Collection, MCC-3445.

Lungers

Not all who came to Colorado were looking for gold. Some came for other opportunities, following Horace Greeley's admonishment, "Go west, young man, go west." Many came because of poor health.

Before the discovery of gold in the area, trappers and traders noticed that sickness and disease—other than the effects of hair loss due to Native American knives–were much less common than they were back east. Colorado's pristine air seemed to be good for those with respiratory problems. Soon doctors in the eastern states were prescribing a move west. Once here, they were known as "lungers."

Fifteen doctors were listed in the 1867 *Denver-Auraria Directory*, and each mining camp had a doctor or two. People who could afford it went to the doctor's office, or possibly a doctor would make a house call if they could pay. Those who were indigent did without. Life expectancy in the second half of the nineteenth century was much lower than now—47.3 years versus 77.8.

Doctors specialized in a particular field, as did Dr. L. F. Preston, consumption specialist, with offices at 808 Sixteenth Street in Denver. Many people came to the area with respiratory ailments, and doctors like Preston did a good business. Here are patients in the waiting room. Courtesy Colorado Historical Society, Buckwalter Collection, CHS-B1403.

The society in new population centers tended to divide into recognizable groups based mainly on nationality, occupation, or religion, and it was natural for these groups to look after their own. Hospitals were built by church groups; for instance Catholic Bishop Machebeuf completed St. Vincent Hospital in 1873. The Episcopals followed, with St. Luke's hospital in 1881. The Jewish Hospital Association completed its building in 1893 but could not fund its opening until 1899. The Swedish population opened Swedish Hospital in 1905. The Denver and Rio Grande Railway opened a hospital in Salida for railroaders.

During the time these hospitals were built, much more was learned about tuberculosis, or consumption, as it was called. Many of the new hospitals were built exclusively to treat the large number of consumptives moving into the area. The treatment regimen included lots of fresh, cold air (patients always slept outside, even in cold weather), nutritious foods, and clean and hygienic living conditions.

As tuberculosis became better understood and antibiotics such as streptomycin decreased the need for long-term hospitalization, most hospitals easily switched to the treatment of other diseases. However, the Jewish Hospital Association grew over time to become the national leader in the treatment and research for all respiratory ailments, changing its name to National Jewish Hospital in 1925 and National Jewish Hospital and Research Center in 1965.

It did not take John and his son long to earn enough profit to buy a horse and wagon and then, later, expand the business into other food-canning products. In 1873, John's brother, Max, came to Denver, working at his watchmaking trade and lived with John at Tenth and Lawrence.[12] In 1883, John asked Max to help with the pickle business, and in 1884 the business was incorporated as the "Kuner Pickle Company" by John, Randolf, and Max. John relied increasingly on Max after John's wife and son died in 1886 and 1887. John sold his remaining interest to Max in 1892,[13] and by the time he died in 1902, the Kuner Pickle Company had grown to become the fourth- or fifth-largest pickle company in the country. The company canned other items also; in 1891 it purchased more than one million pounds of tomatoes from Weld County farmers.[14]

Because he had no sons, Max Kuner brought his grandson, Karl Kuner Mayer, into the business in 1900. Karl hired his brother, Emile, several years later, and by the time Max died in 1913, Kuner remained a family-owned business with strong leadership for many more years.

While the Kuners were growing their pickle business, another multigenerational family was preparing to enter the food preservation business along the Front Range. John Empson, a candy maker from Cincinnati in deteriorating health, came west at the urging of his doctor and his seven-year-old daughter, Alydia, in 1884. He and his daughter settled in Denver at first, but he soon journeyed to Estes Park to regain his health with the help of Enos Mills and Colorado's clean, cold air.

During trips from Denver to Estes Park, Empson and Alydia passed through Longmont several times, and after John was healthy, again, they settled there. On July 13, 1889, he started a food-canning business, opening his factory with financial help from Longmont citizens and businessmen.[15] The business struggled during the start-up phase as most small businesses do. But in the early fall of 1891, the harvest was exceptional and their canning processes were in good running order. It was obvious to John and Lida, as his daughter was known, that they were going to succeed. Then, on the morning of September 18, 1891, a fire broke out in the engine room of their factory, and the entire operation and warehouse were destroyed in a few short hours. Cans of tomatoes and peas exploded as the water inside them turned to steam, and the site seemed like a battlefield of fire and small explosions.[16]

John was stubborn; he told Lida, "The harder you are thrown, the higher you bounce." With renewed vigor and encouragement from the Longmont community, Empson raised the necessary capital and rebuilt at the same location, although he considered moving the operation to Pueblo.

Empson was an extraordinary salesman. He knew how to sell, and the story of the silver jelly kettle is a perfect example. The lore of housewives who put up their own preserves was that jelly was not good if it was made in copper bowls and kettles.

John liked jams and jellies and decided to sell Colorado currant jelly as one of the company's products, buying and leasing farmland planted with currants, strawberries, and raspberries. He knew Colorado was famous for its silver production and was hailed as the "Silver Queen of the West." He bought a silver-plated kettle from the Gorman Company, a well-known silver company in Rhode Island. The kettle, the largest silver-plated kettle Gorman had ever made, was supposedly plated with silver dollars. It was a double kettle, four feet in diameter and four feet high, with steam providing the heat to process the jams and jellies; it would become a Colorado silver kettle from silver-dollar currency for Colorado currants. After Lida graduated from Wolf Hall, a Denver finishing school for young women, John and Lida incorporated another company, Empson patented and & Daughter Cannery, to produce the Silver Kettle Jelly, with Lida as vice president. This took advantage of the advertising benefit of a slight difference in business names. Women involved in businesses were a rarity at this time, and the local newspapers gave free advertising and column space to this novel idea.

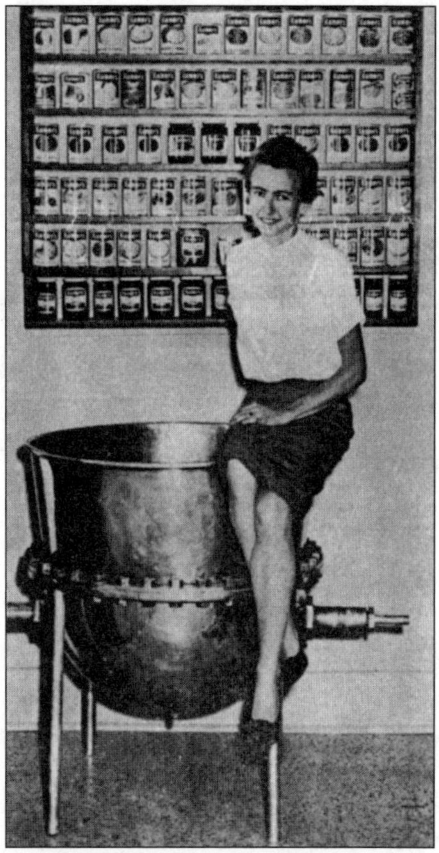

The silver kettle was last shown at the Kuner-Empson centennial celebration in the lobby of a Denver bank. The kettle was four feet tall by four feet in diameter. From "Kuner-Empson Company First 100 Years."

Empson promptly shipped the kettle to the Midwest and East Coast on its own private railcar to show prospective customers the "Colorado Silver Kettle," which was good enough only for Empson's Silver Kettle Jelly. He sold a tremendous amount of it on the strength of that advertising campaign. The Silver Kettle is still part of Longmont's founding lore. It was last exhibited in 1964 at the centennial celebration of the Kuner-Empson Corporation.

John Empson was a fierce negotiator whom no one was able to get the best of. His dealings with town officials, vendors, and other canning companies were always difficult, emotional, and troublesome. For example, in 1890 he decided to can peas, so he bought two farms and planted acres of this hand labor–intensive crop. An eastern company, Chisholm and Scott, had patented and developed a pea viner, a barrel-like device that removed peas directly from the vines. Pea-loaded vines were pitchforked into one end, and paddles inside the barrel batted the pods just hard enough to split the pod and release the peas. Peas rolled out an opening in the bottom into containers or boxes, and the vines and pods came out the far end to be used as fodder for local farm animals. John Empson leased two of these pea viners but grumbled about how expensive they were. Chisholm and Scott charged about nine cents per one dozen cans of peas. Empson demanded that Jack Chisholm train his crew in all aspects of the pea viner: how to assemble it, repair it, and replace its parts. The next year, Chisolm found that there was no repeat business as Empson had built his own pea viner during the off season, copying exactly what he had learned the year before. Chisholm and Scott sued him, and harsh words and physical threats went back and forth for years. But Empson patented and built more machines, even incorporating the "Empson Pea Threshing and Machinery Company," building pea viners and leasing them to other canners for three cents per one dozen cans of peas. The lawsuit was finally settled many years later for very little money, with the lawyers on both sides being the eventual winners.[17]

In 1907, John expanded his canning business in northern Colorado by negotiating with the cities of

Top: A Chisholm and Scott pea viner is shown here to prospective canning companies. Pea viners reduced the labor of harvesting peas enough that canners could profitably process and sell cans of them to the American public. From the August 25, 1924, *Canning Trade Journal.* Above: It took a lot of pea vines to produce enough peas for Empson's yearly pea campaign. These are not haystacks but pea vine stacks awaiting their turn at the pea viners. Courtesy Longmont Museum.

Top: Many women were hired for canning work. It was temporary, lasting only until the harvested produce was in cans. Here, a group of Kuner-Empson employees pose inside the factory. Courtesy Longmont Museum. Above: Empson's first factory was located in Longmont at Third and South Martin Street. It was destroyed by fire in 1891 but rebuilt immediately. The building was finally closed in 1970 and later turned into an apartment complex. Some pieces of canning equipment remain on display inside the complex. Courtesy Longmont Museum.

Loveland and Greeley for the placement of factories there. Both offered lucrative land and tax incentives, similar to today's deals between towns and businesses. Greeley wanted some relaxation of the terms in later years but found John Empson a hard-nosed negotiator unwilling to give an inch.[18]

In the early twentieth century, Empson contracted Luther Burbank, the famed plant wizard, to develop a better variety of pea, one that matured early, was small, and would be in greater demand by housewives. He placed Burbank's name on the labels of his peas for many years and used the name in his advertising as well. From then on, Empson was known as the pea king of Colorado.

Empson expanded into many northern Colorado towns in the years between 1905 and 1920 by building either canning factories or pea-vining stations. In 1920 he sold the business to his Longmont managers and friends, after which he and Lida traveled extensively.

Despite John Empson's complexities, he showed a public service side early on. He was the driving force behind Longmont's Pumpkin Pie Days, a summer festival for the region. He was very proud of the pumpkins he canned for sale to the general public, and annually furnished thousands of fresh pumpkin pies to the festival that cost him thousands in pumpkin and in labor to prepare. When John Empson died in October 1926, two years before Empson and Kuner joined forces in a business arrangement that would dominate Colorado's canning industry for the next four decades, the income from his estate was given to charities, including the Longmont Library.[19]

Lida Empson and Minnie Lohr were best friends. This photo is from a Lohr family album. The Lohr farm, on U.S. Highway 66 between Longmont and Lyons, is now a Longmont Parks and Recreation Agricultural Heritage Site.

In 1928, Lida Empson purchased part of the Macintosh farm northwest of Longmont, where she spent the rest of her life near her good friend, Minnie Macintosh-Lohr.

Farmers on Colorado's Western Slope found the climate and soils excellent for raising fruit crops. Apple, peach, and pear orchards soon dotted the landscape from Fruita to Montrose. It was not surprising, then, to find canneries and packinghouses built to move the produce to market. The Arkansas River Valley also had perfect conditions and irrigation water available for high-quality produce. Almost every town along the river had a canning factory or processing station of

Colorado's Western Slope had rich agricultural lands and several towns had canning factories, including Grand Junction, Paonia, Montrose, and Delta. This Delta factory processed a large volume of tomato products. Its temporary workforce was mainly women, here busily peeling tomatoes. Courtesy Denver Public Library, Western History Collection, X-7680.

some sort, and each had a summer harvest festival, such as Rocky Ford's Melon Days, where watermelons were served free to visiting crowds. The canning and preserving industry was a major part of the prosperity of Colorado before the Great Depression of the 1930s.

During the first thirty years of the twentieth century, Colorado's agricultural communities drew large national concerns into the state. Libby, McNeil, and Libby of Chicago opened two factories and ten salting works, mostly on the Eastern Slope. H. J. Heinz operated thirteen pickle-salting sites at one time or another. Illinois Pickle Company also used Colorado cucumbers at their pickling plant in Denver around 1908. Local companies with specialty products were also started up, such as the Stokes family restaurant and Ellis's restaurant, which canned their own chili con carne and sold it in and outside of the Rocky Mountain region. Both brands survive to the present day.

Strawberries have always been a Colorado favorite. A group of strawberry pickers stop to have their picture taken in a field in northern Colorado. The photo later became a postcard. Courtesy Longmont Museum.

The canning companies had a wide range of relationships with the state's farmers. Some businessmen, like John Empson, purchased land to grow specific crops or experiment with different vegetables. The canners also leased land and held the farmers to contracts for all of a specific crop. Most farmers, however, listened to the prevailing information to plant the crops they thought would bring the most revenue, and they sold to the highest canner bidder. Food-canning companies also competed against sugar beet factories for cropland—the sugar companies using more contracts signed the winter before to ensure enough beets for the upcoming campaigns. Both farmers and canners needed and hired temporary workers to harvest crops and work in the canning factories.

The canning process improved with steam-jacketed kettles that provided even, controllable heat to products that required it before being placed in cans. Empson's

Silver Kettle was a good example of this system, although silverplating was not required. The U.S. Agricultural Department and agricultural colleges like Colorado A&M continued research in order to improve canning's results. The cans themselves changed, as manufacturability was of prime importance. John Empson vertically integrated his business by opening a can-manufacturing business in Longmont in 1915. He added a second floor to his factory for can manufacturing and storage, producing enough cans to supply his own requirements as well as those of other canneries. The can department could manufacture twenty million tin cans per year. The tin-plated steel also improved when tin plating became thinner but tougher and more uniform. The entire operation was done by machine, eliminating any hand labor.

A fire at the Longmont factory on June 21, 1917, caused $100,000 in losses, severely damaging the can-making equipment and the tin plate.[20] John quickly surveyed the damage, had crews clean and repair the equipment, and set it up in another part of the factory. The tin-plate sheets that survived the fire were cleaned, and Empson was able to produce enough cans for the 1917 season.

John Empson vertically integrated his business into can making. He set up this can shop on the second floor of his Longmont factory. He was able to provide cans for his own business as well as for others in the area. From *The Mining Camps Speak*, Sagstetter Collection.

The process for the commercial canning of foods in 1912 was as follows:

1. Raw materials, produce, or meats should be fresh as possible and in first-class condition. Care needed to be taken to prevent handling degradation, bruising, wilting, or spoilage.
2. Grading—the product should be graded as to quality, size, or other characteristics important to the ultimate consumer. Size was of primary importance as items needed to be of similar size so that the heating processes that followed would cook or sterilize consistently.
3. Washing—then as now, it was important to thoroughly clean the product to eliminate unwanted debris and unhealthy matter.
4. Preparation and blanching—most vegetables required some preliminary preparation, such as removing corn kernels from the ears and removing the silk. Peas were softened by parboiling them briefly, as were beans.
5. Washing and filling the can—the can itself was prewashed and then filled mainly by machine. Almost every crop or item has a filling mechanism designed especially for it as the size or shape requirements dictated special control of the filling machines. Most machinery filled a can by volume, but later most were filled by weight. Almost all canned goods of today are filled by weight.
6. Exhausting—after the can was filled, the can and contents were heated to 180 degrees Fahrenheit as it passed through a steam box. This was not required if the item was already hot from the previous step.
7. Capping the can—in 1912, when this process was specified, open-top cans were sealed by a double-seamer machine. The lid was pressed into place, and steel rollers crimped the can shut without the use of acid fluxes or solder as was done to tin cans in the nineteenth century. After sealing, the cans were submerged in a bath of boiling water where any leaks would show up as columns of air bubbles.
8. Processing and cooling—next the sealed cans were placed in retorts that heated them and their contents to particular temperatures for a specific length of time, depending on the item being canned. Both time and temperature control was critical and closely regulated.
9. Afterward, the cans and their contents were quickly cooled in water baths to stop any further cooking of the fruits or vegetables. After cooling, the cans were run through a label machine where each canning company added its own company logos, advertisements, and instructions. These labels brought instant recognition of the product to the consumer, both for what was in the can but also how it was grown, patented, processed, or any other characteristic that the canner wished to emphasize.[21]

So in 1912, John Empson's business would have worked as follows:

1. During the winter and early spring, Empson and his managers would have been planning which current and new produce would be taken to market the following fall. They would then contact local farmers and sign contracts if they could agree on terms for whatever produce the farmers would like to grow. In this period, the Lohr-Macintosh family northwest of Longmont produced peas for Empson. The company probably furnished the seed developed by Luther Burbank for Empson's special variety of small, petite peas.
2. Plant managers would ready the cannery for the harvest, adding modern equipment as it became available and repairing present machinery as required.
3. Once the harvest began, both farmer and canner were very busy, hiring temporary labor as necessary to complete the tasks. George Lohr would have harvested his pea vines and hauled them to the Longmont factory, although Empson had pea-vining stations in Berthoud, Ault, Mead, and Johnstown.
4. Once the peas were inside the cannery, they would be graded and washed, then sent to a steam-jacketed kettle for parboiling to soften them.
5. Peas would then proceed to the canning area where they would be placed in various-sized cans, depending upon the current market demand. Cans would be sealed and sent to the retort area where the pasteurization would occur.
6. Full cans would be cooled quickly and sent through the label machines to place Empson's green and yellow label, showing mouthwatering peas on the front. Luther Burbank's name would figure prominently somewhere on the label.
7. Cans were put into cartons, and cartons were stacked onto pallets for shipment by wagon to local Longmont grocery stores, or by rail to New York City.

The Depression caused most of the smaller canning companies to fail, with only those large enough to weather the financial storm making it to the 1940s, when the Second World War again created a large demand for canned food. Some things never change. After the war, Colorado canning companies continued to process Colorado agricultural products in the Arkansas and Platte river valleys, as well as on the Western Slope. The eventual consolidation by larger national corporations continued with Kuner selling to Stokley–Van Camp in 1960. Stokley sold the Kuner division to Faribault Foods in 1983. The Minneapolis-based company retained the rights to the Kuner name but closed the canning factory in 1984.

Notes

[1] *Liberty Weekly Tribune*, October 22, 1858, 4.

[2] *Rocky Mountain News Weekly*, April 18, 1860, 3.

[3] A. W. Bitting, *The Canning of Foods: A Description of the Methods Followed in Commercial Canning,* Bulletin 151 (Washington, DC: U.S. Department of Agriculture, 1912), 7.

[4] Ibid., 8.

[5] Ibid., 10.

[6] Accessed at http://www.Underwoodspreads.com.

[7] *Liberty Weekly Tribune*, October 22, 1858, 4.

[8] *Rocky Mountain News,* April 18, 1860.

[9] *Rocky Mountain News,* May 1, 1861.

[10] *Boulder County News*, November 12, 1871, 4.

[11] Ibid.

[12] *Denver Directory*, 1873.

[13] John Kuner, "Memoirs of John C. Kuner." Manuscript at Denver Public Library, Western History Department.

[14] *Greeley Tribune*, October 17, 1891.

[15] J. Empson biography, Longmont Museum Archives.

[16] *Boulder Daily Camera*, September 19, 1891.

[17] Pioneer Canning Industry in Colorado, 37–38.

[18] LeRoy Hafen, *Colorado and Its People* (New York: Lewis Historical Publishing Co., 1948), 402.

[19] Empson biography, Longmont Museum Archives.

[20] *Fort Collins Weekly Courier,* June 29, 1917, 7.

[21] Bitting, 20.

CHAPTER 9

Sawmills

The historical records are explicit that D. C. Oakes had purchased and placed a steam-powered sawmill in his wagons for the trip to the the Pikes Peak region. Several kinds and manufacturers of steam-driven mills were available to him in 1859. There was also a plentiful supply of fast-moving streams in the area that could produce enough power to turn sawmills without steam for an entrepreneur who had less capital.

Because of the low cost of sawmill equipment and the large number of experienced operators back east, it is not surprising that entrepreneurs such as Oakes would bring this equipment to the Pikes Peak region. What is surprising, though, was how quickly it happened. Oakes left his home in Pacific City, Iowa, on March 20, 1859, with several ox-drawn wagons full of heavy equipment. He arrived at the "diggings" in mid- or late May, but by that time at least one other sawmill was busily providing planks to the early builders at the mouth of Cherry Creek. Wyatt & Cooper's steam-powered sawmill was in place, set up, and running on April 1, 1859, in Russellville, at the head of Cherry Creek. In a diary entry dated June 10, 1859, Dr. George M. Willing, a Fifty-Niner from St. Louis, wrote the following:

> In camp at last on the head waters of the long sought, anxiously looked for Cherry Creek. Saw three men working on a tom. They were washing only the surface sand, and as a result of the day's labor took out about five dollars. Not very encouraging. Washed out a pan full myself and got about three cents. This would pay. All about us is another pine forest. And in the midst of it is a new town called Russellville. Here there is a steam sawmill in operation, which cuts about 4000 feet a day. Since the first of April when they commenced operations, they have sold 60,000 feet of lumber, at $8 per hundred, which considering the abundance of the material and its convenience, is a pretty tall figure.

> Persons having claims here represent that they are making about eight dollars a day, and profess themselves satisfied. No proper prospecting has yet been done. The bedrock has nowhere been reached. It is our purpose to reach it. The formation here is of conglomerate and drift, intermixed with porphory, hornblende, crystalized quartz, iron pyrites and mica—there are also indications of granite. Am very sleepy—good night.[1]

The diary of Charles C. Post records the same sawmill at Russellville sixteen days later on June 26, as he and his party neared the goldfields:

> Sunday June 26th. We arose at two o'clock, rode twenty-one miles to the head of Cherry Creek by eight o'clock and breakfasted, cooking our "Old Ned" on coals and making tea in a tin cup. At ten o'clock we rode down creek four miles and found some miners camped. They told us they were averaging two dollars or three dollars per day, not water enough to run sluices, with cradles being the only chance. They seemed quite cheerful. We went about four miles more and came to a sawmill in full blast, managed by N. J. Wyatt. It was a small rotary engine mill, but cuts some three to four thousand feet per day, which sells readily for one hundred dollars per thousand in Auraria and Denver or eight dollars a thousand at the mill. It made me feel quite at home.[2]

This illustration is from the J. I. Case Company, a manufacturer of sawmills and, later, tractors. The actual woodcut engravings were reprinted by the company in 1942 as an example of the printing technology of the time. Courtesy Archives, University of Colorado at Boulder Libraries, PAM files.

This photograph of a steam-driven sawmill was given to the Denver Public Library photo collection by Hazel Bennett Kettle, D. C. Oakes's granddaughter. It is probably D. C. Oakes's mill at Huntsville, near Larkspur. Courtesy Denver Public Library, Western History Collection, X-22256.

Evidently, Wyatt's mill was a circular sawmill powered by a small steam engine similar to the one shown above.[3] Russellville was southeast of present-day Franktown and situated on the historic Cherokee Trail between the Arkansas River settlements and what would become Denver. Most historians credit Wyatt with providing the first sawn lumber for a frame house in Denver on April 21, 1859.[4]

Sawmills tallied their output in board feet of lumber. This standard is the measure of the volume of lumber that passes through the mill. One board foot of lumber was a one-foot by one-foot plank one inch thick. Or it might be one foot long by one-half foot wide by two inches thick. Modern sawmills could produce two hundred thousand board feet of lumber per day. Most small, portable sawmills produced two to four thousand board feet each day, as did the first one near Russellville.

Oakes set up his first mill along South Boulder Creek at Deadwood,[5] so named because of the large quantity of fallen timber in the area. It is close to present-day Pinecliff. He had another mill producing lumber shortly thereafter, located twenty miles south of Denver near the territorial road (now Daniels Park Road) two miles north of Plum Creek. An article in the *Rocky Mountain News* on July 9, 1859, states that production was in full blast at Oakes's sawmill. He placed another sawmill shortly thereafter at Huntsville, near Larkspur, forty miles from the mouth of Cherry Creek; advertising in the *Rocky Mountain News*[6] helped the business a great deal until it was flooded by Plum Creek in 1864.[7] Oakes and his partner, Dr. Street, had at least three mills in operation by the early 1860s.

Other mills quickly sprang up in Empire, Central City, Boulder, Idaho Springs, Fairplay, and Twin Lakes—anywhere there was a market for wood planks. It was truly a market-driven industry. The first mills were freighted by wagon across the Sangre de Cristo and San Juan mountain ranges to Silverton in 1873, only months after the treaty was signed restricting the Ute Indians from the area. Another mill was shipped by wagon across the San Juans and into Parrott City in 1876, the year that Colorado became a state.[8]

Sawmill technology had only recently changed in the early nineteenth century from waterpowered sash saws to water- and steam-powered circular saws. Sash saws were straight saws pulled and pushed from the ends, either by human power or by other mechanical sources. Such human-powered saws had

Top: An early mountain sawmill usually was a crude affair, cheaply capitalized and built without permanency in mind. These picture of an HO gauge model mill built by Jim White for Art Lohr's Marshall Pass layout perfectly represent such a mill. The proprietor wrestles a log to the head frame to cut planks with the wooden structure, providing a measure of shelter and a place to hang the power pulleys turning the blades. A narrow-gauge track offers transportation both to and from the mill. In the third picture, both the cutoff saw and the edger show how planks were finished. The last picture depicts the steam boiler and engine turning waste boards to power. Author photo, 2004.

Boulder County sawmills. The top two photos are Leon Van Horn's sawmill below the Fourth of July mine above Eldora. Bottom left is Frank Lounsberry's mill in Boulder at 6th and Walnut. Bottom right is the E. B. Hill mill located near Ward. Courtesy Carnegie Branch Library for Local History, Boulder, Colorado.

This mill located in the San Juan Mountains was probably owned by the nearby mine and its mill. Power is supplied to the turbine-type waterwheel from the stream above. The sawmill is shown in the lower center of the photo. Courtesy Center of Southwest Studies, Fort Lewis College.

been used since before recorded history, but the evolution of other power sources sped the development of rotary saws that were more easily combined with the rotating power wheels, either waterwheels or steam flywheels. There is one historical reference to a waterpowered sash saw in Colorado, immediately south of Twin Lakes, that was built by Tom Cameron in 1866. It took thirty minutes to cut one board and four days to cut up a wagon of logs.[9] Rotary saws were much more efficient.

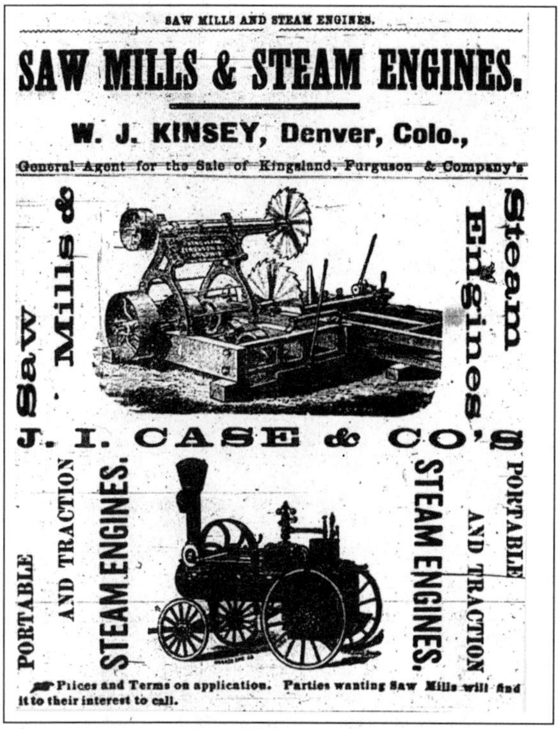

Top: The April 23, 1879, *Rocky Mountain News Weekly* ran this ad for J. I. Case sawmills and traction steam engines. The steam engine had power supplied to the wheels for traction as well as to the flywheel for supplying power to the sawmill. Above: When the Rocky Mountain Lumber Company built the mill at Monarch Lake, it used a Pelton wheel (shown here in construction) to power the facility. Water from the nearby stream turned the wheel, which turned the electrical generator in the far corner through a belt that's yet to be installed. The generator supplied electrical power to the rest of the buildings. Courtesy Archives, University of Colorado at Boulder Libraries.

The state's first mills were considered portable sawmills, as they were easy to tear down, transport, and set up. There has always been a conflict between the availability of power and the availability of trees. Early loggers cut timber and then planks from the logs where the tree fell because the tree was generally too difficult to move until it was cut into smaller parts. With the advent of the sawmill, it was easier to drag the logs to mills, located near streams that provided power to the mill's saws. However, these mills were permanent structures built to house a waterwheel, gearing, and the saws. The steam engine reversed this trend and once again allowed a small mill to be set up in the forest, close to the timber supply.

Logs are large and heavy. A sawmill required a host of workers and equipment to cut down the trees and move them where the pits or mills were located. Teamsters with

This set of big wheels with a log chained to its axle is being dragged by a team of horses probably to a loading area. Big wheels were a common tool for moving heavy logs over relatively level ground. Courtesy U.S. Forest Service.

both oxen and horses dragged the logs into position or later loaded them on wagons or railcars. Sets of wheels were used, with the end of the log tied to the axle and an oxen team attached to the same end, which dragged the log to the mill. Other ingenious transportation schemes were used too: wooden slides, flumes, and, of course, rivers. More than one railroad tie contractor or lumberman floated his ties down one of Colorado's rivers.[10]

The railroad industry did a good business moving lumber to markets, but trains were also used to move the logs to mills. Some early railroads used wooden logs as rails with concave wheels to track on the logs. History reports a logging railroad north of Blackhawk that used wooden rails, although no remnants remain. Log rails do not last as long as iron ones. Common to all sawmills was the difficulty of loading logs onto wagons or railcars. Usually the logs were precut to a length dictated by the mill, then rolled up an incline or more often pulled up using ropes attached to horse teams, with the log acting as a movable pulley.

Basic sawmills were designed to cut logs into planks or squares. Thin planks and lath were used for residential homes and other structures such as barns. It was not easy to cut planks to a consistent thickness, and many a sawmill earned the name "The

Top: A team of two horses pull a log up skids onto a rail flatbed soon to be headed for the mill. Photo by George Beam. Courtesy, Colorado Railroad Museum, Jackson Thode Collection. Middle: This photo shows timber being loaded aboard a logging tram. The horsedrawn tram rolls on light mine rails spiked down on flattened lengths of timber without crossties. The location is above the Hessie townsite near Eldora. Fred Feilding's sawmill at Woodland Flats would be the destination of the logs. Courtesy Carnegie Branch Library for Local History, Boulder, Colorado. Above: A four-foot-diameter log needed four horses to bring it down into Boulder, as shown by this photo by J. B. Sturtevant in the 700 block of West Pearl Street. Courtesy Sagstetter Collection.

Thick and Thin Lumber Company." The market requirement for more uniform, smoother planks created a demand for secondary operations on the rough-sawn lumber, such as planing. Planer mills took planks from a basic sawmill and planed them down to the consistent sizes we would recognize today.

Planer mill businesses might be vertically integrated into the sawmill itself or, more likely, set up as an independent business that bought planks from many sawmills

Four different options were available with this planer matcher, according to the 1902 Mine and Smelter catalog. With this equipment one could plane or shave down lumber to the thickness needed to match boards the owner already had.

and then planed and trimmed them to size. On June 13, 1860, two fellows named Smith and Collier established a steam-powered planing mill in Denver, selling boards, lath, and shingles.[11] Soon advertisements for planers were commonplace in newspapers and business directories throughout the state.

In 1866 the Hallack brothers, Erastus and Charles, advertised their lumberyard at Fifteenth and Lawrence streets and a planing mill in partnership with John Morrison on Holliday Street. Morrison owned a sawmill at the town in the foothills, southwest of Denver, that was eventually named for him. He provided the raw material and the Hallack brothers provided the planing mill, the retail lumberyard, and the building contracting business. E. F. Hallack's name appeared all over the Denver business scene in conjunction with the new waterworks; the Denver, South Park and Pacific Railroad; and other business interests. The association with the railroad yielded a contract to build railcars for the DSP&P in 1874. In 1875 the Hallacks were awarded and completed the entire Aspen Block in Aspen, Colorado.

The Hallack brothers went through several more partnerships as their business grew in parallel to Colorado's growth. They secured a more reliable source of lumber by opening a mill in La Madera, New Mexico, supplying lumber to the entire western United States. They also had lumber interests in Idaho and, in 1920, sold their business to Boise-Cascade. From immigrant labor, through local business, to national and international concerns, it was the perfect example of the evolution of a Colorado business.

A similar story could be told of the Hallacks' strongest competition, when in 1869, Charles McPhee set up a carpentry shop in Denver. His work was high-quality and his organizational skills strong. McPhee first expanded into the building contracting business to secure more work, then vertically integrated into lumberyards and sold building materials of all sorts. In 1872 his yard, with a planing mill and offices, was located at Eighteenth and Wynkoop streets. The new mill was of the latest design and driven by a fifty-five-horsepower steam engine; such a large power source indicated a large and complete mill. He probably supplied dimensional lumber to other builders to keep his equipment running at full capacity. McPhee also partnered with others to supply technical experience, capital, and business associations during the early growth of Denver. He received contract bids on large jobs, such as a hotel in Estes Park for Lord Dunraven, the Inter-ocean Hotel in Cheyenne, and the Old Main building of the University of Colorado in Boulder.[12]

McPhee's continued growth soon required a larger supply of timber, so in 1896 the company approached Edgar Biggs, a successful lumberman in the forests of northern New Mexico, with an offer to capitalize a large mill and logging railroad in the north-central part of that state. Together they incorporated the New Mexico Lumber Company and built a new mill in Lumberton, New Mexico, and then in Edith, Colorado. Edith, named after Biggs's daughter, is located close to the state's border, so close that there was doubt in the 1898 election whether the citizens should be voting for New Mexico or Colorado state officials, one of whom was Biggs himself. The mill at Edith could produce sixty thousand feet of dimensional lumber a day and employed hundreds of laborers.

In the 1920s, McPhee and the New Mexico Lumber Company again began searching for more forests for their retail concerns, which had become national in scope. In October 1924 they opened a large, well-equipped sawmill west of Mancos, Colorado, and shipped lumber everywhere in the United States except the West Coast. The mill had its own logging railroad into the nearby hills, which was used to bring logs to the saws. McPhee and the lumber company owned about ninety million feet of pine stumpage in the area, with contracts for another seventy million with the federal government for timber on national forest and Bureau of Land Management (BLM) land. The company named the logging camp after its president, William McPhee, Charles's son. In 1927 this mill was sawing and finishing ten to twelve carloads of lumber each day. The business paid out healthy and consistent dividends to

This Colorado shingle mill may be small, but it has everything needed to produce shingles, bolts of timber to saw, and bundles of shingles to sell. E. T. Walker and Charley Louk set this mill up in 1879 in Pagosa Springs. Courtesy Colorado Railroad Museum, Gordon O'Neil Collection.

its owners until the stock market crash of 1929. Because of the subsequent depression, the mill at the McPhee logging camp closed temporarily in January 1930. It opened periodically with new management and fresh capital, until it burned down in 1944 while operating as the Montezuma Lumber Company. A more detailed version of these two lumber companies—the New Mexico Lumber Company and Sullenberger's Pagosa Springs mill—and their logging railroad subsidiaries can be found in Gordon Chappell's *Logging Along the Rio Grande*, published by the Colorado Railroad Museum.

McPhee and his Denver accountant and partner John J. McGinnity bought an ally when they partnered with Edgar Biggs, but in so doing they also gained a strong competitor. Alexander T. Sullenberger also held timber interests in northern New Mexico and had his eye on the pine forests across the Colorado state line. He mimicked successfully the actions of Biggs, courting Front Range capital from the Newton brothers, a successful lumber concern that originated in Pueblo but expanded north through Colorado Springs, Denver, Boulder, and Fort Collins. In April 1899, Newton and Sullenberger joined with the Denver and Rio Grande to incorporate and begin construction on a logging railroad, the Rio Grande, Pagosa and Northern Railroad. They planned to lay tracks from Chalma, New Mexico, north to Pagosa Springs, where Sullenberger would build a large mill to supply dimensional lumber to Newton's retail yards to the north. The Denver and Rio Grande

The Rocky Mountain Lumber Company used this artificial millpond to transport logs to its mill saws. The building was constructed in 1904 and burned down in 1908, shutting down the company. Courtesy Archives, University of Colorado at Boulder Libraries.

also purchased lumber for ties and bridges for construction in the area. The mill at Pagosa Springs supplied lumber for the Newtons until 1912. This successful Colorado family eventually moved to Denver and supplied lumber to Denver citizens and the sons and grandsons of the Front Range business community including a Denver mayor who later became president of the University of Colorado in Boulder, James Quigg Newton Jr.[13]

The abundance of wood in some areas meant that it would be used for the roofs and sides of dwellings. At first, people hand-split thin pieces from logs and overlapped them on the roof. But it wasn't until the shingle mill came along that the product became inexpensive enough for general use in the housing industry. If the product was handmade, it was called a "shake" and if it was machine made it was a "shingle."

The shingle mill started with a log called a bolt that was sixteen, eighteen, or twenty-four inches in length. The bolts were sent to the quartering saws, where they were cut along their axes into quarters, opening the internal faces to the shingle machines. Next, all bark and surface defects were removed. Blocks were placed on the carriage of the shingle mill so that the opened faces were presented to the saws. The carriage advanced after each cut such that the top of the cut was slightly closer to the face than the bottom for one cut and the bottom one closer to the saw on the next. This offset action resulted in slight tapers on the shingles so that they lay flat on the roof after installation. Usually shingles were cut with a one-eighth-inch taper over their entire length. The cut shingles were sent to the packing area, where packers inspected and bundled them together to be sent to market. Millions of shingles were made by sawmills in the United States, and one can still buy them today processed in much the same fashion as in the nineteenth century.[14] Shingle mills were located in Boulder, Denver, and elsewhere as early as 1860.

More specialized mill equipment also appeared as savvy businessmen looked for profitable niche markets for wood products. There was a box factory in Middle Park, in 1904–1908, as Boulder businessmen Charles Walcott, T. S. Waltemeyer, and A. M. Waltemeyer incorporated the Rocky Mountain Lumber Company to harvest the forests on the eastern side of Middle Park. Although the business offices were in Boulder, the sawmill and box factory were built a little south of Grand Lake in what is now the southernmost bay of Lake Granby. A small settlement called Monarch was built close by as well as a manmade lake created by damming the nearby Roaring Fork Creek. Monarch Lake is the remaining sign of the endeavor. Logs were cut from the nearby forest and dragged into the lake. A short flume or wooden chute was also used, not too successfully, to drop the logs down the mountain into the water. From there they could be floated to the mill, where they were processed into lumber and boxes. The lumber was either taken to the box factory or sold directly to retail yards. The business probably began in 1904 because that was the year David Moffatt's Denver and Salt Lake Railroad traveled over Corona Pass and through Middle Park. Even with the D&SLRR close by, the principals had to build a twelve-mile railroad of their own to move the boards and boxes to the mainline.[15]

George Eastom operated another sawmill six miles south of Monarch around the same time. The settlement was named for him, but was finally incorporated as Fraser in 1953. Although it was closer to the D&SLRR, Eastom still built a small logging railroad to help move logs from the forests around St. Louis Creek to the mill. George's son, Frank, did not follow in his father's footsteps and instead earned degrees in the new discipline of electricity and later became the dean of the Department of Electrical Engineering at the University of Colorado in Boulder.[16]

Neither sawmill was very successful, probably because they did not control their own markets by retailing into the cities where the greatest demand existed. The two merged in 1907 as the Consolidated Lumber Company. In the fall of 1908, the box factory at Monarch burned to the ground, all operations at both sites came to a halt, and all workers were let go. The sawmills and railroads were sold to an Omaha group of businessmen who tried to turn them into a going concern, but were unsuccessful. The equipment was finally sold for scrap. Later, after the Second World War, another mill was built in nearby Tabernash and the whine of the mill's saws and the smell of sawn timber once again filled the little valley along the mainline railroad, which was then owned by the

Railroads needed huge quantities of ties for rails. This picture shows the Galbreath Tie and Timber Company's yards in Baxterville in Rio Grande County. The Denver and Rio Grande Western tracks supply transportation and demand for the ties. Courtesy Denver Public Library, Western History Collection, X-13612.

Denver and Rio Grande and used the Moffatt Tunnel to bypass the storms on Corona Pass.

The South Platte drainage in Jefferson County became an especially hot area for lumber products driven by the demand from Front Range cities. In 1867, C. J. McDevitt and Isaac Stevens set up a mill at the mouth of Deer Creek on the South Platte near Estabrook. In 1873, John Jones brought to the area a 24,000-pound sawmill costing $3,000 from the Jackson Foundry in Michigan, and three years later he tried to talk W. A. H. Loveland, C. C. Welsh, Edward Berthoud, and others into incorporating the Deer Creek Flume Company, chartered to build a six-mile flume up Deer Creek costing $1,600 per mile. It would have opened to logging the Deer Creek area all the way to present U.S. Highway 285. There is no record, however, of the flume being built or of the company being incorporated.

Farther south, Woodland Park became a major supply town for lumber in Colorado Springs to the south and in Denver and the suburbs to the north. A ten-mile logging railroad there brought the logs to the towns of Woodland, Divide, and Florissant.[17] Beulah and Rye, southwest of Pueblo along the eastern edge of the Wet Mountains, were the forest center that provided lumber to Pueblo and Cañon City. Grand Junction's need for lumber spawned sawmills to the east in Plateau City, Colbran, and Moline, and to the south at Whitewater and on the Uncompaghre Plateau at Pine Hill and Kelso.

One of the largest users of logs was the railroad. Colorado's rapid expansion to its booming population centers created a demand for railroad ties and bridge structures. Ties had to be nine to eleven inches wide by eight to nine feet long. Flat surfaces on two sides were finished with a broadax. The work was subcontracted usually to small, independent "tie hacks"—woodmen who cut ties. Usually a two-man operation would go into a forest and pick out the trees they intended to harvest. Trees were labeled one-tie, two-tie, or three-tie. Thus a particularly tall, straight tree that maintained a diameter of nine to eleven inches for twenty-six feet was a three-tie tree. The hacks preferred two-tie trees, as they were easiest to handle after cutting. The woodmen cut down the tree usually with a one- or two-man crosscut saw, cut off the branches, and then with broadax flattened two opposite sides of the log. A hack could do fifteen ties a day. Ties were then moved to a predetermined location by any means available and cut to the proper length, if necessary. A second subcontract group of teamsters usually moved the ties by wagons pulled by horses, mules, or oxen from the collection point to a central tie camp or possibly directly to the location designated by the railroad for installation. Larger tie camps sprang up throughout the country near railroads, with the ties cut and squared to the required dimensions on-site by a sawmill especially designed to shape the logs to tie dimensions. Each mile of railroad track requires 3,200 ties, which means there are about one billion wooden ties currently in use in North America. One estimate set the number of tie hacks for the railroad during its westward expansion in the last half of the nineteenth century at twenty-five thousand and others were required for transportation and handling.[18]

Mines wanted timbers with the ends milled to a constant shape to serve as supports for shafts, tunnels, and stopes. Machines were designed to do such work, including the shaping of joined ends. In Colorado, mines were one of the major users of

The Brunton Round Timber Framer was advertised as the largest and most complete timber framing machine of its time. This machine was featured to have many advantages over other timber framing machines such as the ablilty to handle logs from 8 inches to 20 inches in diameter and also boasted having twice the strength and double the life at half the cost. From The Mine and Smelter Supply Company catalog.

lumber; larger, better-financed mines had their own sawmills on-site. Such an operation would be a prime candidate for the Mine and Smelter salesman to pitch a Brunton timber framing machine as shown in the company's catalog.

Other uses for wood could and were integrated into the mill—a business strategy called vertical integration. Most sawmills furnished poles debarked and turned to a consistent diameter for fences or corrals. As vertical integration continued, almost all uses of wood became part of the mills: plywood, particleboard, excelsior, doors, sashes, lath, trim, and even matches.

Aspen wood is still preferred for the manufacture of wooden safety matches, and there was a match factory in southwestern Colorado as late as 1990. Western Development and Timber Corporation was located in Mancos and manufactured matches and wood shavings from aspen trees. The company still provides aspen shavings for such products as swamp cooler pads and pet cage shavings. The towns of Buena Vista and Golden both had sawmills that produced matches for the growing population of the Rocky Mountain region. The Buena Vista match factory was owned and operated by George Weaver and was listed in Polk's 1884–1885 *Railroad Gazette and Business Directory* for Colorado, New Mexico, and Arizona. An article in the local Buena Vista newspaper in 1893 refers to a Mrs. Stuart, who lived with her children in the "old Match Factory," indicating its possible demise as a business.

The matchstick process is an interesting one, here described by Blake Mitchell of Western Timber.

Match-Making Process, 1946–1990

1. Green poplar wood is preferred: poplar, birch, or aspen. Green wood holds together better during the veneering process.
2. Up to thirty-inch-diameter logs were cut into twenty-seven-inch bolts.
3. Logs were turned on a veneer lathe. Two veneer ribbons the thickness of a matchstick—about one-tenth of an inch—thirteen inches wide, and about twenty feet long were pulled off the lathe by two people and stacked on a table to the height of about fourteen inches. The lathe (Merritt) was a ruggedly built piece of equipment, fifteen feet long by ten feet deep.
4. The stacks of veneer were taken to the chopper—a guillotine-type machine, about three feet long by three feet wide by four high—that chopped the ribbons into strips about the thickness of the matchstick. The chopper also had lances that cut the thirteen-inch slices to the finished two-inch length of the stick.
   a. The ribbons were advanced automatically on the cutting blade's upstroke, chopped on the downstroke, then repeated until the twenty-foot ribbon was completely finished.
   b. The sticks, now called splints, fell off the chopper into a pneumatic conveyor. A pneumatic conveyor uses forced air in large tubes to move the lightweight sticks around the plant, process to process.

5. The conveyor moved the splints to the treatment room, where they were emptied into a hopper and dropped onto a shaker table tilted at twenty degrees, which shook enough to move the splints down the angle, aligning them in the same direction. The splints moved across slots that allowed short sticks to fall through first, and then another set, eliminating the long ones. This table acted as a quality control sorter, allowing the correct-size sticks to pass to the next process.
6. Properly sized splints were treated in vats of ammonium phosphate. This chemical is a glow inhibiter that does not allow an extinguished match to glow and possibly start a fire. These splints were wet both from their chemical bath and from their own water moisture because they were green.
7. The splints were dried in a two-stage dryer, a process that took about thirty minutes.
8. After drying, the splints were moved to the polisher, a tube tumbler six feet in diameter and forty feet long, set at about a five-degree angle with internal paddles to move the splints down the tumbler. The tumbling action of millions of sticks, the paddles, and wax inside would deburr and polish the splints to a smooth finish.
9. The splints were again transferred via pneumatic conveyor to the seeder process, in which small, broken pieces were removed from the good splints. This tumbler tube—about four feet in diameter and sixteen feet long—had a hard rock maple inner surface with 0.875-inch diameter holes through which the smaller broken pieces would drop, leaving finished splints ready to move to the next step.
10. Again, pneumatic transfer was used to move the splints to a holding bin, then to a hopper that dropped the splints into packing boxes that were shaken as the final product was dropped in. This maximized the number of splints in a box.
11. The splints were sent to tipping facilities, some of which were associated with the splint business. In the case of Western Timber in Mancos, they originally were part of Ohio Bluetip Match. After Ohio Bluetip went out of business, Western was able to find another customer for its matchsticks: Universal Match, whose tipping facility was in Louisiana.
12. The tipping process consisted of dipping one end of the splint into a red phosphorous compound and allowing it to dry. Red phosphorous replaced the more dangerous white phosphorous at the beginning of the twentieth century. After the final year of production in 1990, all of Western's matchstick equipment was either sold to Diamond Match or scrapped.[19]

The number of sawmills that operated in Colorado was staggering: nearly 2,500 in a one-hundred-year period. They were easy to set up, relatively inexpensive, and the state provided a ready supply of free raw material. Most mills were small operations run by two to five men. Many were family involved, as indicated by the use of "Bros." or "Sons" in their names. The 1900 census reported 159 sawmills operating in the state, employing 732 workers, an average of 4.6 men per mill. The 1890 report listed 120 mills with 1,156 wage earners, an average of 9.6 men per mill. Probably the 1900 census counters did a better job of documenting the numerous but remote smaller mills as the transportation and communication systems improved. These small mills did not stay in one location very long, moving to better timber or fast-developing mining boomtowns with a demand for sawn lumber for houses, saloons, and mining timbers.

As with other Colorado industries, sawmills were gradually consolidated into larger, better capitalized, more efficient mills that could supply cheaper material to the retail markets. These mills were, in turn, gobbled up by national concerns that continued the trend, aided by cheaper methods of transportation. Today Colorado's building industry is supplied by large national and international companies whose sawmills are located in other states.

■ ■ ■

Notes

[1] George Willing, "Diary of a Journey to the Pikes Peak Gold Mines in 1859," *The Mississippi Historical Review*, edited by Ralph P. Bieber (Denver Public Library, June 10, 1859).

[2] Ibid., June 26, 1859.

[3] J. I. Case, *Case Wood Engravings: Reminders of a Past Art* (1942), University of Colorado Archives.

[4] Jerome S. Smiley, *History of Denver* (Denver: Denver Times Publishing Company, 1901), 247.

[5] D. C. Oakes, "The Man Who Wrote the Guide Book," *The Trail*, December, 1909.

[6] *Rocky Mountain News*, February 28, 1860.

[7] Hazel Kettles, personal manuscripts, including D. C. Oakes's handwritten account of the trip to Auraria in 1859, Denver Public Library Western History Records.

[8] *Denver Field and Farm* magazine, No. 1644 (August 11, 1917): 8.

[9] Griswold, *History of Leadville*, 67.

[10] *Rocky Mountain News*, July 28, 1875.

[11] *Rocky Mountain News*, June 13, 1860.

[12] Dolores C. Renze, *Brief Study of the Lumber Industry in Colorado* (Denver: Colorado Historical Society, 1949), 25–26.

[13] Mark Foster, *Citizen Quigg: A Mayor's Life of Civil Service* (Golden, CO: Fulcrum, 2006).

[14] Ralph Andrews, *This Was Saw Milling* (Seattle: Superior Publishing Company), 132–133.

[15] Charles Wolcott, *Monarch of Grand County* (Brand Book of the Denver Posse of the Westerners, 1954).

[16] Dr. Frank Eastom, *Enterprize at Frazer* (Denver: Brand Book of the Denver Posse of the Westerners, 1954).

[17] Renze, 19.

[18] William Wroten, *The Railroad Tie Industry in the Central Rocky Mountain Region*, Ph.D. diss. (University of Colorado, Boulder, 1956).

[19] Blake Mitchell, oral description of the matchmaking process from 1846 to 1990.

CHAPTER 10

Saddles and Spurs

D. C. Oakes did not mention saddles in his list of supplies, but since he rode a horse to the Pikes Peak region, must have used a saddle and horse tack. Because Oakes was a seasoned traveler, having gone to California and back ten years earlier, he was undoubtedly familiar with California-style saddles as well as saddles from midwestern centers such as St. Louis and nearby St. Joseph. The Colorado Historical Society exhibits the double-barreled rifle Oakes carried with him on his first trip to the Denver area in 1858, but not his saddle.[1]

Horses were difficult to transport in the small ships of Columbus's day. They had to be both supported and restrained. They could easily do damage to themselves, to others, and to the ship. Illustration by Lienzo de Tlaxcala. From *Man, Made Mobile,* ed. Richard E. Ahlborn.

The Spanish brought cattle, sheep, goats, and horses to the New World, an event that had lasting repercussions within the western United States. After an absence of ten thousand years, horses returned to the land of their origin.

Columbus transported Spanish horses to the Caribbean islands on his second trip there, late in 1493, and twenty-eight years later Cortes used sixteen horses in his invasion of the Aztec empire.[2] Those horses, along with Columbus's stock in the Caribbean, were enough to transplant the horse on this side of the Atlantic.

These illustrations show both types of Spanish saddles, the Jineta at top and the Estradiota at bottom. The riders in both use the Spanish-style spike spur to goad their mounts into action. Illustration by Lienzo de Tlaxcala. From *Man, Made Mobile,* ed. Richard E. Ahlborn.

Coronado's northern expeditions later in the sixteenth century into the Great Plains region, including Colorado, and the development of California in the eighteenth century by the mission padres, hastened the migration of the horse into Mexico and what would become the western United States. The horse would change the cultures of most American Indians from walking hunter-gatherers to mobile hunters who could more easily chase and kill their prey, including the American buffalo.

With their horses, the conquistadores brought Spanish war bridles and saddles. These saddles had been developed over more than five centuries by their European and Moorish ancestors,[3] and included the heavy Spanish *estradiota* and the lighter *jineta* styles. In the New World, these saddles were modified as the changing conditions of their use dictated; those used more for stock tending than for war were lighter. A vaquero and his horse roamed over vast areas of the semiarid northern Mexican plains, tending cattle, sheep, and goats owned by dons of the hacienda. Lighter gear was easier on a horse.

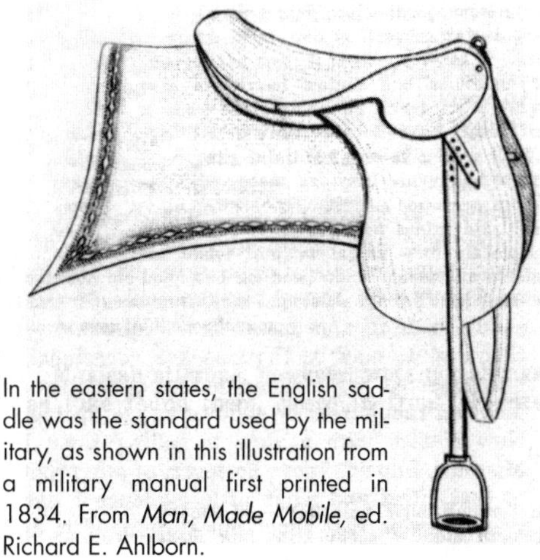

In the eastern states, the English saddle was the standard used by the military, as shown in this illustration from a military manual first printed in 1834. From *Man, Made Mobile,* ed. Richard E. Ahlborn.

The early Puritan settlers brought English riding gear—tack—along with horses to the colonies in the seventeenth century. This riding gear was designed for the needs of a more densely populated land, as transportation of people from farm to farm and town to town was more important than handling cattle and other stock animals.

As European colonists migrated west and Mexican horses and tack moved east, individual users chose the best gear for the task at hand. The Mexican saddle, with a saddlehorn that allowed a rope to be attached for stock work or stump pulling, eventually became the saddle of choice. Mixing of the two cultures in Texas and California, and then on the Santa Fe Trail in the nineteenth century, led to further modifications to individual and regional tastes, but the basic form remained the same. The saddlemaker in Santa Fe furnished saddles to customers returning over the Santa Fe Trail to the Missouri River supply towns of Westport, Independence, and St. Joseph. Makers like Israel Landis had provided saddles since 1844 in Westport, and his son, John, who ran a popular saddlery in Independence, started modifying the design to satisfy the needs of westward-moving customers.

The basis for the western saddle is the saddletree, originally carved from the fork of a tree. A saddletree has four major parts: a front fork, a back bridge called the cantle, and two sideboards called bars that rested on the top sides of the horse's back centered over its strongest vertebrae. The tree provided a seat that more closely conformed to the rider's anatomy, allowing a more stable and comfortable ride. The inside of the

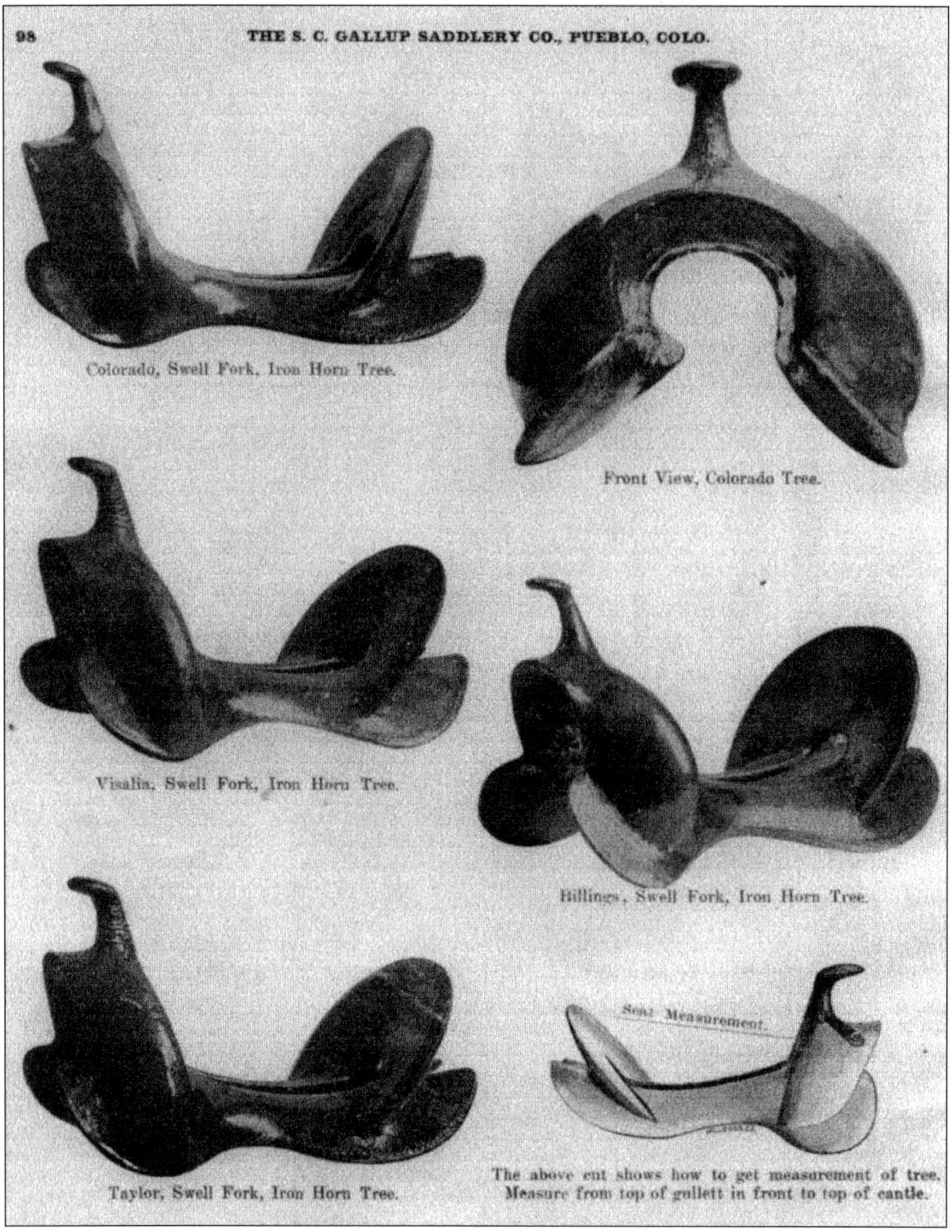

These saddletrees in the Samuel Gallup Catalog No. 15 were also available for sale to other saddlemakers throughout the country. Courtesy www.cabincreekcds.com.

front fork did not touch the horse's withers but distributed the load down to the bars.

Saddletrees have progressed from one piece carved from a single tree fork, to several individual pieces dowelled and fastened together with screws, to a variety of materials assembled together. White pine replaced hardwoods as a good wood for the tree because it was fibrous and a little flexible so that it could withstand harsh jerks with less fractures, and yet was considerably lighter.[4] At first the wooden part was completely covered with wet rawhide that upon drying shrank tightly to the form of the tree, providing much additional strength. This step also allowed the use of individually shaped pieces resulting in a greater number of saddletree types, each with its strengths, weaknesses, detractors, and proponents. Saddlemakers might make the tree themselves or buy it from a specialist. Both specialization of labor and recognition of the increased merits of a particular saddletree style were responsible for the development of separate businesses for their production. In 1860s Colorado, E. L. Gallatin had one of his nephews build saddletrees for all three of his saddlery shops in Denver, Cheyenne, and Nebraska City. Other saddlemakers also purchased trees from his shop. Saddles were often named and recognized by the type of tree, such as the Hope saddle in Texas, the Visalia in California, and the Colorado Swell Fork.

Originally saddletrees were carved by hand in one piece. Later, building the saddletree from four separate parts made for easier manufacturing as well as more options in the final shape. The sideboards could be planed to the proper thickness and then cut and shaped by using a scroll saw and drawing knives, technology that was easily available to saddlemaking shops throughout the West at that time. The cantle and front fork might still be carved, but the shapes were simpler to make and could be roughed out with saws and other machinery.

The most conspicuous part of the tree was the saddlehorn, which protruded from the top of the front fork. The saddlehorn was the major difference between English- and Mexican-style saddles and the major reason why the Mexican saddle was preferred in the West. It was the attachment point for one end of the rider's lariat or rope; the other end attached to a variety of loads, including steers, other animals, or any item the rider wished to drag or hold using a single horsepower. The lariat increased the cowboy's arm length by thirty to fifty feet, and the saddlehorn increased his strength by adding his horse's strength to his own.

A saddletree's horn was required to hold the jerk of a full-grown cow through the rope and was prone to breaking. A broken horn rendered the saddle useless and the rider had little choice but to buy another. Therefore, much work was done to strengthen the horn with thicker forks and forks of different materials, including iron, nickel, and bronze. An enterprising saddlemaker invented a repair kit that would attach a new horn to the front fork, and soon all saddlemakers were offering this repair.

The back fork of the tree held the cantle—the seat. This had the basic shape of the rider's buttocks, but with many variations for individual sizes and preferences for support. Perfectly made saddletrees must be individually fitted to horse and rider. Custom-fitted saddles, obviously, were more expensive, and compromises in fit were made to bring the cost within reach of the ordinary cowboy.

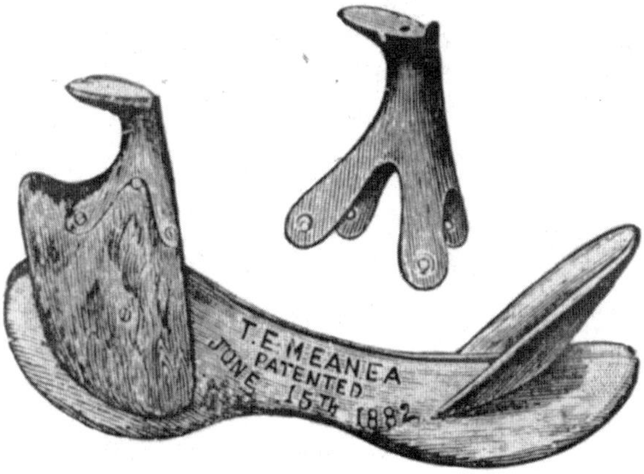

Theodore Meanea patented this saddletree with a replaceable saddlehorn in July 1882. Meanea would have been at the height of his business success in Denver at that time. Courtesy U.S. Patent Office.

The second basic part of a saddle is the cinch, which secured the tree on the back of the horse. In its earliest form it was merely a strap across the tree and around the horse's girth. It remains essentially the same, except the material and attachment points have changed. There has always been argument over the proper location for the cinch, but actually this depends on how the saddle is used by the rider. If little or no use is made of the saddlehorn, the cinch is best situated directly under the rider in the middle of the saddle, center fired. Heavier loads on the front are better held with a more forward cinch, and very heavy loads need a saddle with cinches front and back to keep it from pivoting off the back of the horse around the first attachment point. Vaquero and cowboy alike paid particular attention to tightening the cinch. A loose cinch would allow the saddle to slide to one side or the other, a dangerous position. Too tight a cinch might make a horse angry, or at least uncomfortable. Even now there are rules of thumb for tightening the cinch, and for how soon to retighten it.

The Spanish spelling for *cinch* was easily recognizable by R. T. Frazier's customers. In his catalog he had *cinchas* in five styles as well as bridle reins and saddle trimmings. Courtesy www.cabincreekcds.com.

Cinch straps called latigos, or any other piece of leather of a constant width, were cut from hides by hand or by using a draw gauge, a sharp knife with an edger attached. Most edgers were adjustable, although a saddlemaker might own an entire set of draw gauges, each permanently built to a specific width of up to about four inches.

If the strap was not too long, a die press called a clicker die could be used to cut the entire piece from a hide, including punching the holes in the strap ends used to adjust the length. If the cinch was made of hair, cotton, or wool, it was hand-braided, braiding being one of the occupational skills of leather workers.

The third important part of the saddle was the stirrups, consisting of adjustable straps on both sides that attach to the saddletree and to wooden bands at the end that support the rider's feet. Length adjustment depends primarily on the height of the rider and secondarily on his or her preferred riding method. Some riders preferred the bent knee, or *jineta*, position, while others liked their legs fully extended. Stirrups were usually open at the toes for simplicity, or might be covered for protection of the foot from the rough brush or cactus so prevalent in the southwestern and Mexican deserts. Stirrups could also be covered for decoration, allowing the horse's owner a chance to show off his status or sense of style. They were originally carved from a single piece of wood. Later, wooden strips were soaked in water to soften them, then bent to shape and allowed to dry, maintaining the closed U shape desired. In the twentieth century, metal stirrups were forged for greater strength. Stirrup straps were cut from leather hides by hand using a draw gauge.

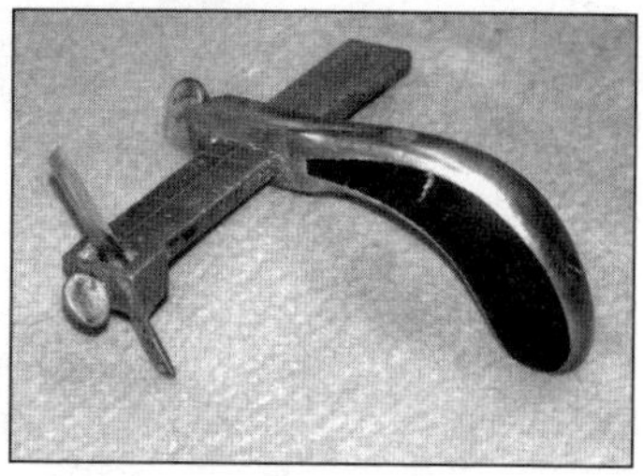

The draw gauge above is a pre-1834 tool manufactured by H. Huber. To adjust the width of the piece of leather to be cut, the steel rule moved in and out of the handle, which in this tool is made of brass with rosewood-inlaid handles. The cutting knife is at the end of the steel rule, and the leather moved over the top of the rule during cutting. Courtesy Dick Sherer Collection.

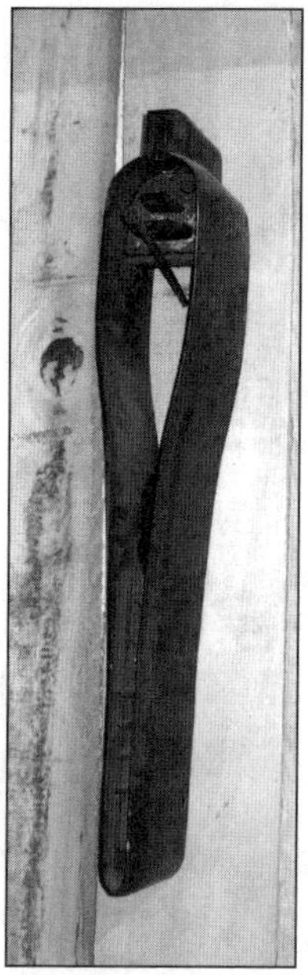

This clicker die would have been for higher-volume production of a latigo strap. The die was placed in a mechanical punch, and many straps of this size were cut. Hole punches inside the narrower end made holes at the same time. Courtesy Donald Bailey.

A saddle consisting of only a saddletree, cinch, and stirrups was known as the Mexican–Santa Fe saddle. It was both functional and inexpensive. One saddlemaker[5] claims that the Mexican–Santa Fe saddle had a tendency to wander around a horse's back during use unless a skirt was included. Skirts of leather lined with sheepskin or felt protected the horse's sides from brush and timber. They were often part of the padding used under the saddletree to cushion the tree's bars where they rested on the horse and provided more stability to the entire rig.

Fenders were longer pieces of leather attached to the saddletree and extended down the horse's flanks between the rider's legs and his or her mount and were often part of the stirrup straps, acting as sweat protectors for the rider. Both skirts and fenders also offered the saddle's owner the opportunity to show off decorative style and worth. Saddlemakers could express their leatherworking artistry to differentiate their saddles from those of other makers. Decorations varied, and still do, from leaf or flower patterns to geometric patterns, with infinite possibilities. More decorations required more handtooling, which increased the cost of the

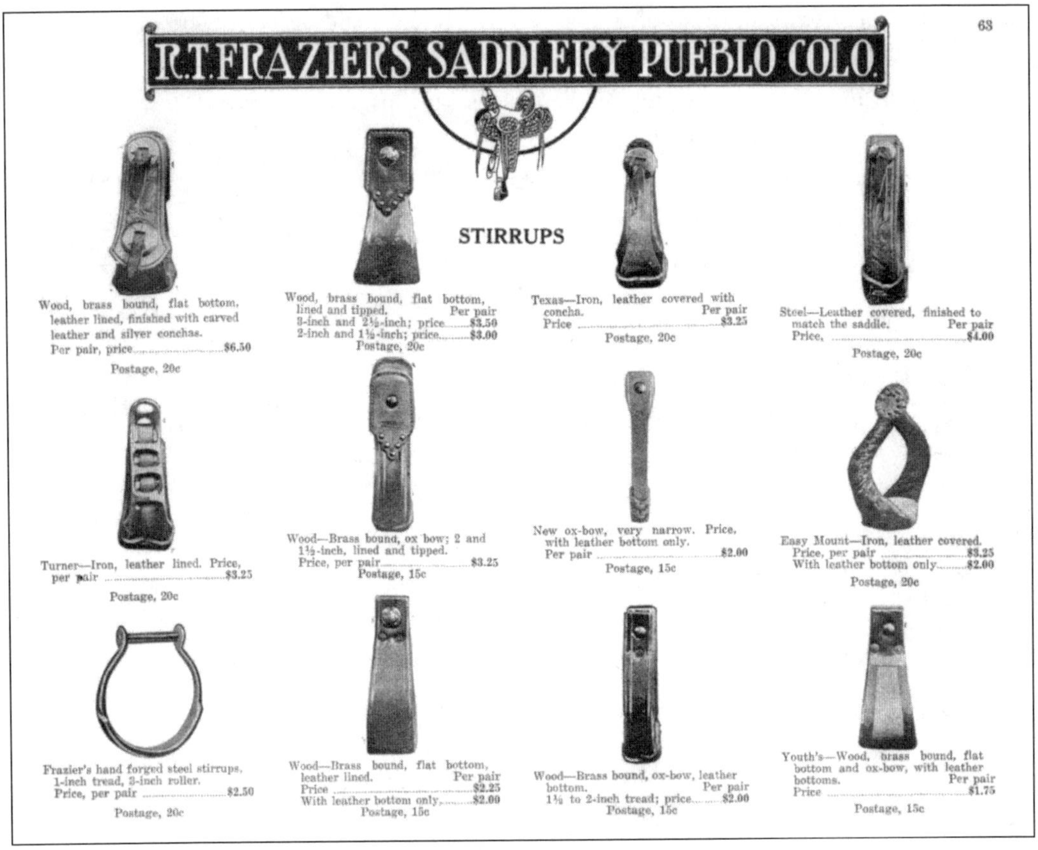

A cowboy could buy any type of stirrup he wished from R. T. Frazier's catalog. Gallup, Flynn, and many other shops relied on catalog sales to expand their market. R. T. Frazier's Catalog No. 29. Courtesy www.cabincreekcds.com.

finished product. Leather tools for making decorations are still the majority of a saddlemaker's personal selection of tools.

Other pieces, such as bags or pouches for carrying loose items, could be added to the saddle if the owner desired. A large leather covering over the tree, jockeys, and skirts was called a *mochila*, which had slots through which the horn and cantle protruded. Riders for the Pony Express used a special *mochila* with four lockable pouches attached for carrying the U.S. mail. The entire *mochila* was transferred from horse to horse, with the mail remaining in the pouches. Longer straps and reins were made by cutting strips from hides, first by hand, and later by using a draw gauge. Pieces were joined together to achieve the proper length, using rivets or stitching.

Saddleries used the apprenticeship system to train those who wished to enter the trade. They also had a structured division of labor. The foreman who ran the shop usually wore a tie and white shirt to work. If he did any handwork, he usually was the main cutter, cutting all the pieces for a saddle. Leather comes in "sides," or sides of a cow's hide. Making a saddle takes two sides, with many small, odd-shaped pieces remaining as scrap. Properly sizing and shaping leather pieces while minimizing the amount of scrap were the most important tasks for a profitable saddlery business.

The foreman handed the pieces to a saddlemaker, whose job was to assemble the saddle. The maker might ask for help with some parts of a saddle, but its assembly was his responsibility and livelihood. Stampers were next in the pecking order; they tooled the leather designs onto parts of a saddle or other leather products such as belts, billfolds, and bags. They might create their own designs or might copy other design motifs. They worked at piece rate, as did all employees except the foreman and owner. A saddlemaker could ask a stamper to design and tool the fenders or skirts of the saddle he was working on. These tradespeople also laced billfolds and assembled belts. Women worked at this level, although few, if any, were saddlemakers. Leather oilers stained and oiled the saddles and other leather products. The oiling bench was usually in a far corner of the shop to prevent new leather from being stained and to keep the fumes away from other workers. Sweepers were at the bottom of the pecking order. They swept the floors of dirt and leather scraps. These small pieces of leather were used to make the smaller parts of a saddle, as well as rosettes, billfolds, and thongs. A saddlery was more a leather-working company than a saddlemaking business: smaller items made from scraps paid the bills.[6]

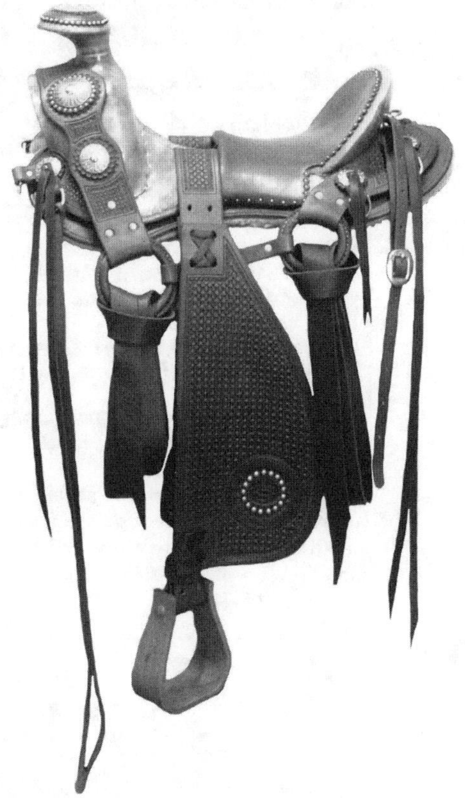

This modern replica of a Santa Fe saddle shows its simplicity. It was light and functional. Courtesy Sawtooth Saddles, Jerry Stewart Sawtooth Saddle Company, www.sawtoothsaddle.com.

The Pikes Peak gold seekers created a demand for goods and supplies as they streamed into the area, looking for quick wealth but finding mostly slow, tedious work. They needed many things to survive and prosper, including saddles, harnesses, and other riding hardware. Those who decided to cash in on the rush by providing agricultural goods needed farming equipment, including horse and oxen collars and harnesses. The early general merchants in the Pikes Peak region freighted in saddles from the Missouri River supply towns and sold them at their stores.[7]

Saddlemakers started their own shops, selling saddles and offering repair services for horse, mule, and oxen harnesses and hardware. By 1860, Denver had three saddle and harness shops: J. A. Hills, Wood and Railey, and John Landis.[8] The latter, a well-known Missouri River saddlemaker who operated out of Independence, and one of his employees, E. L. Gallatin, came to Denver in June 1860 and opened a shop on Blake Street. Landis returned to Missouri but left Gallatin in charge of the store. In 1863, Gallatin purchased the store from Landis with capital supplied by a German watchmaker named Francis Gallup.[9] Gallatin expanded the business by opening shops in Cheyenne, Wyoming, and Nebraska City, Nebraska. Both Gallup and Gallatin also brought relatives into the business, sending Gallup's younger brother, Samuel, to open a shop in Pueblo and Gallatin's nephew, Frank Meanea, to run the Cheyenne operation. Another nephew, Theodore Meanea, was put in charge of a saddle-tree-manufacturing company in Denver, supplying trees to the firm's other locations.

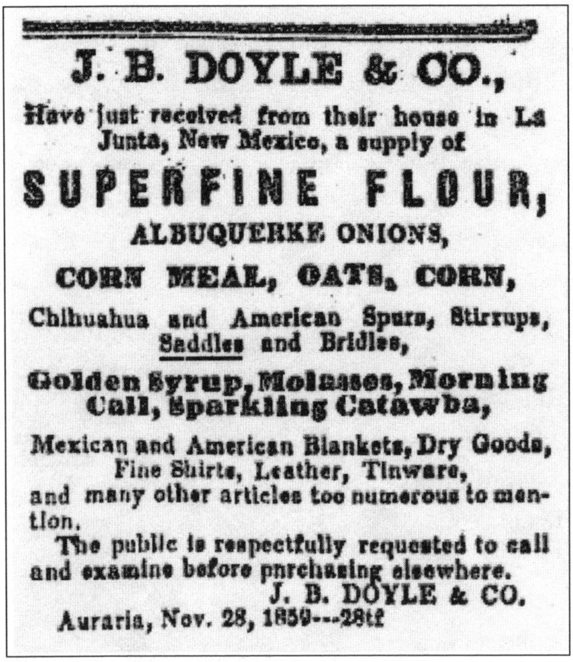

J. B. DOYLE & CO.,
Have just received from their house in La Junta, New Mexico, a supply of
SUPERFINE FLOUR,
ALBUQUERKE ONIONS,
CORN MEAL, OATS, CORN,
Chihuahua and American Spurs, Stirrups, Saddles and Bridles,
Golden Syrup, Molasses, Morning Call, Sparkling Catawba,
Mexican and American Blankets, Dry Goods, Fine Shirts, Leather, Tinware, and many other articles too numerous to mention.
The public is respectfully requested to call and examine before purchasing elsewhere.
J. B. DOYLE & CO.
Auraria, Nov. 28, 1859---28tf

Doyle's in Auraria was one of the largest and best-supplied general stores in the Pikes Peak gold region. Late in 1859, he advertised a new shipment received. Food was the first priority, but saddles were next. From *Rocky Mountain News Weekly*, November 28, 1859.

The Theodore Meanea Saddle Tree shop in North Denver, employees on the balcony. Courtesy Millard Meanea.

Other saddlemakers followed with the incoming gold seekers providing a steady market for their products. Herman H. Heiser arrived along the Front Range late in 1865. He opened shops in Denver and in Central City before settling permanently in Denver. In 1870 he bought the Gallatin and Gallup store at 1538 Blake, and his company remained in business until his

PRICE LIST

		Per Dozen
Billings,	Malleable Iron Neck, 14 inch to 16½ inch Seat,	$ 69.00
Portland,	" " " "	66.00
Visalia,	" " " "	66.00
Taylor,	" " " "	66.00
Funston,	" " " "	66.00
Ladesma,	" " " "	66.00
Nelson,	" " " "	66.00
Oregon,	" " " "	66.00
White River,	" " " "	66.00
Pueblo,	" " " "	66.00
Lehman,	" " " "	66.00
Goodell,	" " " "	66.00
Los Angeles,	" " " "	66.00
Half Breed,	" " " "	66.00
Schamel,	" " " "	66.00
Citizen,	" " 14 in. to 16 in. Seat,	57.00
Youth,	" " 13 in. to 14 in. Seat,	~~45.00~~ 48.00
Boys,	" " 12 in. Seat,	~~39.00~~ [illegible]
McClellan,	15 inch to 16 inch Seat,	54.00
Park,	" "	51.00
Side,	17 inch to 19 inch Seat,	72.00
Rawhide Pack Trees,		~~45.00~~ 48.00
Pack Trees, Common,		15.00
Repair Horns,		6.00

Rerawhiding, or Double Rawhide Trees, $3.50 Extra.
Double Rawhide Cover on Horn, 50c Extra.
Sterling Silver, Brass Polished, Solid Copper, Nickle or Silver Plated Horns, $1.50 Extra. "Meanea" Beveled Sterling Horn, $2.50 Extra.
Full Fork Trees, 13 inch to 15 inch, 50c Extra.
Special Trees, 25c to 50c Extra.
Above 16 1-2 inch; 25c Extra for each 1-2 inch in Length per Tree.
DIFFERENT LENGTH NECKS BY NUMBER: No. 5, Short; No. 7, Medium; No. 6, Long; No. 9, Extra Long.

Saddletrees sold by the dozen and were surprisingly inexpensive. As in any business, Ted Meanea offered enough options to satisfy even the most particular customer. Courtesy Millard Meanea.

sons sold it in 1947.[10] Saddles marked with an HHH, one of the first Colorado trademarks registered, continued to be made into the late 1970s and were one of the most recognizable saddle brands in the country.[11]

As other towns sprang up in Coloado Territory, each had its own harness shop, and most made saddles to order. There were shops in Colorado Springs, Leadville, Del Norte, and Monte Vista. As Western Slope towns grew, shops sprang up in Delta, Ouray, Durango, Montrose, Grand Junction, and others. The mining towns also required tack and saddles. Like car parts dealers and auto repair shops of today, harness and saddle shops were absolute requirements, and it is easy to see why immigrants with other skills, such as watchmaking, would seize opportunities to fill this increasing and steady demand.

Slowly the center of the saddle and harness business shifted south from Denver to Pueblo. In 1870, Francis Gallup's younger brother, Samuel, took over the shop of Joseph Hart in the 300 block of North Santa Fe Avenue in Pueblo.[12] Over the next twenty years, Samuel Gallup developed a variant of the northern plains saddle that became

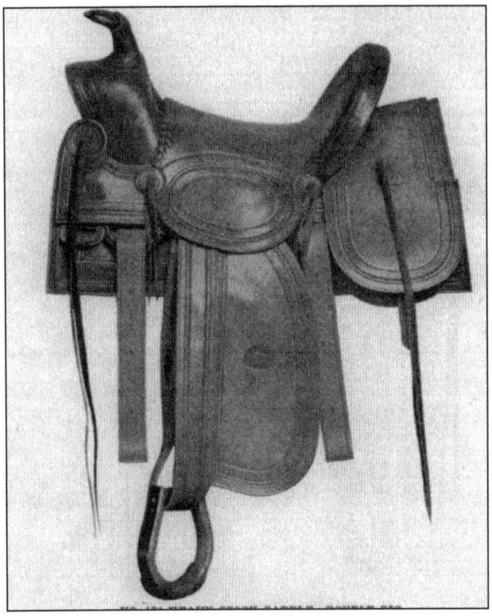

Over the last two decades of the nineteenth century, Pueblo became the saddle capital of the nation, and this saddle was the reason. Cowboys across the West wished this rig sat upon their horse. From Gallup's Catalog No. 15. Courtesy www.cabincreekcds.com.

Samuel Gallup's trademark, a Pueblo saddle on a longhorn steer, became as recognizable as a Chevrolet chevron. From Gallup's Catalog No. 15. Courtesy www.cabincreekcds.com.

known as the Pueblo saddle, with larger skirts and slightly wider forks than its predecessors. The seats were deeper, and the rigging was under the fork instead of wrapped around it.[13] Gallup formed a partnership with his foreman, Robert Frazier, in 1892, which lasted until 1898.[14] Frazier started his own saddlery in Pueblo that year, with both promoting the Pueblo saddle as the best in the world.

Thomas Flynn opened his shop on Union Avenue in 1889,[15] adding to the competition but also increasing Pueblo's reputation as the nation's saddlemaking center. All three used catalog advertising to expand their market geographically. Frank Flynn, Tom's son, claimed that ninety percent of their business came from catalog sales. Pueblo was a railroad center at the time, linking the east-west transcontinental rails from the Missouri River cities with the north-south rails along the Rockies from Montana to Texas—all cowboy country. Every ranch hand had access to these catalogs, also called "cowboy bibles." Thousands of saddles shipped out of Pueblo by rail to ranches around the country. Forty-seven saddlemakers called Pueblo their home at one time or another.[16]

R. T. Frazier had help with his Pueblo business. During his partnership with Gallup he entered into another, more permanent partnership with Katherine (Kitty) Henley. They married in 1893, and Robert gained a business partner. They never had children, but

Kitty worked in the business every day, handling slow or difficult customers and all of the mail order business. Along with their longtime foreman George Willock, they made Frazier's Saddlery the largest saddle producer in the nation, and in the world, by 1917. Frazier died in 1931, but Kitty continued to head the firm until 1958. She died in December 1959.[17]

Saddlemakers made saddles not only for cowboys but also for cowgirls and Victorian women. The latter did not ride astride a horse but sat with both legs to one side, sidesaddle. Makers made and sold sidesaddles; Samuel Gallup created one of the most recognizable, designed by famous cattleman Charles Goodnight. The Goodnight was slightly less dangerous than other sidesaddles, and it was not as safe as riding astride a horse—a fact understood by ranch women everywhere. Not only Annie Oakley and Calamity Jane rode horses with western stock saddles, perhaps built a little smaller for their specific use. Colorado saddlemakers understood this and provided an assortment of women's stock saddles in their catalogs.

R. T. and Kitty Frazier were marriage and business partners from 1892 until his death in 1931. Kitty maintained the business for another twenty-five years before retiring. Frazier's was the largest saddlemaking company in the world in 1918. Courtesy Don Bailey Collection.

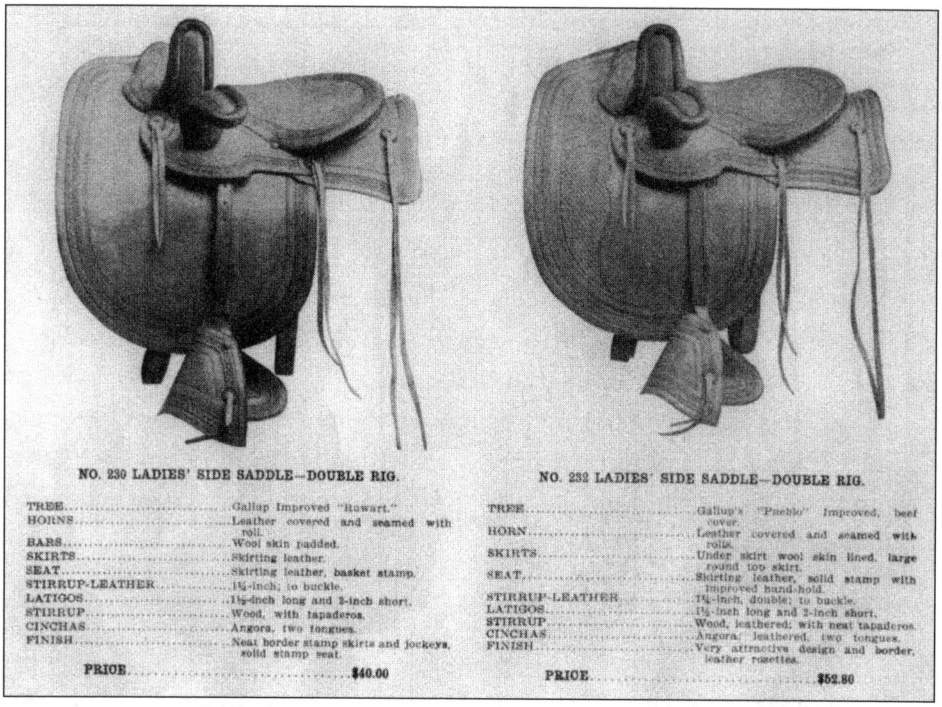

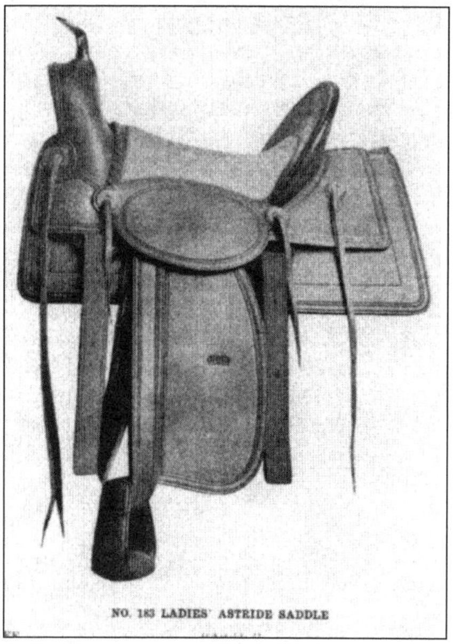

Top: Victorian women rode sidesaddle, so saddle shops made this type for their use. This one was offered by Gallup for $88, a mid to high price for a saddle. From Gallup's Catalog No. 15. Courtesy www.cabincreekcds.com. Left: Western women did not ride sidesaddle. This ladies' astride saddle was not only safer but less expensive—a bargain that western women appreciated. From Gallup's catalog No. 15. Courtesy www.cabincreekcds.com.

A saddle shop such as the well-known Burkhard's Saddlery in Trinidad (on the northern branch of the Santa Fe Trail), sold not just saddles, harnesses, and other leathergoods but also bridles, bits, and spurs—these tools of the cowboy's trade were only a little less important than his saddle.

Spurs had been used by the Spaniards almost as long as saddles had. Early spurs were single spikes for prodding the horse's sides. Later, spurs came to include the rowel circular parts commonly used even today. Saddlemakers in the leather-working trade usually did not make spurs or the metal parts of bridles but instead bought them from companies that specialized in the metalworking trades. Colorado had its share of spur and bridle manufacturers; the Crockett Spur and Bit Company probably was one of the best known.

Display Horses

The saddlery business obviously had very close ties to the horse and more distant ties to the ox and mule. It isn't surprising, then, that horses were used to advertise saddlemakers' businesses.

E. L. Gallatin, an important Denver businessman who was trying to expand his market, wasn't the first saddlemaker to set up shop in Cheyenne, Wyoming, but he captured a large share of the market by placing a full-sized, stuffed horse on a platform that was twelve feet high in front of his shop on the city's Main Street, in 1867.[18]

People would walk down the street to see the "high horse," and since a majority of them needed saddlery goods at some time, Gallatin's Saddlery became a popular store. He was able to hand over a healthy business to his nephew, Frank Meanea, who turned it into one of the premier shops west of the Missouri River.

J. H. Wilson had a similar horse in front of his shop on Larimer Street in Denver,[19] and other large shops had a display horse inside to show off different kinds of tack, just as clothing stores use mannequins to show off the latest in fashions.

S. C. Gallup[20] and R. T. and Kitty Frazier[21] had display horses in their Pueblo shops, too. Frazier's, from the turn of the century, remained until Kitty sold the business in 1958. The horse had gained notoriety after it washed out of Frazier's store during the 1921 Pueblo flood and was recovered fourteen miles downstream in a tree. The McConnells of Mack's Saddlery asked and received permission to purchase and move this popular member of the Pueblo saddlery community to their shop when Kitty shut down the business in 1958.[22] In 1989 the building that housed Mack's Saddlery caught fire. Pueblo citizens urged the fire department to break the front window and save the horse; it was one of the few items that was saved before the building burned to the ground.

Frank McConnell retired after the fire and gave the horse to the Southeastern Colorado Heritage Center in Pueblo, where it stands today in front of the Pueblo saddle exhibit. The local children have named it "Lucky," and with any luck it should be around for another hundred years.

Oscar Crockett originally started making spurs and bits in his Kansas City, Missouri, home at night after working a day job as a blacksmith. In 1916 he opened a small shop in Oklahoma, but later closed it to work in Washington State during the remainder of the First World War. He reopened it in Lenexa, Kansas, in 1920, but moved the business again in 1943 to Boulder, Colorado. Crockett Spur and Bit Company became one of the largest suppliers of spurs, bits, and cowboy belt buckles in the world by 1948. It had as many as 125 employees in the Boulder shop at 944 Pearl Street.[23] Crockett died in 1949, and his widow sold the business to a Denver competitor, James Renalde, in 1951.[24]

After the First World War, the saddlery business slowly declined. The passenger car replaced the horse as the main means of individual transportation, and the tractor

J. H. Wilson Saddlery was located at 1721 Lawrence Street in downtown Denver. It was a medium-sized shop with a reputation for high-quality saddles. James Hunter Wilson died in Denver in 1921. Courtesy Don Bailey Collection.

eliminated the farmer's need for harnesses and tack for his plow horses and wagon stock. Saddles had always been the draw to showrooms and on the first pages in the catalogs, but it was the harness, horse collars, and other mundane items needed on a horsepowered American farm that kept the saddlemaker in business.

Currently, saddlemakers in the Pacific Rim supply inexpensive production saddles for nondiscriminating American riders. There are some American-made production saddlemakers in the country, including Colorado Saddlery in Denver

These four photographs from Frazier's catalog provides an idea of the size of its manufacturing space. It was the largest saddlery in 1918, making bridles and harnesses as well as saddles. Courtesy Don Bailey collection.

Top: The interior of Frazier's showroom contained anything a cowboy or rancher might need. There was also a display horse to display new or unusual equipment. Photograph courtesy Don Bailey Collection. Above: I. R. Swennes opened a shop in Hugo in 1908, and it closed in 1931. His son John is pictured above at work in the shop. Almost every town in the state had a saddle shop; many were one-man shops or family-owned and -operated. Courtesy Don Bailey Collection.

CROCKETT *Sterling Silver Overlaid* **SPURS**

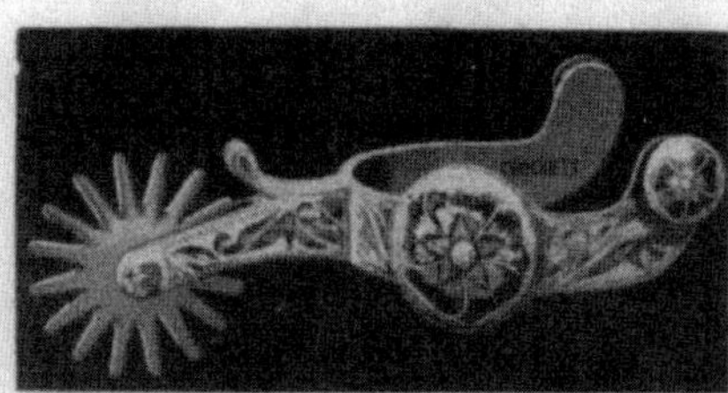

¾" Band 2½" Shank 2½" Rowel
No. 1610 as shown .... 38.00 Pr.

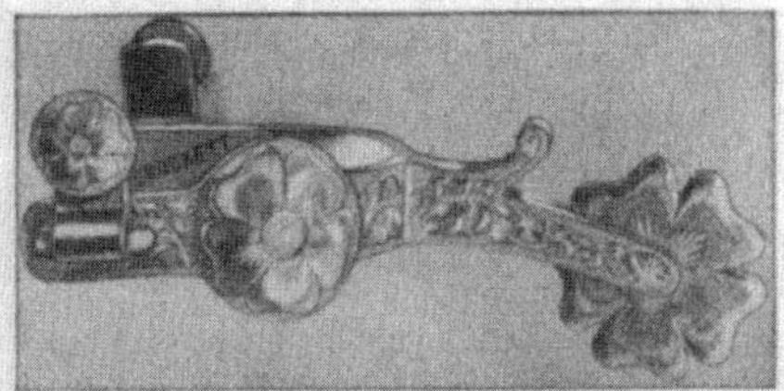

¾" Band 2¼" Shank 2" Rowel
No. 1614 as shown .... 38.00 Pr.

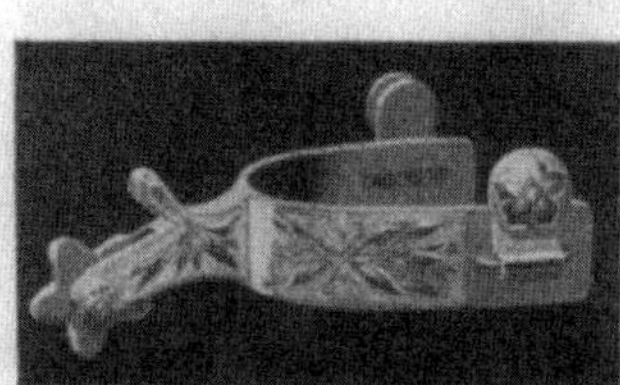

1" Band 1¾" Shank 1¼" Rowel
No. 1611 as shown .... 36.00 Pr.

1" Band 1¾" Shank 1½" Rowel
No. 1612 as shown .... 36.00 Pr.

⅞" Band 2" Shank 1" Rowel
No. 1613 as shown .... 36.00 Pr.

1" Band 1¾" Shank 1¼" Rowel
No. 1615 as shown .... 36.00 Pr.

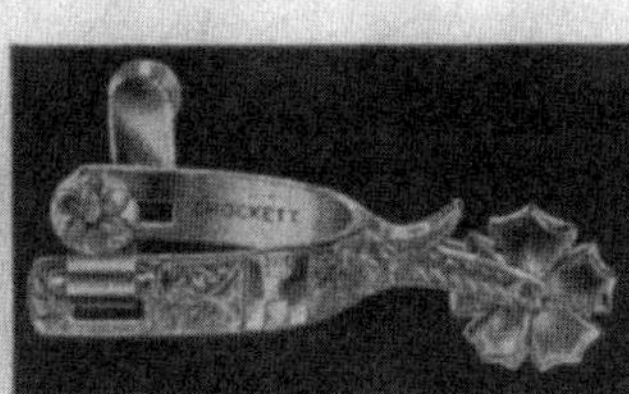

Any One Letter Engraved
¾" Band 2" Shank 1¾" Rowel
No. 1616 as shown .... 34.50 Pr.
Without Letter .... 33.00 Pr.

1⅛" Band 2¼" Shank 2¼" Rowel
No. 1617 as shown .... 42.50 Pr.

WOMEN'S or BOYS' SPUR

¾" Band 1¼" Shank 1¼" Rowel
No. 1608 as shown .... 32.00 Pr.

Made of Stainless Steel
Overlaid with Pure White
Sterling Silver.
Beautifully hand-engraved
by master craftsmen.

Beauty plus Quality

WOMEN'S or BOYS' SPUR

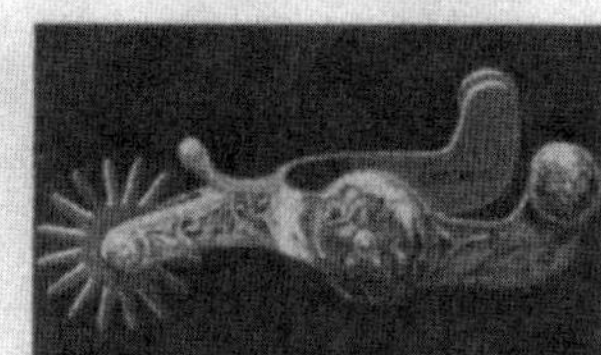

⅝" Band 2" Shank 1¾" Rowel
No. 1609 as shown .... 34.00 Pr.

Page 3 of the Crockett Catalog No. 48 illustrates the high degree of workmanship that went into handmade spurs. The motto near the bottom, "Beauty plus Quality," reflected the company's strengths. Courtesy www.cabincreekcds.com.

Samuel Gallup was famous for Pueblo saddles, but like all saddlemakers, he kept the lights on and the doors open by selling more mundane ware. His horse collars and harnesses are displayed in the harness showroom of his Pueblo shop. From Gallup's Catalog No. 15. Courtesy www.cabincreekcds.com.

(production takes place at the Colorado State Reformatory in Buena Vista). Most saddlemakers in the state are custom makers, contracting for a specific customer and his or her horse. This is the only way a perfect fit can be guaranteed. Most make four to twenty-five saddles per year. The cost is higher than that of noncustom saddles and also depends on the amount of handtooled decoration a customer desires. As with most products, you get what you pay for.

■ ■ ■

Notes

[1] Colorado Historical Society, Artifact H.865.1.

[2] Richard E. Ahlborn, ed., *Man, Made Mobile* (Washington, DC: Smithsonian Institute Press, 1980), 21.

[3] Ibid., 5.

[4] Lee M. Rice and Glenn R. Vernum, *They Saddled the West* (Cambridge, MD: Cornell Maritime Press, 1975), 80.

[5] Dave Mattson, *Santa Fe Saddles,* 2007.

[6] Author's interview with Richarnd Sherer, September 11, 2007.

[7] *Rocky Mountain News*, December 14, 1859, 3.

[8] Donald Bailey, *Saddle Strings* (Simla, CO: Bailey Ranch Publishing, 1995), 3.

[9] Ibid.

[10] Ibid., 10–18.

[11] Bailey, 10–13.

[12] *Colorado Weekly Chieftain,* August 11, 1870, 3.

[13] Rice and Vernam, 67.

[14] Ibid., 59.

[15] Ibid., p.74.

[16] George Williams, verbal discussion with the author, July 2007.

[17] Ibid., 72–73.

[18] Rice and Vernam, 38.

[19] Bailey, 21.

[20] Ibid., 58.

[21] Ibid., 69.

[22] Ibid., 84.

[23] *Boulder Daily Camera,* June 23, 1949.

[24] Cabin Creek.com CD for Crockett Catalog No. 53.

CHAPTER 11

Sugar Beets

In 1859, D. C. Oakes's list of provisions for his trip to the Pikes Peak gold region included two hundred pounds of sugar. Because he was provisioning four men for a six-month period, this quantity was enough for about one-half cup per man per day. That is more than double the 2005 U.S. per capita usage of about forty-five pounds per year.[1]

By the mid-nineteenth century, sugar was no longer considered a luxury item enjoyed only by the wealthy. It's unlikely that Oakes thought about the possibilities of sugar beet factories all along his route up the South Platte River Valley, but only forty-five years later they would become a dominant industrial and agricultural reality.

Although the sugar industry in Colorado, and for that matter North America, depended on sugar beets, it was originally made from sugarcane, a tropical plant native to the East Indies.[2] Probably people first experienced the sweet flavor by chewing a stalk, as is still done today. It would have been an easy and natural progression through the elemental steps of sugar refining: boiling the cane in water and then allowing the syrup to evaporate, leaving sugar crystals.

Unlike sugarcane, sugar beets—namely the white beet, *Beta vulgaris*—can be grown in temperate zones. A German apothecary, Andreas Marggraf, first crystallized sugar from beets in 1747.[3] The success of the beet sugar industry in Europe and the United States was based on four factors:

1. The development of a beet with high sugar content, fifteen to eighteen percent. (Marggraf's beetroot contained only four to five percent sugar.)
2. The improvement of farming methods that lowered the amount of labor required for planting, weeding, harvesting, and improving the soil by rotational crop planting.
3. Improvement in the manufacturing process to minimize sugar loss while producing a higher-quality, purer product.

4. The presence of protective tariffs to keep lower-cost, imported cane sugar out of the market.[4] (Competition between the beet sugar and sugarcane industries has continued since beet sugar was first processed.)

One of Oakes's contemporaries, Peter Magnes, a Swedish immigrant, had grown the first sugar beets in Colorado at his Littleton farm in 1859. Sugar beets and other vegetable crops were not suited for the arid western plains climate. But farmers like Magnes soon learned they would grow well if irrigated along Colorado's Front Range and in western Colorado valleys. No refineries were nearby to process the beets, but sheep and cattle would consume as many beets as they could get as fodder. Greeley's Union Colony and Fort Collins's farmers grew sugar beets for exactly this reason in the 1870s.[5]

The scientists at Colorado A&M in Fort Collins experimented with sugar beets at nearby Larimer and Weld County farms in the 1880s and determined that with proper irrigation and crop rotation, beets with up to fifteen percent sugar content could be grown in Colorado soils. All that was needed was a factory.

In 1899, John Campion and his partners, Charles Boettcher and Molly's husband J. J. Brown, erected Colorado's first sugar beet factory in Grand Junction. The plant showed good promise but was not the moneymaker the owners had hoped for. The problem was lack of beets during the harvest. There were not enough farmers to work the fields, and the local cowboys wanted nothing to do with beet fieldwork. Charles Boettcher's wife, Fanny, noted that "cowboys won't grow sugar beets," and her husband complained that growers were trying to raise beets while on horseback.[6]

The first sugar beet refinery in the United States had been built in 1838 in Northampton, Massachusetts, and processed beets grown from French seeds. It was followed in 1852 by a Mormon effort in Utah. Both were unsuccessful financially.[7]

Sugarcane needs a tropical climate to grow. It was native to Southeast Asia; Christopher Columbus brought it with him to the Caribbean on his second trip. Courtesy Wikipedia.

Sugar beets could grow in more temperate climates, which allowed them to be grown in most of the lower 48 states. This Colorado field was photographed by Lewis McClure in the early 1900s. Courtesy Denver Public Library, Western History Collection, MCC-2683.

A young man shows off harvested beets on the way to the factory. The beets, their tops cut off, are ready for the cosset slicing machines at the factory. Photo by Lewis McClure. Courtesy Denver Public Library Western History Collection, MCC-3210.

From then until 1879, thirteen factories were built across the United States, all of which failed except for one in Alvarado, California, built in 1879. American farmers had yet to understand the intricacies of beet growing: It required a great deal of hand labor to thin and weed, and crop rotation was essential. Refining equipment had to be imported from Europe—a costly expense. When the equipment arrived, there were no knowledgeable workers to operate it.[8]

At the end of the nineteenth century, the tariff for cane sugar entering the country was drastically increased, and the sugar beet industry became one of Colorado farmers' favorite crops and an industry giant that generated factory jobs and revenue for the state and the country. By 1903, new factories were being built in sixteen other states as well. The U.S. Congress continually passed protective tariffs and quota laws that allowed the sugar beet industry to thrive through most of the twentieth century.

Cultivating beets was labor that the kids of the family, as well as adults, could do. The beets are being thinned—the weakest removed along with any weeds in the rows. Courtesy Denver Public Library, Western History Collection, Z-29.

The same factors driving Campion and his partners were present in Colorado's lower Arkansas River Valley. As the Grand Junction plant struggled with its first harvest and processing campaign, two other groups were building plants and contracting acreage, one at Rocky Ford and another at a site near Ordway. The American Sugar Company, with principals from California (owners and operators of the first successful sugar mill, located in Alvarado), and the National Sugar Company, with principals from Baltimore, also thought beets would be a good investment. Both built their plants in 1900, with National not only building a factory but an entire town—Sugar City.[9] The National Sugar Company was the smallest sugar company in the United States and competed tenaciously with the sugar giants by using the lure of landownership and a guaranteed crop for eastern European immigrants. Their original business plan was predicated upon selling real estate plots to the farmers as much as on profits from the sale of refined sugar. In this they were successful, and many immigrants began their life anew in the Arkansas River Valley, owning their own farms and raising and selling sugar beets to national companies as well as the two sugar companies with factories in Holly and Rocky Ford.

Campion and his partners decided to build a second plant on the South Platte River drainage, locating it at Loveland. Boettcher managed the Loveland plant, which was built in 1901. Additional factories were built near the South Platte in Brush, Eaton, Greeley, Sterling, Fort Morgan, and Windsor and near the Arkansas River at Swink, Holly, Lamar, and Las Animas. By 1909, Colorado had become the leading beet sugar–producing state in the nation. Continued expansion resulted in factories in Brighton, Fort Lupton, Johnstown, and Ovid. In 1910, sugar beet production in the South Platte River Valley averaged 806,000 tons.[10]

John F. Campion came to Leadville in 1879, just in time to cash in on the rich discoveries of silver in the area. He earned millions by buying, consolidating, and selling mines and mining claims. Noting the boom-and-bust cycle associated with mining, he and his partners, Boettcher and Brown, decided to diversify into businesses associated with agriculture, and they did so by building the Grand Junction sugar factory and then others that would become part of the Great Western Sugar Company. These factories were built using Portland cement from the Ideal Cement Company, also owned by all three partners. Campion started the Great Western Meat Packing Company to provide beef, lamb, and pork to the rapidly growing Rocky Mountain population. He continued to diversify into other businesses, always based in Colorado and loyal to his adopted state. A town south of Loveland is named after him, although he and his wife spent most of the rest of their lives in Denver. He died there in 1916.

It is opening day at the Monte Vista sugar factory, November 15, 1911. Beets grew well in the irrigated soils of the San Luis Valley as well as the bottomlands of the state's rivers. Photo by O. T. Davis. Courtesy Denver Public Library, Western History Collection, X-11062.

Campion, Boettcher, and Brown were no match, however, for the East Coast robber barons, and in 1902 the National Sugar Trust, directed by the Overmeyer brothers, Henry and Theodore, tried to squeeze the beet sugar manufacturers out of business in Colorado by selling below cost. When that was unsuccessful, they sent their representatives into each community with a factory and threatened to set up their own factories if the independent operators, including the Great Western Sugar Company, didn't sell out to them. The state's growers were ecstatic at the thought of two companies competing for their beets. In 1905 the consolidation was complete along the South Platte, with all the purchased factories under the Great Western Sugar banner but now owned by the Overmeyers and their financial backers.[11] Added capitalization from eastern financiers allowed further expansion into other towns at the discretion of the directors on Wall Street. Along the Arkansas River, however, the story was slightly different, as the Holly Sugar Company and National Sugar held out against the trust and remained independent. They were already competing against each other, and the threat of a third factory wasn't very credible. The National Sugar Company was America's smallest sugar corporation until it closed in 1967.

The sugar beet industry is actually two distinct industries tied together by a negotiated contract between the farmer who raises the beets and the factory that processes them. The contract was often contentious but necessary: Both parties wanted the same result—a healthy market for high-quality sugar and sugar beets at a competitive price—the transfer of the beet from one to the other was always a point of disagreement. The factory wanted a perfect beet, harvested at exactly the right time to maximize its sugar content at the lowest possible cost. Harvesting too early or too late could lower that content. The beet should have no bruises or cuts, or it would quickly degrade, losing its sugar content. The farmer spent many hours in the fields thinning, weeding, and harvesting and did not want to worry about every bruise. The factory wanted the beet clean, and the farmer wanted the factory to clean it.

The contract between the two parties specified not only how many beets the factory would buy but also how much it would pay for their sugar content (how much it would subtract if part of the weight was dirt) and the quality of the beet.[12] Each load delivered by a farmer was sampled in the company's laboratories using the latest technology to figure the contractual points, just as gold and silver had been sampled for the purpose of negotiating terms.

To prevent farmers from believing that the laboratory sampling procedure was only a fancy way to cheat them, the company hired their wives during the beet season to work in the laboratories and run the samples, thus making them mediators between the two parties and keeping the relationship more of a family affair.

Certainly from the farmer's perspective, growing beets *was* a family affair. In the days before child labor laws, young children were encouraged to work the fields with

Moving beets from field to factory was an enormous undertaking as thousands of tons were involved. A wagon of beets from the field dumps its load into a Colorado and Southern railcar for the final trip to a factory. Overpass ramps were common at beet dumps throughout the region. Courtesy Longmont Museum.

their parents, and thinning and weeding were tasks even children could do. Some children were forced to work. Such forced child labor in beet fields was one of the reasons why child labor laws were originally passed. Colorado child labor laws still allow children over twelve years old to work in their family's fields. Beets were a labor-intensive crop, planted not one plant per hill, but four to seven plants per hill. They were thinned, usually twice, to retain the healthiest beets only. For many years, preventing weeds from overrunning the beets was a laborious task done by hand. Depending on the weather, beets needed to be irrigated a minimum of three times between spring planting and harvest after the first frost.

Harvesting a beet was not easy either. Being a root crop, it clung tenaciously to the soil around it. A worker had to loosen it from the soil, pull it out of the ground, knock off the clinging dirt without bruising or cutting the beet, cut off the top foliage, and place the beetroot in a wagon to be taken to the factory. The top of the beet could be no larger than 4.25 inches in diameter or it would not pass through the slicing station. The factory would buy the beet; the farmer still owned the top foliage,

The factory hired temporary office help during campaigns. Seven office workers pose with their supervisor, with piles of beets and the factory in the background. Courtesy Longmont Museum.

which he fed to his livestock or sold to his neighbor. The farmer and his family and work crew had many acres of beets to tend and harvest—a tough row to hoe. After harvest, the farmer often worked at the factory as temporary labor, processing the piles of beets. The longer a beet sat in storage, the lower its sugar content.[13]

For eight months of the year, a sugar factory was a relatively quiet place to work—no hurry, no overtime, no beets. Management negotiated the coming year's contracts, and the plant's personnel installed new equipment and repaired the old. But when the harvest started, things changed dramatically. During the four-month "campaign," as it was called, factories operated around the clock. Beets were moved from field to factory by wagon, train, and later, truck. After the farmer had delivered his contracted beets, the factory owned the crop, and any subsequent loss in sugar content was now the factory's problem. Beets were stored in silos, storage bins, and big piles. Big piles turned out to be best because they allowed for greater airflow through the mass, slowing degradation. From piles in the factory yards to the cleaning and slicing equipment, beets were moved by running water through a flume about two feet wide by three feet deep.

Sugar refining in a sugar beet factory was essentially the same as at a cane factory. Beets were sliced and soaked in hot water to extract the sugar, the sweet juice was purified of nonsugar substances, and the water evaporated, leaving sugar crystals. The trick to making a sugar factory into a commercial success, however, lay in the details.

A sugar factory processed a lot of beets all day, every day, until there were no more. Here beets are piled around the factory. A factory also used limestone in the process, piles of which are present in the lower right of the photo. Courtesy Longmont Museum.

The flume of water that carried beets to the slicers helped clean them. Eliminating dirt and trash from the beets also protected the knives and kept their maintenance cost down. Slicers were designed to cut the beets not into flat slices but into pieces with small V-shaped ripples. These slices were called cossets and would not stick together, allowing the diffusion water to better access their surfaces.

The diffusion process included soaking the beet cossetts in vats of hot water and controlling the water flow so that it moved counter to the movement of the cossets. Juice with the highest sugar content passed through fresh cossets and proceeded until pure, hot water passed through them, with most of the sugar removed, just before they were dumped from the cells as waste pulp. This maximized the amount of sugar and minimized the time required to extract it.

Diffusion vats were enormous tanks holding 450 cubic feet of water—about 3,300 gallons. The diffusion "battery" might have fourteen to fifteen vats side by side.

Beets were moved from piles to the factory in flumes of water, providing not only transportation but also cleaning before they went through the cosseting machines. This photo shows the flumes being built the summer before their first use. Courtesy Longmont Museum.

Water was heated to 130 degrees F and then circulated from vat to vat. Heat was added to maintain the temperature.

The diffusion battery was the heart of a sugar factory. The most senior and competent personnel were in charge of loading the beet cossets into vats and moving the juice from vat to vat. If the slices did not remain long enough in the battery, too much sugar would be lost in the pulp. If they remained too long, the juice extracted more nonsugars and plant material, which would cause problems further down the line.

In ancient times the juice was boiled down and evaporated and the sugar crystal collected, but in factories of the twentieth century, more steps were added. Research by sugar industry scientists had found that treating the juices with quicklime and carbon dioxide gas purified the juice by removing many of the nonsugars, clearing the liquid and keeping the sugars in the juice until a higher percentage could be recovered by evaporation. The lime combined both chemically and in colloidal solutions to precipitate out unwanted acids and organic material. The CO_2 gas then combined with the excessive calcium (lime) in the juice to form calcium carbonate (chalk), which further helped remove unwanted material.

A factory used so much quicklime that most had limekilns. Large quantities of limestone and coke were shipped by train to the factory's kilns. Coke was the kilns' heat source because its chemical-reducing qualities also aided in the generation of CO_2 gas. The Great Western Sugar Company moved hundreds of thousands of pounds of beets, limestone, and coke to its many western factories. In northern Colorado the company owned its own railroad to help with this task.

After purification, the juice was repeatedly filtered to remove the precipitates and the beet pulp that was still in the juice. This pulp, however, was much lower in sugar content than it was before the purification step. The sugar water was now called "thin juice" and was ready for evaporation. Great Western used quintuple evaporators to heat the juice to sugar saturation with the least amount of energy, saving on the cost of coal. A sugar factory had a large boiler room, and efficient use of boilers to heat water and steam was a primary concern for profitability. In 1920 a standard sugar factory processed twelve hundred tons of beets per day, and to do so the evaporators had to evaporate fourteen hundred tons of water using lots of water, steam, and coal. This process removed water from the thin juice to make "thick juice."

The thick juice was, by then, pure, containing as much dissolved sugar as the water could hold. At this point the thick juice was fed to the crystallizers and seeded with fine sugar crystals, which grew from the thick juice formed around them. The resulting sugar crystal and syrup mix was called *massecuite,* French for "cooked mass," and was passed to a centrifuge, where the sugar crystals were removed from the liquid and dried in a granulator with warm air.

The remaining syrup was fed twice more through the crystallizers, from which second and third batches of sugar were produced. These sugars were of successively lower quality, having impurities as well as a brownish color. The remaining syrup was molasses, which still contained sugar, but had too many impurites to be economically processed further. Colorado sugar factories sold everything they could: top-quality white sugar, brown sugar, and molasses. They also sold beet pulp to local farmers as high-quality cattle and sheep fodder. Great Western also established and owned cattle and sheep feedlots near the factories to ensure a market for the pulp.

For most of America's past, this was the form sugar came in: loaves. The paper cover was blue, and the sugar was very hard. A tool called a sugar nipper was used to break off pieces. Courtesy Jas Townsend and Son Internet Sales.

The best description of the sugar process in the industry's heyday is recorded in *Technology of Beet Sugar Manufacturing*, a book published by Great Western Sugar for its employees in 1920. It includes details of every step with examples of the difficulties faced and homework problems for employees to do in order to learn the trade.[14]

As with any business, the importance of marketing and selling the product cannot be overlooked. Earlier in the nineteenth century,

Thousands of tons of beets yielded thousands of one-hundred-pound sacks of sugar, here stored in the warehouse to be shipped to customers all over the country. One ton of beets yielded about three hundred pounds of sugar. Courtesy Colorado Historical Society, CHS.X6724.

sugar was sold in large lumps called sugar loaves and sugar cones. Both were wrapped in blue paper, which reflected light in a way that made the sugar look whiter and thus of higher quality.[15] This sort of branding—the shape of the loaf and the color of the paper—helped the general public instantly recognize a sugar loaf. In fact, early settlers named more than twenty mountains and buttes in Colorado "Sugarloaf."

At most Colorado sugar factories, sugar came in cloth sacks of different sizes. This Great Western sugar sack held ten pounds of sugar. After the sack was filled, it was sewn shut. Author's collection.

Loaves of sugar were made by packing the wet sugar and molasses combination at the end of the refining process into a conical or loaf-shaped mold. The mass was squeezed and packed down into the upside-down mold, which had a hole in the bottom from which the molasses and liquids drained. The molds were often heated to bake out as much molasses as possible. The mass was then dropped out of the mold, leaving a loaf of solid sugar that was whiter and purer at the base and yellower and browner at the top where the drain hole had been.[16]

These loaves came in various sizes, ranging from one-pound loaves that could be held in the hand to forty-pound loaves that were difficult to lift. Special sugar cutters—much like lopping shears—were used to cut off more easily handled pieces. The cook would scrape small, granulated amounts of sugar off the loaf with a knife.[17] Whiter, purer sugar was used for frostings and presentation cooking, while the browner, less pure sugar was sufficient for dark puddings, wines, and beermaking.

The following is a recipe for frosting for a spice cake circa 1742:

> —take a pound of doubly refined Suggar, pounded and sifted thro a silk sieve, take 2 or 3 white of egg beat them up in a Delf bowl, mix yr. Suggar in it by Degrees, beating it continually till all yr. Suggar is in, if it should be too dry, add some more whites, beat it up very well, you must not make it too thin but fine and smooth, and also thick, when yr. cake comes out of the oven, you must let it ly a little before putting on the Frosting, then lay yr. Frosting on smooth with a knife on top and side till all is on, then set in yr. Oven, till yr. Frosting is a little hard, so keep for use.[18]

"Doubly refined, pounded, and sifted" meant that the cook had to spend as much time preparing the "Suggar" as she did to make the frosting.

Better transportation decreased the time required to move products, including sugar, to the homemaker. Sugar loaves eventually gave way to granulated sugar, easing the handling burden, and the packaging changed from blue paper to sugar sacks. One-, five-, ten-, fifty-, and hundred-pound sacks were filled and sewn shut at the end of the lines at the factory. Cloth sugar sacks and flour sacks were often reused by pioneer women to make garments for the family. Later, paper sacks replaced the cloth sacks, and cardboard boxes were used as a basis for colorful advertisements and recipes as much as for sugar protection. The only solid chunks of sugar a person can buy these days are sugar cubes.

Only the Fort Morgan sugar beet factory remains in operation in Colorado, as the demand for sugar has decreased thanks to changing tastes and the use of corn syrup as the primary sweetener in processed foods.

Factories

Location	Owner	First Campaign
Grand Junction	Colorado Sugar Manufacturing	1899
Sugar City	National Sugar	1900
Rocky Ford	American Beet Sugar	1900
Loveland	Great Western	1901
Greeley	Great Western	1902
Eaton	Great Western	1902
Fort Collins	Great Western	1902
Windsor	Great Western	1903
Longmont	Great Western	1903
Lamar	American Beet Sugar	1903
Sterling	Great Western	1905
Holly	Holly Sugar	1905
Brush	Great Western	1906
Fort Morgan	Great Western	1906
Brighton	Keyes Syrup	1906
Swink	Holly Sugar	1906
Las Animas	American Beet Sugar	1907
Monte Vista	Independent, then Great Western	1911
Brighton	Great Western	1917
Grand Junction	Holly Sugar	1918
Fort Morgan	Industrial Sugar	1919
Delta	Holly Sugar	1920
Fort Lupton	Fort Lupton Growers	1920
Ovid	Great Western	1926

Notes

[1] U.S. Department of Agriculture, Economic Research Service, Sugar and Sweetener Yearbook series, Tables 50–53, 2005.

[2] Food Timeline, "About Refined Sugar," accessed at http://www.foodtimeline.org.

[3] *Technology of Beet Sugar Manufacture* (Denver: Great Western Sugar Company), 3.

[4] Ibid., 4.

[5] William May, *The Great Western Sugarlands* (New York: Garland Publishing), 2.

[6] Ibid., 13.

[7] Leonard Arrington, *Beet Sugar in the West* (Seattle: University of Washington Press, 1966), 6.

[8] Harry Austin, *History and Development of the Beet Sugar Industry* (Washington, DC: UYS Sugar Beet Association, 1928).

[9] Dena Sabin Markoff, "The Beet Sugar Industry in Microcosm: National Sugar Manufacturing Co., 1899 to 1967," master's thesis. (University of Colorado, 1980).

[10] Watrous, 1911, 21.

[11] May, chapter 4.

[12] *Technology of Beet Sugar Manufacture*, 34–38.

[13] Ibid., 35–37.

[14] Ibid.

[15] David, *English Bread and Yeast Cookery*, 138.

[16] Ibid., 137.

[17] Food Timeline, "Sugar Cones and Loaves," http://www.foodtimeline.org.

[18] David, 459.

Bibliography

Chapter 1, Flour Mills

Bakker, Jan Theo. *The Mills-Bakeries of Ostia*. Amsterdam: J. C. Gieben Publisher, 1999.

Cabe, Carl. *Flour Milling*. Lawrence: University of Kansas School of Business, 1958.

Convery, William. *Pride of the Rockies*. Boulder: University Press of Colorado, 2000.

Hayes, A. A. *New Colorado and the Santa Fe Trail*. London: C. Kegan Paul & Co., 1881.

History of Brighton, Colorado and the Surrounding Area, 1887–1987. Curtis Media Corp., 1987.

Kuhlmann, Charles B. *The Development of the Flour-Milling Industry in the United States*. Ph.D. diss. Cambridge, MA: The Riverside Press, 1929.

Moritz, L. A. *Grain-Mills and Flour in Classical Antiquity*. New York: Arno Press, 1979.

Pickle, Charles. Manuscript. Denver Public Library, Western History Collection.

Shwayder, Carol Rein. *Weld County Old and New*. Greeley, CO: Unicorn Ventures, 1983.

Steinel, Alvin T. *History of Agriculture in Colorado*. Fort Collins, CO: State Agricultural College, 1926.

Chapter 2, Breweries

Banham, Russ. *Coors: A Rocky Mountain Legend*. Lyme, CT: Greenwich Publishing Group, 1998.

Baron, Stanley. *Brewed in America*. Toronto and Boston: Little, Brown and Co., 1962.

Cochan, Thomas, ed. *Pabst Brewing Company*, Business History Series, Graduate School of Business Administration. New York: New York University, 1948.

Coel, Margaret, Jane Valentine Barker, and Karen Gilleland. *The Tivoli: Bavaria in the Rockies*. Denver: Colorado and West, 1985.

Collyer, Robert. "History of Brewing in Pueblo, Co," *The Walter Brewing Company American Breweriana Journal*, 2000.

Hennich, Mike. *Brewing in Trinidad Colorado*. Irving, TX: Ale Publishing Company, 1992.

Kostka, William. *The Pre-Prohibition History of Adolph Coors Company, 1873–1933*. Golden, CO: Adolph Coors Company, 1973.

Love, Ed. *Colorado Breweries*. Western History Department of Denver Public Library. Albacor, Colorado Springs, CO, 1982.

125 Years of Memorabilia. Golden, CO: Coors Brewing Company, 1998.

Rahne, Paul M. "Zang's: The History," *American Breweriana Journal* (77): 1995.

Rich, H. S. *One Hundred Years of Brewing*. New York: Arno Press, 1974; reprint of 1903 edition.

Yearbook of the United States Brewers Association. New York: U.S. Brewers Association, 1909.

Chapter 3, Ice

Anderson, Oscar Edward, Jr. *Refrigeration in America: A History of a New Technology and Its Impact*. Princeton, NJ: Princeton University Press, 1953.

Brockett, L. S. "Ice: Its Formation, Peculiarities, and Uses—Its Commercial Value and Importance—The Ice-Harvest, How Gathered and Marketed," *Appletons' Journal* 5 (100): 228–232.

Cummings, Richard O. *The American Ice Harvests: A Historical Study in Technology, 1800–1918*. Berkeley: University of California Press, 1949.

David, Elizabeth. *Harvest of the Cold Months: The Social History of Ice and Ices*. New York: Viking Penguin, 1995.

Dugan, John. *Greeley and Weld County: A Pictorial History*. Norfolk, VA: Doning Co., 1986.

Fickel, Helen. *Personal Recollections of Berthoud's Icehouses*. Unpublished notes. Berthoud Historical Society, July 2002.

Greeley, H., et al. "The Ice Trade," in *The Great Industries of the United States: Being an Historical Summary of the Origin, Growth, and Perfection of the Chief Industrial Arts of This Country.* Hartford, CT: J. B. Burr & Hyde, 1872.

Halsted, B. D. *Barns, Sheds and Outbuildings: Two Hundred Fifty-seven Illustrations.* New York: Orange Judd Co., 1881.

Harney, G. *Stables, Outbuildings and Fences: Illustrated with a Series of 120 Original Designs and Plans, with Descriptive Matter.* New York: Geo. E. Woodward, 1870.

Harper's Weekly 28 (August 30, 1884): 562.

"The Ice Houses of Grand Junction," *Journal of the Western Slope* 5, no.4 (Autumn 1990).

Jones, J. C. *America's Icemen: An Illustrative History of the United States Natural Ice Industry 1665–1925.* Humble, TX: Jobeco Books, 1984.

Magoffin, Susan Shelby. *Down the Santa Fe Trail and into Mexico: The Diary of Susan S. Magoffin, 1846–1847,* ed. Stella Drumm. Lincoln: University of Nebraska Press, 1982, c. 1962.

Noel Hume, Ivor. *Historical Archaeology.* New York: Alfred A. Knopf, 1969.

Trowbridge, J. T. "Among the Ice-Cutters," in *Lawrence's Adventures Among the Ice-Cutters, Glass-Makers, Coal-Miners, Iron-Men, and Ship-Builders.* Boston: Fields, Osgood, & Co, 1871.

Weightman, Gavin. *The Frozen-Water Trade.* Waterville, MA: Thorndyke Press, 2002.

Chapter 4, Millinery and Dressmaking

Ferretti, Kate. Interview by Nancy Whistler for the American Association of University Women's Centennial-Bicentennial Oral History Project, August 4, 1975. Manuscript, Denver Public Library.

Gamber, Wendy. *The Female Economy.* Urbana and Chicago: University of Illinois Press, 1997.

Harris, Beth. *Famine and Fashion: Needlewomen in the Nineteenth Century.* Burlington, VT: Ashgate Publishing Company, 2005.

Hewitt, Margaret. *Wives and Mothers in Victorian Industry*. Westport, CT: Greenwood Press, 1975.

Hood, Thomas. "The Song of the Shirt," *Hoods Monthly Magazine*, 1844.

Kidwell, Claudia B. *Cutting a Fashionable Fit.* Washington, DC: Smithsonian Institute Press, 1979.

Salmon, Marylynn. *Women and the Law of Property in Early America.* Chapel Hill: University of North Carolina Press, 1986.

Chapter 5, Carnations

Besemer, Stuart. *An Economic Analysis of the Carnation Industry in the United States.* Master's thesis, Colorado State University, Fort Collins, 1966.

Kingman, Dick. *A History—Colorado Flower Growers and Its People.* Denver: Colorado Greenhouse Growers Association, 1986.

Meyer, Linda M. *Guide to the Records of the Colorado Flower Growers Association.* Fort Collins: Colorado State University, Morgan Library, Agricultural Archives, 2005.

Taylor, Frank J. "The Great Carnation Lottery," *Saturday Evening Post,* October 9, 1954.

Chapter 6, Mining Precious Metals

Agricola, Georgius, and Herbert Clark Hoover. *De Re Metallica.* New York: Dover, 1950; originally published in 1556 in Latin.

Barba, Alvaro Alonzo. *El arte de los metales.* Translated by Ross E. Douglas and E. P. Matheson. New York: John Wiley and Sons, 1923.

Breitling et al. *Gold.* New York: Alpine Fine Arts Collection Limited, 1981.

Coghlan, H. H. *Notes on the Prehistoric Metallurgy of Copper and Bronze in the Old World.* London: University Press at Oxford, 1951.

Egleston, Thomas. *The Metallurgy of Silver, Gold and Mercury in the United States,* Vols. 1 and 2. New York: John Wiley and Sons, 1887.

Eissler, M. *The Metallurgy of Silver*. London: Crosby Lockwood and Son, 1889.

Faulk, Terry H. *Simple Methods of Mining Gold*. Palmer Lake, CO: Filter Press, 1981.

Fell, James E. *Ores to Metals*. Lincoln: University of Nebraska Press, 1979.

Fossett, Frank. *Colorado: Its Gold and Silver Mines*. New York: C. G. Crawford, 1879.

Hofman, H. O. *The Metallurgy of Lead*. New York and London: The Scientific Publishing Company, 1901.

Hollister, Ovando J. *The Mines of Colorado*. New York: Promontory Press, 1974; reprint of 1867 edition, originally published by Samuel Bowles & Co.

James, Alfred. *Cyanide Practice*. New York: Engineering and Mining Journal, 1902.

Jura Furnace and Engsbachtal Furnace. *Stahl und Eisen*. 56 Jahrg., no. 9 (February 27, 1936).

Kemp, Donald C. *Quicksilver to Bar Silver*. Pasadena, CA: Socio-Technical Publications, 1972.

Lohse, Joyce. *First Governor, First Lady: John and Eliza Routt of Colorado*. Palmer Lake, CO: Filter Press, 2002.

Mathews, Alfred E. *Pencil Sketches of Colorado*, Denver, 1866.

Mine and Smelter Supply Company Catalog No. 15. Denver: The Merchants Publishing Company, 1902.

Nichols, Maureen. *Gold Pan Mining Company and Shops*. Breckenridge, CO: Quandary Press, 1994.

Niebur, Jay. *Arthur Redmond Wilfley*. Denver: Western Business History Research Center, Colorado Historical Society, 1982.

Pettem, Silvia. *Red Rocks to Riches*. Boulder, CO: Stonehenge Books, 1980.

Rickard, T. A. *A History of American Mining*. A.I.M.E. Series. New York: McGraw-Hill, 1932.

———. *Journeys of Observation*. San Francisco: Dewey Publication, 1907.

Smith, Duane A. *Song of the Hammer and Drill*. Golden: Colorado School of Mines Press, 1973.

Wheatley, Mary W. "Reminiscences of the Early Sixties," *The Trail*, January 1911.

Wilson, E. B. *The Chlorination Process*. New York: John Wiley and Sons, 1897.

Young, Otis E. *Western Mining*. Norman: University of Oklahoma Press, 1970.

Chapter 7, Cigars

Bati, Anwer. *The Cigar Companion*. 2nd ed. Philadelphia: Running Press, 1993.

Castle Rock Tribune, various dates.

Colorado Business Directories, various publishers, 1872–1940. Carnegie Library, Boulder, CO.

Colorado Field and Farm, June 27, 1903; September 9, 1911.

Colorado Rancher and Farmer, November 26, 1949.

Cooper, Patricia A. *Once a Cigar Maker*. Urbana and Chicago: University of Illinois Press, 1987.

Denver Business Directory, various publishers, 1866, 1872, 1876–1950.

Directory of the Tobacco Trade. New York and Philadelphia: The Tobacco Leaf Publishing Company, 1874–1875, 1885, 1887, 1893, 1905.

Douglas County Portrait and Biographical Record, 1898. Douglas County Library, Castle Rock, Colorado.

Fort Collins Courier, August 19, 1882; March 25, 1985.

LeCompte, Janet. *Pueblo, Hardscrabble, Greenhorn, the Upper Arkansas*. Norman: University of Oklahoma Press, 1978.

Noel, Thomas. *Growing Through History with Colorado: The First 125 Years, 1862–1987*. Denver: Colorado National Banks and the Colorado Studies Center, University of Colorado at Denver, 1987.

Rocky Mountain News, June 28, 1973.

Shoemaker, Len. *Saga of a Forest Ranger*. Boulder: University Press of Colorado, 1958.

Trinidad Business Directory, various publishers, 1880–1932.

Winter, Joseph. *Tobacco Use by Native North Americans*. Norman: University of Oklahoma Press, 2000.

Chapter 8, Food Canning

Bitting, A. W. *The Canning of Foods: A Description of the Methods Followed in Commercial Canning*, Bulletin 151. Washington, DC: U.S. Department of Agriculture, 1912.

"Cooked Tomatoes," *Boulder Daily Camera*, September 19, 1891.

Counter, Marguerite Frink. "Pioneer Canning Industry in Colorado," *Colorado Magazine* 30, no. 1 (January 1953).

"The Empson Packing Company," *Longmont Ledger*, September 4, 1903.

"Empson's Silver Jelly Kettle," *Longmont Ledger*, July 15, 1898.

Hafen, LeRoy R. *Colorado and Its People*. New York: Lewis Historical Publishing Co., 1948.

Kuner, John C. "Memoirs of J. C. Kuner," 1895. Manuscript at Denver Public Library, Western History Department.

"Kuner-Empson Co, First 100 Years," Kuner-Empson company newsletter. Longmont, Colorado, Historical Museum archives, 1964.

New Orleans Passenger Lists, 1820–1945. http://www.ancestry.com.

Revealing our Routes: A Biography of Lida Empson. http://www.wowmuseum.org. Women of the West Museum, 2002.

Rhoads, Douglas H. *Labels, Leadville and Lore.* Blair, NE: Rhoades Publishing, 2005.

Chapter 9, Sawmills

Andrews, Ralph W. *This Was Saw Milling*. Seattle, WA: Superior Publishing Company.

———. *This Was Logging*. Seattle, WA: Superior Publishing Company.

Appleby, Susan Consola. *Fading Past*. Master's thesis, University of Colorado at Denver, 2001.

J. I., Case, Company. *Case Wood Engravings: Reminders of a Past Art*. 1942.

Chapman, Arthur. *The Story of Colorado*. New York: Rand McNally, 1925.

Chappell, Gordon S. *Logging Along the Denver and Rio Grande*. Golden: Colorado Railroad Museum, 1971.

Defebaugh, James Elliott. "History of the Lumber Industry of America, Vols. 1 and 2," *The American Lumberman*. Chicago, 1906 and 1907.

Denver Field and Farm magazine, no. 1644 (August 11, 1917): 8.

Eastom, Frank A., Dr. *Enterprise at Frazer*. Denver: Brand Book of the Denver Posse of the Westerners, 1954.

Foster, Mark S. *Citizen Quigg: A Mayor's Life of Civil Service*. Golden, CO: Fulcrum, 2006.

Johnston, Hank. *They Felled the Redwoods*. Fish Camp, CA: Stauffer Publishing, 1996.

Kettles, Hazel Bennet. Personal manuscripts, including D. C. Oakes's handwritten account of the trip to Auraria in 1859. Denver Public Library, Western History Records.

Marr, Josephine Lowell. *Douglas County: A Historical Journey*. Douglas County (Colorado) Historical Society, 1983.

Mitchell, Blake. Verbal description of match-making process, 1846–1990.

Oakes, D. C. "The Man Who Wrote the Guide Book," *The Trail*, December 1909.

Post, Charles C. "Diary of Charles C. Post," in *Overland Routes to the Gold Fields*, edited by LeRoy R. Hafen. 1859.

Renze, Dolores C. "Brief Study of the Lumber Industry in Colorado," graduate paper. Denver: Colorado Historical Society, 1949.

Wheatley, Mary W. "Reminiscences of the Early Sixties," *The Trail*, January 1911.

Willing, Dr. George M. "Diary of a Journey to the Pikes Peak Gold Mines in 1859," *The Mississippi Historical Review*, edited by Ralph P. Bieber, Vol. 14.

Williston, Ed M. *The Design and Operation of Sawmills and Planer Mills*. San Francisco: Miller Freeman Publications, 1976.

Wolcott, Charles A. Manuscripts, including information on the Rocky Mountain Lumber Company, at the University of Colorado Western History Archives.

Wolcott, Frank H. *Monarch of Grand County*. Denver: Brand Book of the Denver Posse of the Westerners, 1954.

Wroten, William H. *The Railroad Tie Industry in the Central Rocky Mountain Region*. Ph.D. diss. University of Colorado, Boulder, 1956.

Chapter 10, Saddles and Spurs

Ahlborn, Richard E., ed. *Man Made Mobile*. Washington, DC: Smithsonian Institute Press, 1980.

Bailey, Donald A. *Saddle Strings*. Simla, CO: Bailey Ranch Publishing, 1995.

Crockett Spur and Bit Company, *Catalog No. 48*. Reproduced by Cabin Creek CDs. Cascade, ID, 2006.

T. Flynn Saddlery. *Illustrated Catalog and Price List*. Pueblo, CO, 1926.

R.T. Frazier Saddlery. *Illustrated Catalog and Price List. #29*. Pueblo, CO. Cascade, ID: Reproduced by Cabin Creek CDs, 2006.

Samuel Gallup Catalog #15, *Illustrated Catalog and Price List*. Pueblo, CO. Cascade, ID: Reproduced by Cabin Creek CDs, 2006.

Laird, James R. *The Cheyenne Saddle*. Cheyenne, WY: Westerners International, Cheyenne Corral, 1983.

Rice, Lee M., and Glenn R. Vernum. *They Saddled the West*. Cambridge, MD: Cornell Maritime Press, 1975.

Sherer, Richard L. *Horseman's Handbook of Western Saddles*. Franktown, CO: Sherer Custom Saddle Inc., 1988.

Chapter 11, Sugar Beets

Arrington, Leonard. *Beet Sugar in the West*. Seattle: University of Washington Press, 1966.

Austin, Harry. *History and Development of the Beet Sugar Industry*. Washington, DC: UY.S. Sugar Beet Association, 1928.

Food Timeline. "About Refined Sugar," http://www.foodtimeline.org/.

Markoff, Dena Sabin. "The Beet Sugar Industry in Microcosm: The National Sugar Manufacturing Co, 1899 to 1967." Master's thesis, University of Colorado, 1980.

May, William J. *The Great Western Sugarlands*. New York: Garland Publishing, 1989.

Morgan, Gary. *Sugar Tramp*. Fort Collins, CO: Centennial Press, 1975.

Technology of Beet Sugar Manufacture. Denver: Great Western Sugar Company, 1920.

General

Baker, James H. *History of Colorado, Biographical Vols. 1–5*. Denver: Linderman Co. Inc., 1927.

Blair, Edward. *Leadville: Colorado's Magic City*. Boulder: Pruett Publishing, 1980.

Conrad, Howard L. *Uncle Dick Wootton*. Chicago: W. E. Dibble and Co., 1890.

Eleventh U.S. Federal Census. *Report on Manufacturing*. Washington, DC: Government Printing Office, 1895.

Fifteenth U.S. Federal Census, Vol. 3. *Manufactures*. Washington, DC: Government Printing Office, 1933.

Fossett, Frank. *Colorado*. New York: C. G. Crawford, Printer and Stationer, 1879.

Fourteenth U.S. Federal Census, Vol. 9. *Manufactures*. Washington, DC: Government Printing Office, 1928.

From Maces Holes to Beulah. Beulah, CO; Beulah Historical Society, 1979.

Garrard, Lewis H. *Wah-To-Yah and the Taos Trail*. Palo Alto, CA: The American West Publishing Company, 1968; originally published by the Grabhorn Press, 1850.

Hafen, LeRoy R., ed. *Pikes Peak Gold Rush Guidebooks of 1859*. Philadelphia: Porcupine Press, 1974 (Tearney and Oakes).

Hall, Frank. *History of Colorado*, Vol. 3. Chicago: Blakely Printing Co., 1889.

Harrison, Louise C. *Empire and Berthoud Pass*. Denver: Big Mountain Press, 1964.

Hawke, David Freeman. *Nuts and Bolts of the Past: A History of American Technology, 1776–1860.* New York: Harper and Rowe, 1989.

History of Clear Creek and Boulder Valleys, Colorado. Chicago: O. L. Baskins and Company, 1880.

Jones, William C., and Forrest Kenton. *Denver: A Pictorial History.* Boulder, CO: Pruett Press, 1973.

Larimer County Business Directory, various publishers, 1898–1938.

LeCompte, Janet. *Pueblo, Hardscrabble, Greenhorn, the Upper Arkansas.* Norman: University of Oklahoma Press, 1978.

Lohse, Joyce B. *First Governor, First Lady: John and Eliza Routt of Colorado.* Palmer Lake, CO: Filter Press, 2002.

Mathews, Alfred E. *Pencil Sketches of Colorado,* Denver, 1866.

Marshall, Muriel. *Uncompahgre.* Ouray, CO: Western Reflections, 1998.

Ninth U.S. Federal Census, Vol. 3. *Statistics of Wealth & Industries.* Washington, DC: Government Printing Office, 1872.

Noel, Thomas J. *Growing Through History with Colorado.* Denver: Colorado National Bank, 1987.

Oakes, D. C. Letters and manuscripts, 1859–1885. Denver Public Library, Western Historical Section.

———. Letters and manuscripts, 1859–1885. Denver, CO: Colorado Historical Society, Hart Library.

Ramstetter, Charles, and Mary Ramstetter. *John Gregory Country.* Golden, CO: Clazy 3 Press, 1999.

Rifle Shots: The Story of Rifle, Colorado. Rifle: Rifle Reading Club, 1973.

Seymour, John. *The Forgotten Arts.* London: Dorling Kindersley Limited, 1984.

Simmons, Virginia McConnell. *The San Luis Valley: Land of the Six-Armed Cross.* Niwot: University Press of Colorado, 1999.

Smiley, Jerome S. *History of Denver.* Denver: Denver Times Publishing Company, 1901.

Smith, Phyllis. *From Settlement to City.* Boulder, CO: Pruett Publishing, 1981.

Southworth, Dave. *Colorado Mining Camps.* Round Rock, TX: Wild Horse Publishing, 1997.

Stevenson, Thelma V. *Historic Hahns Peak.* Fort Collins, CO: Robinson Press, 1976.

Tenth U.S. Federal Census, Vol. 2. *Report on the Manufactures.* Washington, DC: Government Printing Office, 1883.

Thayer, William M. *Marvels of the New West.* Norwich, CT: The Henry Bill Publishing Co., 1890.

Thirteenth U.S. Federal Census, Vol. 9. *Manufactures.* Washington, DC: Government Printing Office, 1912.

Twelfth U.S. Federal Census, Vol. 8. *Report on Manufacturing.* Washington, DC: Government Printing Office, 1903.

Wentworth, Frank L. *Aspen on the Roaring Fork.* Denver: Sundance, 1976.

Westermeier, Clifford P. *Colorado's First Portrait: Scenes by Early Artists.* Albuquerque: University of New Mexico Press, 1970.

Index

*Page references in **boldface** indicate illustrations.*

D

E

F

G

N

O

P

T

U

About the Author

William Reich is a native Coloradoan and a graduate of the University of Colorado in Boulder. He holds Bachelor of Science degrees in business management and mechanical engineering, two fields figuring prominently in the subject matter of this book.